Christian A. Schwarz

The 3 Colors of Your Spirituality

9 Spiritual Styles:
How do you most naturally
connect with God?

NCD DISCIPLESHIP RESOURCES

ChurchSmart
RESOURCES

What does it mean to be in love?
What does it mean to be in love with God?

What does it mean to be a philosopher, a practitioner, or an artist
who loves to be a philosopher, a practitioner, or an artist?
What does it mean to be a philosopher, a practitioner, or an artist
who is in love with God?

What does it mean to gradually become
whom you have been created to be?

I dedicate this book to my nine spiritual mentors,
Thomas, Gene, and Ian; Victor, Henrik, and Olli; Ole, Jonathan, and Jack.

Every single one of you gave me a hard time.
Through all of you together, however, I could sense God's light—
without burning my eyes.

C.A.S.

The 3 Colors of Your Spirituality
Retail price $12.00 – Quantity discounts available
Call 1-800-253-4276 for current pricing

Also available:
How to Embrace The 3 Colors of Your Spirituality in Your World
A guide for journeying through this book in the context of a group
Call 1-800-253-4276 for current pricing

Published by ChurchSmart Resources
St. Charles, IL 60174
www.churchsmart.com
orders@churchsmart.com

© 2009 by Christian A. Schwarz
NCD Media, Emmelsbüll, Germany

© U.S.A. edition: 2009 by ChurchSmart Resources
3830 Ohio Ave., St. Charles, IL 60174

Layout and artwork by Christian A. Schwarz

Editorial team: Kathy Haley, Adam Johnstone, Ross Johnstone

Printing: Mohndruck GmbH, Gütersloh, Germany • Printed in Germany

ISBN 1-889638-85-0

The 3 Colors of Your Spirituality

Introduction

Are you happy with your spiritual life, with the way your relationship with God is currently expressed? If you are like most people, your answer is: "No, I'm not really happy."

This "No" can stem from a number of different reasons; however, the probability that your reason is described and treated in this book is relatively high. While working on *The 3 Colors of Your Spirituality*, I continually kept in mind those people who aren't truly happy with their spiritual life, but don't really know why. If you happen to be one of them, I am looking forward to accompanying you on a journey throughout which you will gain new and challenging experiences with God.

If you are satisfied...

However, if your answer to my question is "Yes," that could be for one of two reasons:

- Perhaps you regard the times in which you learned new things and curiously explored areas beyond your own comfort zone, as a closed chapter of the past. You don't feel any inclination to change or improve your present situation, let alone to explore new horizons. You prefer that everything remain as it is. If this describes you, I would guess that this book will not really speak to you, at least not in your present state. You may decide to leaf through it, but chances are you will find many of the things you read to be quite annoying.

- However, your reason for being "happy" with your spiritual life may be completely different. You may have discovered so many new and exciting things in the Christian faith that you are full of curiosity to learn what fresh surprises God has in store for you. If this is the case, over the next 188 pages you will find many things that will touch, move, and change you.

Key terms:
Natural Church Development has coined a number of terms that have already become part of the Christian vernacular in many circles. These terms will be explained, if such an explanation seems to be helpful in a given context, in the text boxes below the orange headings found in the outer margin of the page.

Although God is mentioned on almost every single page, the theme of *The 3 Colors of Your Spirituality* isn't God himself, but rather the different ways people experience God. Throughout the course of this book you will identify your personal spiritual style—your spiritual mother tongue, so to speak. You will find out how much you already live in accordance with this style. You will learn how you can continuously grow in this style. And finally, you will come to understand how rubbing shoulders with other styles of spirituality, presently foreign to your experience, can help you release your full spiritual potential.

My own background

Over the past number of years, our Institute has worked with more than 60,000 churches in about 70 countries in order to help them experience qualitative and quantitative growth. This work has shaped me personally. I am not just the author of *Natural Church Development*, but a person who invests all of his energy in helping others implement the very things that the book *Natural Church Development* speaks about.

Throughout my travels on all six continents my job has not been to speak about an abstract science, but rather to work with real people in real churches on real life problems. We have found real solutions, experienced real defeats, had real celebrations, shared real tears, prayed real prayers—and have seen real progress. Of course, all of these experiences have strongly shaped my understanding of God.

A theory "between practice and practice"

The German theologian Helmut Gollwitzer once defined theology as "theory between practice and practice" (see diagram). In other words, theology doesn't begin in the silence of the study. Rather, it starts with concrete questions that have come out of everyday life practice and are waiting for carefully reflected answers. Theologians don't invent these questions. They discover them through attentive listening and observation. In order to answer them, they develop a theory—hopefully a helpful one. It is then the task of this theory to impact practice in such a way that the outcome will be improved practice.

NCD:

Abbreviation for Natural Church Development. It's the name of the approach to Christian ministry that we have derived from our research on all six continents. NCD doesn't feature a specific church model, but is based on universal principles that apply to all kinds of churches, regardless of culture, spiritual tradition, or church size.

This is how theology works, or at least how it *should* work. This is how I understand our work with Natural Church Development. The goal is not to downplay theory in favor of practice. On the contrary, what we urgently need is a theory that begins with practical questions and that aims at improving Christian practice. That is the approach of *The 3 Colors of Your Spirituality.*

Passion, balance, and maturity

Through Natural Church Development, we have increasingly learned to focus on the causes of long-term church growth. Churches don't grow because they improve their entertaining skills, introduce a marketing strategy, or set numerical growth goals. Churches grow—and this is the unambiguous central finding of our research in more than 60,000 churches—if their quality is high.

What determines church quality? When conducting our research to assess the quality of a church, we don't look at the quality of the show on the platform nor at the quality of the pews. Rather, we evaluate the quality in the heads and hearts of the people sitting in the pews. The church is made up of people, and the quality in the heads and hearts of the people is the quality that counts. This quality is determined, not exclusively, but to a large degree by the spiritual passion, balance, and maturity of each respective believer. And those are the three keywords of this book. How do you achieve *passion, balance,* and *maturity*? How do other believers achieve them? How does a whole church achieve them? This is what *The 3 Colors of Your Spirituality* is all about.

Withdrawal from the real world?

This book is being published at a time in which the world is being shaken by economic, political, and ecological crises such as seldom seen before. The world is facing collapse. And precisely at this time, I am choosing to invest several years of my life in a study of spirituality. How does that fit in with current events? Is religion once again going to serve as a suppression of an unbearable reality, as withdrawal from the world's problems, as flight into our inner selves?

These are reasonable questions, since this has been the way Christianity has shown itself, at least in part, throughout history: as the "opium of the people" (Karl Marx), as "platonism for the people" (Friedrich Nietzsche), even as "collective neurosis" (Sigmund Freud). Criticism of these three perspectives may

> ## "Theology is always...
>
> → **theory**
>
> *between*
>
> **practice** *and* **practice"**
>
> *Helmut Gollwitzer in "Liberation to Solidarity"*

In his book, "Liberation to Solidarity," theologian Helmut Gollwitzer defines theology as "theory between practice and practice"—it is triggered by practice (left arrow) and aims at achieving a positive change of practice (right arrow). This twofold linkage to practical concerns characterizes the theological paradigm behind Natural Church Development, which is especially relevant for "The 3 Colors of Your Spirituality."

be, on the whole, unfair, exaggerated, over-generalized, and partly driven by questionable motives; but who would seriously deny that each of them highlights open wounds within Christianity?

My purpose is not to defend this "wounded Christianity," but rather to help identify the wounds and offer a way to heal them. At that point, we can once again ask the followers of the mentioned critics for their opinion about this teachable, self-critical, healed, or at least progressively improved Christianity. I believe their judgment will be a different one.

The dogma of the constant "more"

I see this book as an answer to the economical and political crises of our time, even if this is not its focus. For decades, the pursuit of the material "more" has almost become a dogma of society, questioned only by a small minority. Money is good, more money is better. One car is good, more cars are better. Two hours of TV each day is good, four hours is better. 1000 dollars of welfare is good, 2000 dollars is better. But also: 2000 calories per day is good, 4000 is better. Working out one hour a day is good, working out two hours a day is better. In this way, the unquestioned goal to acquire more has created its own vicious circle.

NCD Survey:

By means of the NCD Survey any church can identify how strongly each of the quality characteristic of growing churches is presently developed, and especially, what characteristic is most holding back long-term growth. The scientific procedure behind the Survey is based on research carried out in more than 60,000 churches. By conducting the Survey regularly, the development of church quality can be monitored with precision.

There is no unlimited growth in a limited world. By God's design, our planet has limits. Growth can only take place within clearly defined limitations before resulting in fatality, as is proven by the study of cancerous growth. In all of God's creation, this seems to be a rule without exception.

Really without exception? Not entirely. There is *one* kind of growth that the Creator himself has designed so that it can continue indefinitely, without ever reaching a natural limitation. That is *spiritual growth*, the ever-increasing intensification of our love for God, which is inseparably linked to an ever-increasing transformation of ourselves.

Why are some aspects excluded?

When studying this book you may notice that while it covers many areas of the spiritual life, other aspects seem to be excluded. There are two particular areas that are touched on in "The 3 Colors of Your Spirituality," but that are not dealt with in any systematic way:

1. The communal dimension of the Christian faith.

2. The command to "love your neighbor," which also includes the topic of social responsibility.

Are these not two essential elements of the Christian faith? Is it even possible to write a book about spirituality without extensively addressing these two areas? Could it be that I want to present spirituality as a purely individualistic affair ("God and I" or even, "God and my soul"), that is detached from both our fellow believers and the people outside of the Christian community?

These questions are justified, since—according to the Bible—both areas are essential aspects of the Christian faith. Why, then, do they play a lesser role in this book?

The reason is not that I deem these aspects unimportant. The exact opposite is true. They are so important that they have received their own place in the overall system of Natural Church Development, where they are given extensive treatment. The communal character of the Christian faith is dealt with in the tools related to the quality characteristic "holistic small groups." The command to "Love your neighbor," including the topic of social responsibility, is dealt with in the tools related to the quality characteristic "loving relationships."

In "The 3 Colors of Your Spirituality" I have deliberately applied a narrow understanding of "spirituality." In this book, the primary focus is the personal relationship of the individual believer with God—and not the effects that this relationship has on different areas of our lives.

If somebody says, "I express my spirituality primarily by striving for social justice," I would respond: "That is wonderful. This is an important part of discipleship, which also has a prominent place in Natural Church Development. However, in our system we don't assign this to the quality characteristic 'passionate spirituality,' but to 'loving relationships.'"

If we defined "spirituality" so broadly as to include almost all of the vital functions of Christianity, it would no longer make sense to distinguish between the individual quality characteristics of growing churches. Every single quality characteristic (for practical reasons in NCD, we distinguish eight of them) would finally become a synonym for "the whole." There would be an enormous overlap of the eight areas. Therefore, it seems to make more practical sense to give each quality characteristic a deliberately narrow definition. Those aspects that go beyond the narrow definitions are not brushed aside, but are given a thorough, user-friendly treatment in other parts of the system.

At the same time, while stating that this book does not focus on the two areas mentioned, this does not mean that they are completely ignored. The third part of this book, in particular, addresses both dimensions without treating them systematically and exhaustively (for example, see the topic of Mutual Mentoring).

> ## These aspects are so important that they are extensively dealt with in other parts of the NCD system.

If you view Christianity skeptically

Perhaps you are *not* among those Christians who are excitedly preparing for a "spiritual marathon." Maybe you approach this book from a completely different perspective. You are fed up with the Christian faith. You don't feel any need for the kind of church life that you have experienced so far. If this is true, I hope you will continue reading nonetheless. Maybe your frustration with Christianity has something to do with the fact that you have never experienced nor observed the dynamics described in this book. Maybe the two of us—you, a critic of Christianity, and I, the author of this book—are both in the same boat.

It may be that your withdrawal from Christianity is rooted in the fact that you have never encountered Christians who were interested in your specific spiritual style, in your spiritual mother tongue, in the unique way you express your faith. Maybe you have been in a church where the favored spiritual styles were simply incompatible with yours. The expressions of faith that you encountered there appeared unnatural, or perhaps even awkward, to you. They did not connect with who you are.

Perhaps you have turned your back on Christianity not because you have been disappointed by God, but simply because nobody has helped you to find a way of connecting with God that considers your own uniqueness. If this is true, I would guess that the contents of the following pages will be of interest to you.

The term "God"

Perhaps your religious skepticism goes so far that you have eliminated the term "God" from your vocabulary. If that is true, I don't want to persuade you to re-introduce this term into your everyday vocabulary as quickly as possible. Very likely you associate so many negative experiences with the idea of "God"—emotionally-loaded experiences at that—that it would be better to completely abstain from this term for a while. Whenever you come across the term "God" (which I am going to use often), please interpret it for the time being simply as a placeholder for "the great unknown," nothing more. At the end of this book you may ask yourself anew if it would not make sense to call this unknown—or unknown one—"God."

8 quality characteristics:

The expression used to describe universally valid principles of healthy churches that have been identified in our research: empowering leadership, gift-based ministry, passionate spirituality, effective structures, inspiring worship service, holistic small groups, need-oriented evangelism, and loving relationships. These principles apply to every church without exception; however, their practical implementation differs considerably from church to church.

Leo Tolstoy addressed this thought in the following way: "If the idea crosses your mind that everything that you have thought about God is wrong, and that there is no God, then don't get upset. Many people have similar thoughts. What you shouldn't believe, however, is that your own unbelief is the result of the fact that there is no God... When primitive people stop believing in their wooden god it does not imply that there is no God, but simply that the true God is not wooden."

In other words, you may be absolutely right in what you have rejected in the past. Perhaps it has been, metaphorically speaking, a "wooden god," as Tolstoy calls it. In that case, it was right to throw that image of God overboard. But you must remember that in throwing away a wooden god, God has neither ceased to exist, nor did you cease to be a person who has been created to have a positive relationship with your creator.

Focus on transformation

The goal of this book is not simply to share information. I don't want to confine myself to describing the "correct theory." Rather, I would like to enable you...

- to really *understand* these principles of spirituality (with your mind as well as with your heart);
- to *apply* them in your own life (even if this may require awkward processes of trial and error);
- to help *other people* join the process (unless this stage has been reached, I, as an author, have failed).

The Trinitarian Monastery

In order to support the implementation process, we have founded a *virtual monastery*: a web-based community of Christians from the most diverse spiritual traditions. While the monastery itself is virtual, the community of believers couldn't be more real. The idea is that you can, just like in a "real" monastery, withdraw to this virtual monastery from time to time in order to find what you most need for your own spiritual growth.

Trinitarian Monastery:

A web-based community in which Christians of all cultures and denominations support each other in spiritual growth: **3colorsofyourspirituality.org**

In contrast to a real monastery, which always promotes a specific spiritual tradition, our *Trinitarian Monastery* functions differently: You have access to exactly those traditions which are most helpful in your present phase of development. The "monastic experiences" that you access online will support the learning processes described in this book (more on page 182).

We have also developed a companion guide, *How to Embrace the 3 Colors of Your Spirituality in Your World,* which offers guidelines for implementing these processes. With these tools and all God has given you, you must seize the opportunity to go deeper and higher.

Christian A. Schwarz
Institute for Natural Church Development

The yellow boxes and the symbol of fire

In every single chapter of this book you will find a box providing additional information. This information comes out of my personal experiences of working with these concepts over the past few years. These texts are not essential for understanding the book, so you may decide to skip them while reading it for the first time. However, they may provide some information that will enhance your own understanding and be helpful to your spiritual growth.

The background graphic of these boxes is the symbol of fire. Both in Scripture and in Christian tradition, this image has been used frequently to symbolize the essence of spiritual passion. The goal of this book is none other than to fan this spiritual flame into a full blaze—or, if your fire has all but gone out, to fuel it anew.

Part 1

God's truth, goodness, and beauty:
The heart of spiritual passion

Who among us doesn't long for a deep spiritual experience? Many Christians hit the road full of expectation, but before long their growth process comes to a halt. Why does this happen? How can it be changed? What does a pursuit of spiritual passion look like that is not foreign or unnatural? A spirituality in which we feel 100 percent natural, authentic, and alive?

Do you express your faith according to your God-given style?

Has anyone ever asked you about your personal spiritual style? Has anyone ever offered to support you in exactly that area, the area of your strongest receptiveness for the divine? Or has it been your experience that most Christians are so focused on their own approach to God that they believe it is the right one, or at least the best one, for everyone else?

Over the past years, in the context of my ministry, I have communicated with thousands of Christians, quite personally with some of them. However, until two years ago nobody ever asked me, "Christian, what is your personal spiritual style? How could I help you to grow in that area?" The reason this changed two years ago is rather trivial. You see, I have spoken so much about spiritual styles of late that it is only natural for people to become curious about my own spiritual style.

Spiritual Style:

The way in which a believer connects most naturally with God. In NCD we distinguish nine spiritual styles that result from their assignment to the three colors of the Trinitarian Compass. Spiritual styles should not be confused with the spiritual tradition, denomination, or movement to which we belong. Each of these movements may prioritize one or more of the spiritual styles, but within their membership, they always encompass all nine of them.

Why so many people leave their churches

In the 1980s, church growth research into evangelistic campaigns revealed facts that were so spectacular they should have resulted in a revolution. Out of all the people who had come to Christ and looked for a Christian community, only 0.3 to 15 percent could be found in a local church one year later. To put it the other way around, out of all the people who started their Christian journey, 85 percent (in the best case) to 99.7 percent (in the worst case) had turned their back on the church one year later.

Some of those individuals may regard themselves as "bad Christians." Others may be convinced that the Christian faith isn't really for them. Still others may continue to attend their church, but have basically withdrawn from church life. They endure it rather than feeling lifted up by it. Or they have looked for another church which they believe would be a better fit.

There are many reasons why people leave a church. These are not exclusively related to an insensitivity toward spiritual styles. One may leave a church because it is unloving, or due to a conflict in theology, or because the church doesn't meet the family situation, or...

However, even in these cases it could be eye-opening to take a look behind the scenes. Could it be that what one perceived as "unloving" had more to do with an insensitivity toward different approaches to God? Could it be that behind the theological conflict there was a conflict between opposing spiritual styles that was merely carried out at a theological level? And could it be that the incompatibility of the church with one's family situation had something to do with the fact that every single family member has his or her unique spiritual style and that it is unrealistic to expect that the same things that are appealing to one member, would touch the others in the same way?

What does a spiritual person look like?

When thinking about a "spiritual person," most of us have a certain image in mind. These images differ considerably depending on the spiritual tradition to

What is the meaning of the three colors—green, red, and blue—in this and other Natural Church Development books? At the core, they symbolize different ways in which God reveals himself to human beings: in creation and the laws of nature (green with the symbol of the rainbow); in the sacrifice of Jesus (red with the symbol of the cross); and finally in our own hearts (blue with the symbol of the dove). Each of the spiritual styles that are portrayed in this book can be described by the intensity with which each of the three colors shapes our approach to God.

which each of us belongs. Take a look at the diagram. The spirituality expected of the members of a given church is markedly tinted toward the same color that church prioritizes: In some cases, it is primarily green (stressing "creation spirituality"); in other cases, it is primarily red (strongly word-oriented); in still other cases, it is primarily blue (focusing on personal experience).

However, in spite of these differences, we always have stored in our minds a certain standard image of a "spiritual person." If this image is appealing to us—great! If we sense that it doesn't fit us, we may perceive ourselves as "bad Christians," or even come to the conclusion that the Christian faith isn't really "our" religion.

A standard-model of a spiritual person

Over the past few years I have read about 400 books on spirituality. Throughout this process I realized that there are certain personality types that are more likely to be labeled "spiritual:"

- Spiritual people aren't "flashy," and they are hardly ever "extreme" (obviously the truly "spiritual" have found a happy medium);

- they are rarely characterized by a provocative, "fighting" attitude (obviously a soft person is more spiritual than one who loves to express him or herself in the midst of conflict);

- they are usually middle-aged or even really old—in most cases they are even dead (obviously, old age has a strong impact on spirituality, and the advantage of being dead is that you can no longer reject the "spiritual" label);

- they are likely to be early risers (obviously, waking up early is a sure sign of spiritual maturity);

A book for God or for human beings?

Some years ago—while I was the editor of a Christian magazine—I met with a group of other Christian editors to share our experiences. At the beginning of our meeting everybody was asked to summarize briefly the purpose of our respective magazines. The most frequent response of my Christian colleagues was: "Our magazine seeks to give glory to God!" My own answer, however, was a different one. "Our magazine doesn't seek to give glory to God. Rather, it's meant to be an instrument that helps as many people as possible give glory to God."

Why was it so important for me to make this distinction? For two reasons:

First, a printed product (such as a magazine or a book) cannot give glory to God. What would that look like in practical terms? Printed products are not personal beings that can connect with God. They are made up of paper and ink.

Whenever we expect of material objects something that is the task of human beings, we are in danger of reducing the Christian faith to a belief in magic. We begin to construct buildings that will exalt God, instead of buildings that will help people exalt God. We create institutions for the glory of God, instead of being effective in supporting people to give glory to God. We formulate "creeds" to honor God, instead of seeing them as helpful tools for people to honor God. This apparently insignificant shift of emphasis has dramatic consequences indeed!

Second, the text of an article or a book that has been written to give glory to God should really address God, not human beings. A text addressing God would be an entirely different text than one designed to address human beings.

When I pray, I speak to God. When I write a book, I don't speak to God, but to human beings. I speak differently to God than I do to human beings, and I speak about different subjects with God than those I discuss with human beings. God doesn't need my instruction, but it might be useful for other human beings. I don't have to wake God up, but for humans such a wake-up call may be quite helpful.

By the writing style, it is easy to detect a book that is trying to give glory to God "directly" (rather than being an instrument that helps as many people as possible to give glory to God). Depending on the spirituality of the author, these books are characterized by a sacralistic, spiritualistic, or "biblical" language; the argument tends to be somewhat indirect and foggy, usually a bit "other-worldly." You won't find any kind of provocation, irony, or humor—all of which are means of communication that may be inappropriate when directed toward God, but can be wonderful and extremely effective means to communicate with people. In the end, these books sound a bit like the Christmas address of the Queen of England. And many readers are convinced that a "spiritual" book has to sound just like that.

To make my point clear, this is a book for human beings, not for God. When people ask me for the "creed" behind this book or behind NCD, my response is: It's not the task of NCD to formulate any creed. Rather, NCD wants to help as many people as possible find personal creeds that they can wholeheartedly identify with, so they can fully give glory to God.

> **This book doesn't seek to give glory to God, but to help as many people as possible give glory to God.**

- their physical movements tend to be slow, perhaps even a bit ponderous (in countless books I have read—no joke!—that quick physical movement is an expression of spiritual immaturity, thus "ponderous" obviously equals "spiritual");

- they can come from numerous professions—preferably pastors or monks—but they are definitely not professional football players, comedians, body-builders, or models (obviously, among these professions spiritual life isn't really possible).

If you don't fit that model?

Of course, I have nothing against people who fulfill all of the above criteria. However, I do believe it is problematic for this personality type to be treated as the role model for spirituality. The result is that those who don't match that profile (and don't even want to match it!), either view themselves as "unspiritual," or feel great pressure to increasingly adapt themselves to that standard role model, an attempt which will never succeed.

For many years of my life I was seriously convinced that I had to adapt to the role model I just described. However, thanks to God, it didn't work. There are countless ways to express your spirituality. There is definitely nothing wrong with the criteria just listed, but they don't have anything to do with spiritual maturity.

Spiritual people can be extreme, passionate fighters, young, late risers, full of body movement, or comedians. They can comply with the criteria mentioned above, be the exact opposite, or anything in between. The fact that many books on spirituality favor a certain personality stereotype has done enormous damage.

The attempt to express your spirituality in a way that does not match your spiritual style leads to spiritual frustration. Dallas Willard accurately observed, "Spirituality wrongly understood or pursued is a major source of human misery and rebellion against God."

Spiritualities:

I agree with the great Swiss theologian Hans Urs von Balthasar who distinguishes between "spirituality" and "spiritualities." According to von Balthasar there is, at root, only one spirituality, whose "one, concrete norm is Jesus Christ who endows each of these forms with its own particular meaning derived from the unity of God's triune love." Thus, an authentic "Christian" spirituality is one that binds us to Christ and leads us through the power of the Holy Spirit to God the Father. Within that essential framework, however, there are innumerable ways of meeting Christ, and von Balthasar describes them as "spiritualities." I refer to them as "spiritual styles."

Do you know your style?

Every believer has a unique spiritual style, but only very few of us know what that style is. Some of us may live in *accordance* with our style having never reflected on it. Others live in *contrast* to their style without being aware of it. In this book I have reduced the plethora of spiritual styles to nine main types and 18 sub-types. Differences in spiritual style are normal. It is not a matter of "good faith" versus "bad faith." Rather we are looking at different ways of encountering God—each of them positive, but in need of being complemented by the others.

While the first part of this book describes the practical implication of this paradigm, the second part will portray every individual style in detail. A test will help you identify your own spiritual approach (page 64). On the basis of this, the third part of the book will then show those who already know their style, how they can continue in their growth process.

What is radical balance?

The message of this book—and of Natural Church Development in general—is the message of spiritual balance. Whenever I mention this concept, it is usually strikingly well received. I am afraid, however, that this applause is based, at least in part, on a gross misunderstanding. Balance, for many Christians, is the very opposite of everything radical. "Passionate faith? No, no, that is something we leave to the cults. We are not fanatics, we are balanced."

In general usage, for many people the term "spiritual balance" has become almost synonymous with mediocrity, with lack of passion, with stagnation. Of course, the concept of spiritual balance has nothing at all to do with that.

From "balance" to "radical balance"

Take a look at the diagram. The horizontal axis displays the range between "nominal" (left) and "radical" (right), where nominalism is the constant peril, and radicalness the desired goal. The vertical axis expresses the degree of spiritual balance, which covers all increments from "imbalanced" (bottom) to "balanced" (top). When we combine the two perspectives, we get four basic positions (and of course every shade in between):

- *Quadrant A:* Here we have the combination of **imbalance** and **nominalism**. People tending to this position may have quite dogmatic views on what is right (namely, their own position) and what is wrong (other positions). They may bluntly reject other spiritual styles or traditions as "sectarian" and will certainly not indicate the slightest willingness to learn from them. However, their own tradition doesn't really mean that much to them either. They may defend it with strong words, but not with inviting passion. Representatives of this position may claim that their way of conducting a worship service is the only correct one. Nevertheless, they only *rarely* attend the worship services, the specific style of which they vehemently defend.

- *Quadrant B:* Compared to Quadrant A this demonstrates great improvement. Although this position is still characterized by **imbalance** (people are not willing or able to learn from other approaches), it is at least marked by **radicalness** and thus by passion for one's own spiritual style. We should never forget that the radical element of this position is not the problem, but solely the fact that radicalness is expressed in an imbalanced way. This is the very position that many have in mind when they react negatively to the term "radical." They have primarily, if not exclusively, experienced radicalness in this imbalanced variety and believe that radicalness is inevitably linked to imbalance and fanaticism.

- *Quadrant C:* This position is marked by **balance**—people approach different spiritual styles and traditions with respect—which appears to be very positive. On closer examination, however, we detect that this balance is not very stable, as it is purely **nominal** in nature. Representatives of this position aren't really concerned with learning from other spiritual approaches or advocating them with passion. Ultimately, they are indifferent toward all of the styles. If church leaders tend to this position (and in this occupational group it seems

Radical balance:

Key concept behind the quality characteristic "passionate spirituality." On the one hand, Christians are encouraged to grow in their own spiritual styles (radicalness); on the other hand, they are encouraged to learn precisely from those styles that at present appear strange to them (balance). This concept applies in the same way to other areas of Natural Church Development as well.

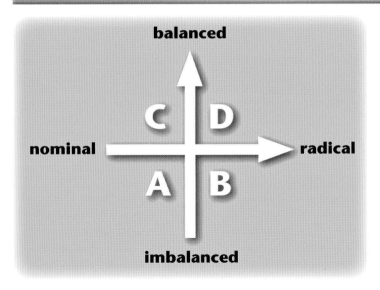

This diagram shows four options that result from one's position on the two axes "nominal – radical" and "imbalanced – balanced." Quadrant A symbolizes spiritual imbalance which is expressed nominally. Quadrant B describes a position where spirituality shows itself radically, but in an imbalanced way. Quadrant C describes those Christians whose spirituality is balanced but nominal. Quadrant D indicates the goal of spiritual growth: radical balance.

to be disproportionately high), we should never confuse their articulated benevolence with active support. In their limitless courtesy toward the most diverse positions, representatives of Quadrant C are usually markedly pleasant people. However, you cannot change the world with them.

- *Quadrant D,* finally, describes the goal of the spiritual journey as outlined in this book: **radical balance**. Here the passion for your own style is combined with respect and the readiness to learn from other styles.

Two steps toward radical balance

How can you achieve this kind of radical balance? Basically, in two steps:

- The *first step* is to identify your own spiritual style, to grow in that style, and to be able to live it out confidently. That is the radical component, which is the theme of part 2 of this book.

- Then, from that strong grounding in your native style, the *second step* is to deal with those styles that are furthest away from your way of experiencing God (the so-called "opposite pole"). This is the step which leads to spiritual balance. Part 3 of this book gives instruction as to how this can be done.

Your starting point and your destination

Which of the four quadrants describes you? Perhaps I should rephrase that. Which of the quadrants *currently* describes you? This is not a set of fixed personality styles, but a description of starting points. Once you have identified your starting point, you can take the appropriate steps that will lead you increasingly to the goal of radical balance.

- Is your spiritual life relatively balanced, but you are missing radicalness (*Quadrant C*)? Congratulations, you have discovered the important dimension of spiritual balance. Your next step is to develop the radical element of your spirituality.

- Are you already radical in your spirituality, but sense that you are lacking balance (*Quadrant B*)? That's promising, as you are already practicing an essential aspect of passionate spirituality, that of radicalness. Now you should work toward spiritual balance.

The peril of nominalism

I have never met a church leader who was happy about nominalism in his or her own church. Most leaders have the desire to see the Christians in their ministry live their faith more passionately, more consistently, and with greater commitment.

However, some of them fear that "passion" would be linked to a specific style (e.g. "charismatic" or "seeker-oriented" or "contemporary") that doesn't fit their own tradition. Though this is not the case. Churches that get involved with Natural Church Development are not prompted to leave their own tradition in order to adopt a style that is foreign to them. On the contrary, Lutherans who get involved with NCD will become more passionate Lutherans; Roman Catholics will become more passionate Roman Catholics; Baptists will become more passionate Baptists; and Pentecostals, more passionate Pentecostals.

Every denomination is endangered by the tendency toward increasing nominalism. The danger that a lack of growth reduces faith to what is on paper applies to a Pentecostal as well as to a Lutheran or a Catholic.

However, it cannot be ignored that some church traditions are more prone to nominalism, while others may be more prone to legalism. While in some churches those who live their faith nominally have to justify themselves, in other church traditions the very opposite is true—those who want to live their faith with passion have to justify themselves. Although they are accepted, they are deemed a sub-culture, even if this sub-culture may be viewed positively (in the best case). It goes without saying that in these church traditions the percent-age of nominal Christians is higher than in others.

While some churches are set up such that they literally cease to exist if the spiritual passion is extinguished, others consider it an advantage that the outer forms, rituals and institutions remain intact, even if spiritual passion may fade away. This may be seen as an advantage or a disadvantage. However, chances are high that a considerable percentage of members in these churches will reduce faith to outer conformity with expected customs, and that the rituals will be fulfilled mechanically, without inner participation.

Nevertheless, for these churches the path to spiritual passion doesn't lead them away from their own tradition, as some may fear. It merely leads them away from a kind of traditionalism that is one of the causes of nominalism. While we had breakfast together in Riga, Latvia, the Lutheran Archbishop of Latvia, Janis Vanagas, told me something that I immediately wrote down on my paper napkin: "Tradition is the living faith of the dead; traditionalism is the dead faith of the living." That's exactly the approach Natural Church Development wants to foster—saying "good-bye" to traditionalism, and "hello" to our own living traditions!

Hardly anything has been more counterproductive for evaluating nominalism (and its counterpart: spiritual passion) than the fact that passion has been so often expressed in an imbalanced way (Quadrant B in the diagram on page 17). Compared to that, many people prefer a nominal balance (Quadrant C). However, neither option is desirable. The goal of spiritual growth is a maturity that combines radicalness with balance.

> **Tradition is the living faith of the dead; traditionalism is the dead faith of the living.**

- Do you feel that your present spirituality is neither radical nor balanced (*Quadrant A*)? That's no reason to throw in the towel. Countless people share this starting point. This is exactly where most of us have begun our spiritual journey. Your greatest asset is a desire to invest in a growth process rather than being content with your present situation.

Radical balance and spiritual passion

The integration of radicalness and balance is the key to spiritual passion. Regrettably, many churches view spiritual passion through critical lenses. Without a doubt, they have the imbalanced version of passion in mind (Quadrant B). From that viewpoint, their skepticism is understandable. However, a critical view of Quadrant B should never be a reason to reject the concept of radical balance as outlined in this book (Quadrant D).

We should never try to justify the lack of passion—maybe even with reference to "balance"—as something desirable. In this area, the biblical warning is crystal clear: "I wish that you were either cold or hot," the risen Christ said to the church in Laodicea. "So, because you are lukewarm, and neither cold nor hot, I am about to spit you out of my mouth" (Rev. 3:15-16).

Countless congregations view passion primarily as a hormonal rite of adolescence, not as the fingerprint of God. "Prevailing wisdom suggests that passion, like algebra and acne, should be endured, not exegeted," writes Kenda Creasy Dean in her eye-opening book *Practicing Passion*. "With nothing left 'to die for' in Christian teaching, it became increasingly unclear whether or not Christianity offered something worth *living* for."

> **Nominalism:**
> *The opposite of spiritual passion. People regard themselves as Christian, but their faith has no life-changing effect. Therefore, it is one of the most important tasks of churches to constantly spark the spiritual passion of their members—not in the sense of simply stirring up emotion, but by strengthening their "spiritual muscles." Nominalism should be accepted as the starting point of many people, but must never be re-interpreted as something normal or even positive.*

Nominalism as the opposite of passion

As described in the box on the opposite page, all churches, regardless of their spiritual tradition, are endangered by nominalism, as this is nothing other than the result of vanishing passion. Every single believer is endangered by it; in fact, every single one of us goes through different phases in our lives in which nominalism prevails, and others, in which radicalness prevails. In other words, nominalism is not a static state ("these people are nominal, and those are radical"), but rather a constantly present peril for all of us. It should be one of the primary tasks of church leaders to support their people in their daily fight to overcome nominalistic tendencies.

However, rather than doing that, a number of churches have started to use theology to justify nominalism. In most cases, they do it in order not to appear judgmental or exclusive. They want to include as many people as possible, nominal Christians as well as committed believers. Ironically, by doing so they achieve the opposite of what they intend. In the end, nominalism turns people away. People who are looking for something "to die for"—and there are many of them—will inevitably look elsewhere. It's no surprise that churches with a high percentage of nominal Christians tend to be declining churches.

The good news is that the state of nominalism can be changed. People who are nominal in their faith—and we should never forget that each of us will go through a phase of nominalism at one time or another—can take practical steps to spark the fire of passion once again.

Spiritual passion and the Trinitarian Compass

What is at the center of the Christian faith? Without a doubt, it is a personal experience of God himself, whom we can see at work in *creation*, approaching us through *Jesus* of Nazareth and in the power of the Holy *Spirit*. That's the New Testament experience *per se*. Originally, the Trinity was not a formula, nor a doctrine, nor even an ideology, but rather an event recounted, an experience witnessed, and a relationship encountered.

The goal of the Trinitarian Compass, the theological core of NCD, is to help people experience God's initiative toward us and the practical consequences of that. The Compass strives to release what we are accustomed to refer to as the "Trinity" from the abstraction of a theological formula. It aims to make our encounter with the triune God part of our everyday life. It seeks to reveal what it means to experience God in three different ways while always meeting the same God.

Trinitarian Compass:

The spiritual key to Natural Church Development. The Trinitarian Compass, in its generic form, reflects God's threefold revelation (as Creator, in Christ, and in the Holy Spirit) and can be applied to different areas of our lives. It always helps us identify (a) the exact stage of the individual believer's or the whole church's development, and (b) the steps that are necessary in order to achieve greater balance.

Once you become familiar with the Trinitarian Compass, you will discover that it is all about the two themes of "oneness" and "threefoldness," and always with reference to God himself. The Compass uses the symbolic language of color— green, red, and blue. The individual colors relate to the creation revelation (green), the salvation revelation (red), and revelation through the Holy Spirit (blue). All three areas share the common reality of an encounter with God, yet they differ from each other in terms of the dimension of God's revelation that is emphasized. In other words, the Trinitarian Compass is all about identity (oneness) and diversity (threefoldness), which has been the predominant theme of the age-old discussion of the Trinity.

However, the focus of the Trinitarian Compass is not targeted on the relationship which the three divine persons have with one another. (I would guess that throughout the history of theology, everything that can be said about this theme, has already been said, and possibly even a little bit more.) Rather, the focus of the Trinitarian Compass is to describe how *we, as human beings,* relate to the divine Trinity. Both questions are important, but neither should be confused with the other. I don't know how much more time God will give me on this planet, but most likely I will invest the rest of my life in nothing other than continuing to work on this topic, both theologically and practically. It seems to me that in this area we have only just begun.

The Trinity as an immensely practical theme

In both Roman Catholic and Protestant churches, we seldom hear sermons explicitly on the Trinity. For some reason people seem to have the impression that, while being an important theme, it is not really relevant to our daily lives. Back in 1798 Immanuel Kant wrote: "It is utterly impossible to draw any practical consequences from the doctrine of the Trinity." With all due respect to Kant, I believe the opposite is true. Once we start to think about our own relationship to the triune God with reference to the most diverse questions of life, trinitarian thinking becomes something eminently practical.

Christian spirituality should fulfill the following three criteria: It should be Word-based (red segment), Spirit-directed (blue) and world-focused (green). If one, or even two, of the three dimensions are underdeveloped, there is a lack of spiritual balance.

My thesis, in a nutshell, is "Tell me how you view God, and I will tell you what kind of spirituality you have." Better yet, "Tell me how you view God and I will tell you how you live." Verbally, almost all Christians appeal to the divine Trinity—in our terminology: to all three colors—but it can be demonstrated that different strands of Christianity give different weight to each of the colors, tending to prioritize one or two of them.

The essence of the three colors

Each of the three colors has a specific focus that, on a practical level, permeates all areas of life.

- Since **green spirituality** relates primarily to God's revelation in creation (Ps. 19:2; Rom. 1:19f), it can be referred to as "creation spirituality." That which can be perceived by the five senses is given high spiritual significance. As Emil Brunner has stated, "God prints the stamp of his character on everything he creates." Therefore, the creation of the world is a revelation of God. The objective side of God's revelation in nature corresponds to the subjective reality that we are created in the image of God. Green spirituality takes seriously the fact that God has made a covenant with all of humanity—God's covenant with Noah, the sign of which is the rainbow. As a result, green spirituality has a universal tendency. The rational penetration of the dynamics of nature is not viewed as being in opposition to faith, but is, in itself, an expression of faith. In contrast to red and blue spirituality, which advocate the objective (red) and the subjective (blue), green spirituality is often expressed in neutral form. In green spirituality, the focus is on **understanding**.

- Since **red spirituality** focuses on the salvation revelation, it has—with good biblical support—an exclusive tendency (John 14:6). Red spirituality is concerned with receiving and sharing the gospel. The Bible is given an absolutely central place. Red spirituality stresses the objective dimension of the Christian faith; its expression is primarily verbal. The "Word" is seen as the center of everything. Faith is primarily understood as **standing firm**, as a solid standpoint, which has a reliable, trustworthy foundation.

• **Blue spirituality** can embrace a variety of expressions (both introverted and extroverted), but all of them are focused on a personal encounter with the Holy Spirit. The supernatural dimension is not excluded from, but integrated into spirituality, sometimes even seen as the essence of spirituality. Blue spirituality has a deliberately subjective tendency: What God has done objectively in Christ becomes a subjective experience "in our hearts." Through the Holy Spirit, "Christ for us" becomes "Christ in us" (Gal. 2:20. 4:19, Col. 1:27). With the focus on the Holy Spirit, a dynamic component comes into play. Faith is not so much viewed as a standpoint, but as **being moved** and moving others.

Both/and rather than either/or

This book is all about spiritual passion that is birthed out of an authentic encounter with the triune God, not an enthusiasm generated by psychological mind-games. The essence of passionate spirituality is a God-centered existence. Encounter with God is the root; passion is the fruit. Just as "passion" encompasses both suffering and enthusiasm, so does a genuine encounter with God.

Each color focuses on one specific, biblical aspect of God: The eternal God, whom we know is "above us" (green segment), is "among us" through the incarnation of Jesus Christ (red), and at the same time produces the knowledge of his presence "within us" (blue). While green spirituality likes to use adjectives to describe God and red spirituality prefers nouns, blue spirituality is characterized by verbs. It is striking to observe that Scripture uses different genders to characterize different aspects of God (more about this on page 24).

If we want to achieve this kind of passion, we cannot afford to bypass any one of the three colors. Take a look at the six graphics at the bottom of these two pages. None of them can be understood in terms of either/or, but only in terms of both/and. The integration of the three colors is not a diplomatic compromise. It is based on the nature of God who reveals himself in three different ways.

Green spirituality views Jesus as the rabbi, the wisdom teacher, the human being; red spirituality focuses on the Jesus who said about himself: "I am the way and the truth and the life" (Joh. 14:6), and who has opened this way through his suffering and death; blue spirituality adores Jesus especially as the

Three locations to encounter God	*Three word categories to characterize God*	*Three genders to describe God*

one who performed miracles, who had power over evil spirits, who not only died for us, but was also raised from the dead. Do these three dimensions have an either/or relationship to each other? Once that is taught, the slippery slope toward heresy has begun.

It has been said that our operating theology (those things that really matter to us) can be found in our favorite songs. Choral hymns and classical music correspond to the color green; gospel songs are typically red; praise and worship songs are markedly blue. This tendency is confirmed when we take a closer look at the lyrics: Hymns and classical music are filled with references to creation; gospel songs point to Jesus as the only way to God; and worship songs emphasize the concepts of Christ in us through the Holy Spirit. We sing what we believe!

My point is simply this: It is perfectly all right to stress certain aspects more than others, but it is not all right to overshadow any one of the three dimensions or to neglect it completely.

God as a person

In the box on page 24, I discuss the three grammatical genders that Scripture uses to describe different dimensions of God's nature. Two of these genders (masculine and feminine) are personal; one (neuter) is transpersonal. Here, again, it is important to realize that we aren't speaking about an either/or relationship, but both/and.

- God is a *person*. Although the term "person" isn't used in Scripture, both the Old and New Testaments communicate this idea continually. God has a name. This means that he can speak to us, listen to us, answer us. "For the biblical God this is essential," writes Pope Benedict XVI, "and if we take this away, we have abandoned the faith of the Bible."

- At the same time, however, God is *more than a person,* and he is definitely not a person in the same way we are, nor as we imagine a person should be. When God is more than a person, he is certainly not less than a person. He is not an object; we cannot manipulate him; "he is not impersonal, not under-personal," as Hans Küng expresses it. "Better than personal or apersonal we should, if we are looking for a term in this category, call him trans-personal."

The very color that primarily tints our image of God (see the three graphics on the left hand page) has practical consequences for different areas of our lives. Three examples of these consequences are displayed in the three graphics below.

First consequence: *Three kinds of knowledge*	*Second consequence:* *Three levels of application*	*Third consequence:* *Three spiritual goals*

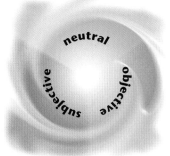

Male, female, and neutral images

Due to my ministry, I am regularly dealing with the most diverse streams of Christianity—some of which are on my wave length, some with which I have more difficulty. In this context, I have learned that the question of which pronoun we use for God—he, she, or it—is an emotionally heavy-laden one (in almost all camps of Christianity). Occasionally, the discussion can be so out of control that the arguments presented cannot even be heard. The sheer use of a pronoun that is believed to be "wrong" from one point of view is sufficient reason to immediately terminate any meaningful dialogue.

We need to realize that this question is not about sexual identity, but grammatical gender. When we mix up the two, perhaps by fighting for an image of God as an anatomically-correct bearded man, we have completely gone outside the biblical boundaries ("You shall not make yourself an image").

What does the Bible contribute to this discussion? Which pronouns does it use for God? I have discovered that depending on which "color" of God is in focus, Scripture uses different genders.

Masculine: Since the red color zone is related to God's revelation in Jesus Christ, it deals, indisputably, with a "man." There is solid biblical evidence that red spirituality can be described as a "masculine" spirituality. The relationship of Jesus with his heavenly father can only be properly understood in the context of a patriarchal society. It explicitly aims at subordination. A son, even an adult son, has to do the will of his father. Thus, red spirituality can be demanding on the giving side, while calling for obedience on the receiving side.

Feminine: In the original Hebrew, the term for "spirit" (ruach) is in almost all cases a feminine expression. In other words, according to the Bible, the spirit is a "she." Only in those cases where the spirit (or the wind, since both realities are described by the same word) acts violently, the masculine form is used. In Greek, then, "Spirit" became neuter (pneuma), in Latin, masculine (spiritus), and as such—in the masculine form—it moved into the English language. It is interesting to note that the verbs connected with ruach are almost exclusively allocated to one of the following two groups: (a) verbs of motion, (b) verbs of setting-in-motion. The Spirit isn't only itself in motion, but sets other things in motion. This dynamic character is the focus of blue spirituality.

Neuter: Apart from these two personal views ("he" and "she") Scripture also uses neutral expressions for God—"the divine." For instance, Colossians 2:9 uses this language. Although it would be wrong to reduce the nature of God to this neutral language, it would also be wrong to dismiss the transpersonal dimension completely. God is person, but, at the same time, he is more than a person. The transpersonal terminology stresses the transcendent, cosmic dimension of God, which plays an important role in green spirituality.

The doctrine of the Trinity, which stresses both the oneness and the threefoldness of God, teaches us not to view these different aspects of God as mutually exclusive (God is "he," God is "she," God is "it"), but complementary. At any rate, Scripture itself uses masculine, feminine, and transpersonal terms to describe the nature of God.

> **Scripture itself uses masculine, feminine and transpersonal terms to describe the nature of God.**

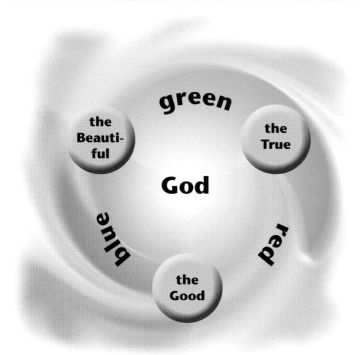

It is characteristic of the biblical account that God's truth, God's goodness, and God's beauty are not separated from each other. However, our own image of God (which we must never confuse with God himself) tends to start with such a separation: Some believers primarily see the True in God; others, the Good; and still others, the Beautiful. Of course, these one-sided images of God influence our relationship with God, i.e. our spirituality.

Maybe you have already been in touch with the transpersonal side of God ("the Divine"). Great! In that case, your next step should be to explore the personal side of God. Maybe you have understood and experienced God almost exclusively in personal ways. Wonderful! In that case, your next challenge is to explore the transpersonal side of God. This book will help you pursue either direction.

God's truth, goodness, and beauty

Take a look at the diagram above. It displays three aspects of God's character that cannot be assigned to one particular color, but have their reference points midway between the individual color segments:

*   *God's truth* rests on the interface between green and red. Christians with a primarily dogmatic orientation focus on this aspect.
*   *God's goodness* rests on the interface between red and blue. Since this word, which is a bit ambivalent in English, points toward God's standards (what he defines as "good"), it is at the center of an ethical approach.
*   Finally, *God's beauty* rests on the interface between blue and green. This is the aesthetic perspective that focuses on the unique splendor of God, for which Scripture has a technical term: "the glory of the Lord."

In a later chapter (page 55), I will deal with the practical consequences of focusing primarily on God's truth, goodness, or beauty. Different church traditions clearly display different priorities. Evangelicals, for instance, prize truth and goodness and tend to neglect the aspect of beauty as an essential part of the gospel.

The true blend of truth, goodness, and beauty is the fully-orbed *shalom* of the kingdom of God. As it is God's desire for us to live in him, we cannot afford to neglect any one of these three dimensions.

Nine ways to encounter God

The graphic to the right identifies nine spiritual styles in relationship to the colors green, red, and blue. A proper understanding of the position of each respective style within the Trinitarian Compass is more important than the terminology used. When dealing with an individual style, you should ask yourself three questions:

1. Which *color(s)* does this style reflect?
2. What are the two *neighboring styles*?
3. Which styles are *opposite* this style?

The answers to these questions will give you significant information about the respective style and also about those people who represent this style.

The ambivalence of terms

When considered outside of the graphical representation, the terms used for describing the individual styles (such as "sensory," "rational," "doctrinal," etc.) may be subject to misunderstanding. Usually the Christians who display a given style tend to regard the term used as positive, while for those who represent other styles the same term may carry primarily negative connotations. That is perfectly normal. The terms have been deliberately chosen such that they can be understood both positively and negatively, depending on whether we are looking primarily at its strengths or its areas of vulnerability.

Passionate spirituality:

One of eight quality characteristics of growing churches. Depending on the spiritual tradition of a church, the way passion is expressed can vary significantly. Spiritual passion is not linked to one specific spiritual style, but is an essential part of every style. Without passion neither spiritual growth nor church growth is possible. Spiritual passion is a synonym for a living, constantly growing relationship with the triune God.

I have worked hard to choose the terms such that they always express what is distinctive, not what they have in common with other styles. For instance I didn't opt for "scriptural" (which applies to all styles) but for "Scripture-driven;" not for "passionate," but for "enthusiastic;" not for "sacrificial," but for "ascetic;" not for "contemplative," but for "mystical," etc. In every single case my goal was to highlight the aspect that makes the respective style unique.

A spiritual style: your antenna to God

In order to understand what a spiritual style is all about, it is helpful first to view it as an "antenna for the divine." Metaphorically speaking, God "broadcasts" on all nine channels, but we may have only set up to receive one or two channels. The reason that we don't receive anything on the other seven or eight channels is not that God doesn't broadcast anything, but simply that we haven't switched on these channels. This is where our nice metaphor breaks down: While on a TV set we can switch to the channel of our choice by a simple click on the remote control, preparation is required on our part in order to activate the reception of any of the nine spiritual channels that are currently deactivated.

There are Christians who have learned to express their spirituality in many different ways. However, there is always *one* style that comes most naturally. This is what we call one's *native style.* We must never forget that this style, while it is the most natural and thus the most "significant" one for us, describes only one of various possibilities for connection with the divine. Most people tend to see their native style as *the* key to spirituality, simply because they have

WORLD

sacramental

sensory

rational

mystical

doctrinal

Scripture-driven

enthusiastic

ascetic

sharing

SPIRIT

WORD

The Trinitarian Compass: At the center of every color zone there are two spiritual styles. One of them is more extroverted, the other, more introverted. In addition, there are three styles located exactly on the borderline between each of the different color segments. The position of each style on the Trinitarian Compass is more important than the terminology used when it comes to understanding the essence of each individual style. For this reason, throughout this book you will find the same basic graphic, with changing stresses and accentuations. The goal is to internalize the image of the Compass, as this image is important for comprehending spiritual dynamics.

experienced it as *the* key in their own lives. They tend to overlook the fact that there are other keys by which the same truth—or different aspects of the same truth—can also be unlocked.

Favorite locations

It is helpful to ask in which environment representatives of each style feel particularly close to God. It's not that God is objectively closer to us in those situations, but that we *feel* his closeness more, we *sense* him to be closer to us. Some people get this feeling at a large charismatic conference when they experience something that is beyond their comprehension. For others, a solemn liturgical atmosphere triggers the feeling of closeness to God. And there are others who experience God's presence most strongly when they are away from the church doing street ministry.

I have assigned a "favorite location" to each of the nine styles covered in this book. An overview of these locations can be found in the table on page 28. I will describe each of the nine locations in more detail in part two of this book.

The green styles: "sensory" and "rational"

The green color zone is home to the sensory and rational styles. The sensory style tends toward "blue" (the sacramental style), while the rational style tends toward "red" (the doctrinal style). However, what both styles have in common is a reflection of the earthiness of Christian spirituality. They both express relationship with God through relationship to God's creation. Even so, each has a different focus. The sensory style relates more to the material, empirically-perceivable side; the rational style, to the mental, intellectual side. Green spiritualities can appear quite earthly. Sometimes they are called "secular spiritualities." People who are not connected to this channel of relationship with God

Name of style	Favorite location	Motto	Focus	Key Scripture reference
sensory		enjoying the works of God	beauty & perception	*The heavens declare the glory of God; the skies proclaim the work of his hands. (Ps. 19:1)*
rational		understand-ing the nature of God	logic & science	*By wisdom the Lord laid the earth's foundation, by understanding he set the heavens in place. (Prov. 3:19)*
doctrinal		thinking cor-rectly about God	truth & doctrine	*See to it that no one takes you cap-tive through hollow and deceptive philosophy, which depends on human tradition and the basic principles of this world rather than on Christ. (Col. 2:8)*
Scripture-driven		applying the Word of God	Bible study & discipleship	*Let the word of Christ dwell in you richly as you teach and admonish one another with all wisdom. (Col. 3:16)*
sharing		passing on the grace of God	evangelism & service	*We are therefore Christ's ambassadors, as God were making his appeal through us. We implore you on Christ's behalf: Be reconciled to God. (2 Cor. 5:20)*
ascetic		developing discipline for God	sacrifice & inner values	*I beat my body and make it my slave so that after I have preached to others, I myself will not be disqualified for the prize. (1 Cor. 9:27)*
enthusias-tic		celebrating the power of God	power & excitement	*For the kingdom of God is not a matter of talk but of power. (1 Cor. 4:20)*
mystical		resting in the presence of God	mystery & devotion	*We do not know what we ought to pray for, but the Spirit himself inter-cedes for us with groans that words cannot express. (Rom. 8:26)*
sacramen-tal		expressing the incarna-tion of God	liturgy & symbolism	*The Word became flesh and made his dwelling among us. (John 1:14)*

Overview of the nine spiritual styles: Each style emphasizes one specific aspect of the bibli-cal message. In other words: Each of the nine styles is "bib-lical," and each one needs to be complemented by the other styles.

frequently misunderstand green Christians' enthusiasm for the senses and reason. For them these two dimensions are purely "worldly." They don't understand that green spirituali-ties strive to encounter God in the midst of this earthiness.

The Bible indicates the perils of green spirituality. The Old Testament reports that Solomon patronized the arts and sci-ences, two interests of green spirituality. The time of Solo-mon was characterized by intense international relationships, extensive trading, the marriage with Pharaoh's daughter, and a huge harem with numerous foreigners whose gods demanded special worship practices. The result was syncretism—the pollution of God's people, of holy Jerusalem.

The red styles: "Scripture-driven" and "sharing"

The red color zone is home to the Scripture-driven and the sharing styles. The Scripture-driven style tends toward "green" (doctrinal style); and the sharing style, toward "blue" (ascetic style). Both styles are strongly "word-centered." The Scripture-driven style is primarily concerned with the personal application of the Word of God; the sharing style, with passing on the Word of God. In the sharing style, the focus on the Word can even be detected when material things are passed on to meet the needs of others. Red believers do it primarily because the Word of God commands them to do it.

Christians with other styles may view red spirituality as "dry" or devoid of feeling. They cannot understand how lively and dynamic red Christians experience their interaction with the Word of God, and how positively this shapes their emotions. Though red Christians tend to speak less about their feelings and attribute less significance to them within their spiritual life than blue Christians, they do have strong feelings, and those feelings are especially responsive to the Word.

The specific peril of red spirituality isn't difficult to identify—legalism. Legalism is the flip side of a commendable and absolutely necessary concern, that of taking the Word of God seriously in your everyday activities.

The blue styles: "enthusiastic" and "mystical"

The blue color zone is home to the enthusiastic and the mystical styles. These are two different ways of approaching the supernatural, one more extroverted ("arms up"), the other more introverted ("head down"). However, in both cases going beyond the rational dimension is key. The mystical style has a closer affinity to green (the sacramental style), whereas the enthusiastic style is closer to red (the ascetic style). The enthusiastic style is frequently found in Pentecostal or charismatic churches, or among Christians in non-pentecostal churches that have been influenced by the charismatic movement.

While green and red spiritualities primarily relate to knowing something "about" God, blue spirituality emphasizes the intimacy of knowing and being known by God *in* the Spirit.

> **Green:**
> *One of the three primary colors of NCD's Trinitarian Compass. Green is assigned to the creation revelation and encompasses, on a practical level, the area of what is accessible through the senses and through reason. Arts and sciences have their place within the green color zone. Christians with a green spirituality often stress ecological awareness and social responsibility. In most cases, green spirituality is marked by a higher level of tolerance than we find in the other color zones.*

People who don't tend toward blue spirituality themselves may quickly accuse blue Christians of "subjectivism." They are unable to understand how much energy blue Christians derive from these subjective experiences and how that energy enables them to fulfill the very responsibilities that are important for red and green Christians as well.

Needless to say, this subjective tendency is not only a strength, but also a peril of blue spirituality: The less their spirituality is influenced by the other colors, the greater the danger of sinking into emotionalism. When this point has been reached, feelings become the ultimate standard to evaluate whether God has spoken. Neither rational (green) nor biblical (red) arguments are able to convince them otherwise.

The three borderline styles: "doctrinal," "ascetic," and "sacramental"

The three styles that are located on the borderlines between the three colors, should be given special attention: the doctrinal style (between green and red), the ascetic style (between red and blue), and the sacramental style (between blue and green). All three styles draw their energy from the two colors they are composed of. At the same time, they are at the center of the three "style families" (the dogmatic, ethical, and aesthetic families) which will be introduced and discussed later (page 55).

Red:

One of the three primary colors of NCD's Trinitarian Compass. Red is assigned to the salvation revelation (the cross of Jesus Christ). In red spirituality, Scripture and evangelism are given higher priority than they are in the other color zones; they are central to the whole spiritual life. Red spirituality stresses the line between belief and unbelief, life and death, light and darkness. Everything is targeted at encouraging people to move to the correct side of this line.

The doctrinal style combines the rational component of green spirituality with the word-orientation of red spirituality. This combination is the direct counterpart to blue spirituality. The ascetic style connects concerns of the red and the blue color segments so as to create a concept of "purity" that can express itself in a more or less "anti-green" attitude. Finally, the sacramental style connects the supernatural dimension of the blue color zone with the sensory, material side of the green color zone, thus representing the direct counterpart to the red, word-centered color zone.

Why nine styles?

I have been asked repeatedly why I distinguish *nine* styles. Why not seven or twelve or 16? Both biblically and empirically it would be foolish to insist dogmatically on a specific number. Even when thinking in terms of the three colors of the Trinitarian Compass we could come up with a different breakdown. We could describe each color zone as one "style" (thus resulting in three styles); or we could define the core of each color as one "style" and the interfaces between the colors as three more styles (thus resulting in six styles); or we could divide each of the nine styles mentioned into two sub-styles—depending on their neighboring styles (thus resulting in 18 styles). All of these would be legitimate options. In this question, there is no "right" or "wrong." It is simply a matter of how many equally-sliced portions we would like to make of the whole pie.

The number nine is not at all important to me. Rather, when developing the spiritual style categories, I was guided by the following three criteria:

1. The slices as a whole must cover the **entire spectrum** of the subject at hand (in this case, of Christian spirituality), as displayed in the Bible. In my study of this theme I encountered other typologies which also distinguished different spiritual approaches to the Divine, but I was given the impression that they encompassed basically different shades of one color (for instance, light red, red, and dark red), rather than the whole.

2. Once "the whole" has been defined, the more pragmatic question of **how to divide** the pie comes into play. Here the important question is which system makes sense when it comes to practical implementation.

3. As I mentioned before, it's important to place the individual segments in the **correct arrangement** so that they form a continuum on the one hand (such as: enthusiastic – mystical – sacramental – sensory, etc.), and display meaningful polarities on the other (i.e. the styles opposite each other really are those that are furthest from each other).

The nine spiritual styles and Jesus

Another frequent request has been to show evidence of every single style in the life of Jesus. At the root of this question is the correct assumption that all nine styles find their unity in Jesus. Nevertheless, I find it more confusing than helpful to present Jesus as the "model" for each of the nine styles. Why?

1. The descriptions of the individual styles are based on human beings and their real-life situations in which there is a mixture of both the spiritual and less spiritual. Every Christian is out of balance, the only exception is Jesus. Not one of us represents "the whole pie," so to speak. When describing and naming the individuals styles, this *mixture of light and shadow* helps to point out the virtues and the vices of each style. That mixture cannot be found in Jesus' life.

2. Jesus really represents the "whole pie" and thus gives us a role model for an ideal relationship with our heavenly Father. However, that ideal is something entirely *different from the summation of nine spiritual styles.* Jesus may have acted, in specific situations, in a way that we could label as "sacramental," "rational," or "ascetic," but he didn't represent the sacramental, rational, or ascetic styles.

3. Representatives of every style tend to draw out of Jesus' example aspects that point to their own style. That is the result of highly selective perception, and of *selective Bible study.* The goal of the Trinitarian Compass is to overcome this sort of selective perception. Therefore, we must not make the mistake of strengthening the very tendencies that we should strive to overcome by providing "nine biblical images of Jesus."

> **Blue:**
>
> *One of the three primary colors of NCD's Trinitarian Compass. Blue is assigned to God's revelation in the Holy Spirit, the revelation in our hearts ("Christ in us"). Blue spirituality focuses on the inner being, including feelings. The supernatural dimension of faith is regarded as essential. Blue spirituality can express itself in a variety of ways; there are both extroverted and introverted forms. However, the common denominator is always a personal encounter with the Holy Spirit.*

One-sided Jesus images

Each of the spiritual styles is based on an imbalanced image of Jesus. Some love to speak about Jesus changing water to wine; others focus on Jesus' fasting in the wilderness. Some take the sharp-witted, debating Jesus as their role model. Others zero in on Jesus as the performer of miracles. Some stress Jesus' withdrawal from people and his intimacy with his father; others, Jesus' approachability and his life in the midst of the crowds. Some highlight the fact that Jesus constantly quoted Scripture; others focus on the incarnation—the Word became flesh. Some claim that Jesus didn't change one iota of what was then the Bible, while others stress the fundamentally new teaching that he brought into this world.

When we wear certain glasses, we only see the things that these glasses allow us to see. Other things are either blurred or not seen at all. We have become accustomed to using the term "paradigm" to describe this phenomenon, but we should never forget when using this scientific sounding word, that it simply refers to the mental blockage that each of us has due to our own way of viewing things.

I am aware that I could be accused of wearing glasses as well. In my case, I am wearing "three-colored glasses," thus seeing the three colors everywhere. My response is: *Each of us* wears some sort of glasses. The question is not whether we wear glasses, but whether the lenses are constructed in such a way that we are able to take in the whole of biblical revelation, rather than just our favorite ideas.

Can we change our style?

When describing spiritual styles (however they are labeled), some authors tend to see specific styles as unchangeable identities, almost like a personality profile. This is often expressed by the authors' terminology. For example, rather than speaking about someone who displays "a sacramental style" or "speaks a sacramental language," this person is called a "sacramentalist."

I am well aware that many readers of this book will use similar labels, in spite of my clearly articulated warnings. However, I strictly avoid this kind of terminology in my teaching. At some point in your life you may display a certain style, such as the mystical or the ascetic style. But that does not make you a mystic or an ascetic. You have a style, but you are far more than that style.

I may write about mystical believers, the mystical style or a mystical faith, but I will not label representatives of that style as "mystics." Such terminology places people in a box, potentially damaging their opportunity for spiritual growth. The starting point of their spiritual journey becomes the destination, so to speak. In my opinion, we should strive to avoid such dangerously static labeling. The language we use should clearly reflect that we believe in the dynamic nature of the system.

As a Christian matures, and discovers new spiritual styles (that which is referred to as "Level B learning" later in this book), his or her native style will not disappear. However, it may be that another spiritual style surfaces as being far stronger than what was perceived as his or her original native style.

When people tell me that they have completely "changed" their spiritual style, I have found that what they really mean is that what they believed to be their "previous style" has never been their native style, but simply the style of their church, their spiritual tradition, or their environment. They have taken for granted that this must have been their native style, since they haven't been aware of any alternative.

Later on, when they encounter a different way of approaching God, and discover how much more natural it is for them to express their spirituality in a different way, they tend to interpret that experience as a "shift" in their spiritual style. For example, someone might say, "For many years I have had an ascetic style, but now I have shifted to the sensory style." What they really should say is, "I used to live in an environment where the only acceptable style was the ascetic style, so I adapted to that. When I encountered the sensory style, however, I discovered that it has always been my native style."

The perceived change has been a shift from living out a style you have believed to be your style, to truly living out your native style. You can only discover your native style after you have had the opportunity to experience it.

Even if it holds true that your most developed style can change over time, this doesn't mean that you can choose which style you would like to have. We don't select our spiritual styles like an item in an online catalogue. Rather, we identify the specific style that God has given to us—and remain open to other options that he may have in store for us.

> **Identify the specific style that God has given to you—and remain open to all that he has in store for you in the future.**

What is your spiritual language?

Throughout this book we have been talking about "spiritual styles," but we could just as well have used the expression "spiritual languages." The analogy between languages and spiritual styles is compelling. Real languages have their vocabulary, their grammar, their syntax, and above all a specific manner of thought that is inextricably linked to the language and only accessible to those who speak it well. Spiritual languages are exactly the same.

Mother tongue and foreign languages

The most important analogy between natural and spiritual languages is probably this one: Each of us has only *one* mother tongue, with the exception of those who have been raised bi-lingually. We are all capable of dealing with many other languages, maybe even to the degree of speaking some of them properly. However, our accent will always reveal our native tongue.

The same applies to spiritual styles: Every Christian has a native style, but we are also capable of dealing with many other styles. In order to do that we have to learn the vocabulary, grammar, and syntax of that style. We will have to accept—in the area of real languages as well as spiritual languages—that no language is purely logical. There are certain rules, and countless exceptions to those rules. Many important things cannot be derived from rules at all. Rather, they are learned by constant listening and imitating, through trial and error. Language learning is not mathematical.

Languages have developed through long, historical processes and encompass different, divergent, and sometimes even contradicting elements. Many things are grossly illogical, some of which could easily be changed or simplified through language reform. However, such reforms will never succeed because native speakers will move heaven and earth in order to preserve their language (as illogical, as contradicting, as difficult as it may seem) because they feel "at home" in their language.

Native style:

The one spiritual style by which each Christian most naturally expresses his or her spirituality, even if he or she has learned different ways of approaching God throughout the course of his or her spiritual life. This native style can be compared to our mother tongue. Even if we have learned different languages, our mother tongue has an abiding significance. It is the language in which we dream, in which we most adequately express our feelings, in which we feel most secure and comfortable.

Different dialects of the same language

Just as you cannot choose your mother tongue, you cannot choose your native spiritual style. You simply accept what you have been given. It's the only language that you will be able to speak without an accent. The accent that shapes one's mother tongue reveals solely the geographical or cultural home of this mother tongue and shouldn't be confused with a foreign accent.

Spiritual styles function similarly. Every style is displayed in different dialects (variations), which differ considerably from one another. This can lead to serious communication problems even within your own spiritual language. My own style, for instance, is the sacramental style. However, since my spirituality has been strongly shaped by the Protestant wing of Christianity, my own "dialect" is different from that which is spoken, for instance, by my Orthodox or Roman Catholic friends, even if we share the same language.

However, the same dynamics can be encountered in the area of real languages. Though being a native German speaker, I have utmost difficulty understanding

Spiritual styles and language learning

Since our Institute works in about 40 different language areas, it has been indispensable for me to learn foreign languages. Over the past 15 years, I have invested almost one third of my time in the study of languages. While working on the project of which this book is a part, I recorded a series of half-hour mini seminars introducing NCD, in eight new languages. Of course, that required that I learn something about those languages beforehand.

Again and again I am asked why I invest so much time doing this, rather than having a native speaker read the seminars for me. I know that in a foreign language I communicate with a strong and partly dreadful accent, but at least I communicate. By making an effort to express the things that are important to me in a language other than my own, I demonstrate that I am willing to invest a lot of energy in order to move into the terrain of another culture. I am not ashamed of my strong accent. Listeners notice how hard it is for me to speak some languages. At the same time, they notice how important it is for me to express myself in their categories, rather than to jabber away in my native tongue.

I confess, however, that my major motivation to study languages is not so much the goal of communicating with others. I don't do it primarily for other people, but for myself. Once I have learned to express the same key term or the same paradigm in different languages, which I do all the time when writing a book like this, I understand myself better. I have discovered that my study of languages has helped me immensely in my work on spirituality, which surprised me at first, but now makes a lot of sense. When studying foreign languages,

I train the same mental and emotional "muscles" that I need in order to connect with God through different spiritual styles.

The analogy between languages and spiritual styles is striking. For instance, I arranged the eight new languages that I explored, plus my native tongue, in a circular way—similar to the layout of the nine spiritual styles of the Trinitarian Compass. In this language diagram, I distinguished three language groups (northern, western, and eastern languages) and placed two of the languages in each category. Then I positioned three languages exactly on the borderlines between the geographical classifications. I distinguished neighbor languages (in my case, Dutch and Danish) and languages that are opposite my native tongue (Indonesian, Korean). All that I learned from this exercise, I could apply one-to-one to the way I deal with spiritual styles.

In language learning I encountered a phenomenon that, in relation to spiritual styles, I would like to call "style projection." When I communicate with someone in a language other than my own, I frequently have difficulty understanding the words, so I have to ask people to explain them to me. Those who have experience with foreign languages are usually quick to express the same thought in other words, or they repeat what has been said at a considerably slower pace. Monolingual people, on the other hand, tend to use exactly the same wording as before, but they increase their volume considerably! And if I should again inquire what they mean, they actually start to shout at me. This same phenomenon of (well-meant) shouting can be encountered in the area of spiritual styles.

> ## In foreign languages I communicate with a strong accent, but at least I communicate.

some of the German dialects. It's remarkably easier for me to understand a foreign language that I have learned relatively well—such as English—than certain dialects of my own native tongue.

The pain of language learning

Your mother tongue is the only language that you will learn without effort, without vocabulary memorization, without grammar drills, without pronunciation training. None of that is necessary, since it comes "naturally" for a native speaker. However, when foreigners attempt to learn your mother tongue, they have to take an entirely different approach to learning. It's painful to learn a foreign language. It requires the courage to humble and expose yourself. If you express your honest feelings in a language that you don't really master, you make yourself vulnerable. Without the willingness to make this sacrifice, without a considerable degree of self-discipline, and without continuity in your learning efforts, you cannot expect to make any significant progress in your language learning endeavor. I need not stress that the same applies in the area of learning spiritual styles as well.

There is no doubt that both in your native tongue and in foreign languages ongoing training is useful. However, in the area of your native tongue this training will be altogether different than in foreign languages. When I want to improve my German, I read poetry, 16th century literature, highly complex textbooks, and study drama and opera lyrics. When I want to improve my Danish, I read the Danish newspaper, watch Danish TV, or repeat relatively simple sentences from a CD. Both approaches are considered language learning, but they follow completely different means.

In the age of globalization there is one dimension of language learning that has much more to do with spirituality than it may appear at first sight. When you communicate with other people, do you expect them to use your native language, or are you willing (and prepared!) to begin to use their language? If we, as a matter of principle, expect others to shift to our language in order to communicate with us, we will almost inevitably develop some sort of imperialistic thinking—"Why on earth is it so difficult for the other person to speak my language? I do it all the time, and it isn't really that hard."

The challenge to discover your mother tongue

However, there is one decisive difference between mother tongues and native spiritual styles. We all know what our mother tongue is. In most cases it is identical with the language of our environment. This is not necessarily true when it comes to spiritual languages:

- First of all, the *spiritual language of your environment is usually not identical with your spiritual mother tongue.* For example, it's illusory to believe that the spiritual language that is spoken in your own church, is automatically your native language. Confusing these two categories is probably one of the greatest blockages to spiritual growth.

- Second, there is no one who doesn't know his or her mother tongue, but only a minority of Christians know their native spiritual style. Nobody would ever imagine investing time in order *to "discover" their own mother tongue.* When it comes to spiritual styles, however, we often have to begin with such a discovery process. The good news is that it is really not that hard to identify your native spiritual language.

The Jesus rule

While it can be confusing to present Jesus as a model for each of the individual styles (see page 31), without a doubt, Jesus taught—and practiced—the very concerns incorporated into the Trinitarian Compass. Did Jesus, then, teach the "three colors?" He certainly did, and he did it both in his words and his deeds.

A prime example is Jesus' answer to the teacher of the law, who asked him for the "greatest commandment" (Mk. 12:28-31). This question—and the answer Jesus provided—is at the center of the whole biblical message. Jesus' answer is: "Hear, O Israel, the Lord our God, the Lord is one. Love the Lord your God with all your heart and with all your will and with all your mind and with all your strength. The second is this: Love your neighbor as yourself."

The creed that God is one

Jesus begins his answer with the creed that every Jew was accustomed to repeating every morning and every evening: "Hear, O Israel, the Lord our God, the Lord is one" (Deut. 6:4). The proclamation of the "oneness" of God is not only central to the Jewish faith, but also to the Christian faith—and it is of utmost importance for understanding the essence of Christian spirituality.

The fact that God is "one" implies that all attempts to "divide" God are not permissible. However, in the course of church history there have been many attempts to do just that. We have to face the fact that if we select our "favorite color" to describe God and push the other colors aside, this is nothing other than "dividing" God. Of course we don't really divide God—no human being could do that—but we do divide our understanding of God and the range of possibilities for encountering God. This is the most important aspect of spirituality: Spelling out what it means, in practical terms, that God is *one*, not just verbally approving a theological reality.

Jesus rule:

The command of Jesus to love God with all our "heart," with all our "will," with all our "mind"— and, accordingly, with all of our "strength" (Mk. 12:30, see diagram). Since this threefold expression of love for God is at the core of the biblical message, it is given a central place in NCD. We cannot choose to love God more with our heart, will, or mind. All three dimensions must be present (balance), and all three of them should be pursued with all of our strength (radicalness).

The first part: Loving God

After this appeal to God's oneness, Jesus answers the teacher of the law's question in two parts: First, loving God; second, loving others. It should be noticed that in both parts the text speaks about "love." Love always implies getting involved in a personal relationship, approaching the other as a person, and investing in a real-life encounter.

It is noteworthy that the Christian tradition has mainly focused on the second part of this dual command ("Love your neighbor as yourself"). This one-sided tendency has serious consequences. Theologian Helmut Gollwitzer wrote in 1964 that it should be made clear that "community with God is not inferior, but superior to community with other people. How else can we avoid the danger that in the end community with other people is seen as the only community that is real for us, and God is only the metaphysical reference point that is supposed to stress the importance of charity? According to this concept, it is no longer possible for love to flow back and forth between God and humans, when God has been reduced to a mere term. On the basis of this,

... with all your mind

**Mark 12:30:
Love the Lord
your God ...**

... with all your heart

... with all your will

In Mark 12:30 Jesus answers the question about the "greatest commandment" by stressing that we should love God with all our heart (blue), with all our will (red), and with all our mind (green). And we should do that with "all our strength." In other words: not a little bit of our heart, or a little bit of our will, or a little bit of our mind, but a balance of all three that displays that we have invested all we have in every single area (yellow arrows).

it is only consistent that some Protestant theologians—in strict contrast to the whole Old and New Testament—have declared that we have to direct our love not to God, but to our neighbor."

Love for our neighbor—charity—is indispensable, but it is never a replacement for loving God. If people claim that they express their "love for God" exclusively through their "love toward other people," they are entrapped in the misconception that Helmut Gollwitzer highlighted. In Jesus' answer, there is not the slightest hint that love for people is supposed to substitute love for God.

Quite the contrary. Jesus specifies how we are to love God. It shall be expressed with "all your heart," "with all your will" (another possible translation: "all your soul"), with "all your mind," and with "all your strength." *Heart, will,* and *mind* are terms that are at the very center of what the colors blue (heart), red (will) and green (mind) are meant to symbolize. It cannot be any other way, as the Trinitarian Compass has been developed around this and other central biblical teachings. It is meant to be an instrument that helps us learn to love God through all "three channels," and with "all our strength," in other words, radically. The concept of "radical balance" (page 16) has its foundations here.

Note that Jesus doesn't say: "The most important thing is that you love God with your heart. Mind and will are less important." Neither does he say: "Some people love God with their heart, others with their will, still others with their mind. How wonderful!" Nor does he say: "Love God a little bit with your heart, a little bit with your will, and a little bit with your mind." Rather, he overtly states that he expects complete commitment ("all of your strength") in all three areas from all Christians. Jesus' command is the greatest motivation for

What's our part, what's God's?

Many Christians have difficulty connecting the word "love" with the command "you shall." Especially in those cases where our understanding of love has been more strongly shaped by Hollywood than by the biblical concept of love, we tend to see love as an overpowering feeling that may emerge, if we are lucky, just in time to disappear in the same mysterious way as it has come. That has nothing to do with our will, and it is definitely nothing that could be commanded.

The biblical concept of love, however, is different. Throughout the whole New Testament, love is something that appeals to our will. Love doesn't consist of overpowering feelings, but of concrete deeds. Thus love—both for God and for human beings—can be demanded of us.

However, it is not just Hollywood that has had a negative effect on our notion of "love for God." Particularly in Protestant groups there can be enormous reluctance to speak about the human part of our relationship with God. Their concern is that paying attention to the human side could deviate us from the reality of God's omnipotence. They fear that this could open the doors to "righteousness by works:" the erroneous belief that we can earn God's grace by our good deeds.

This concern is justified, but the conclusions that these groups have drawn, are not. Jesus himself prompted us to love God with all of our heart, all of our will, and all of our mind. Henri Nouwen expressed it in these words: "Jesus tells us to set our hearts on the kingdom. Setting our hearts on something involves not only serious aspiration but also strong determination. A spiritual life requires human effort." And Richard Foster specifies, "The opposite of grace is works, but not effort." Grace is opposed to earning, not to effort.

In fact, it can be shown that nothing inspires and enhances effort like the experience of grace. Biblically speaking, good deeds don't make "a good Christian," rather, the believer justified by faith produces good deeds, just as a good tree bears good fruit. If good deeds (fruit) are lacking, it is an indication that something is wrong with the tree. It can be demonstrated that those theological traditions that exclusively stress the work of God, while ignoring the work of his children, usually rank relatively low in "passionate spirituality."

It is not our task to produce love in our own strength. Our task is to identify and remove all that which hinders the overflow of the love that God has poured out in our hearts (Rom. 5:5). John Ortberg explains this dynamic with the following analogy: "Think of the difference between piloting a motorboat and a sailboat. I can run a motorboat all by myself. All I have to do is start the engine. I am in control. But a sailboat is a different story. I can hoist the sails. I can steer with the rudder. But I am utterly dependent on the wind. My job is simply to do those things that will enable me to catch the wind when it comes." And he adds, "Spiritual transformation is like piloting a sailboat."

This is a wonderful image that describes both God's and our human responsibility. We cannot make the wind blow, but we do have to hoist the sails if the wind is going to take effect.

> **We cannot make the wind blow, but we do have to hoist the sails if the wind is going to have effect.**

addressing the concept of the "opposite pole," which will be dealt with in the third part of this book. We cannot afford to entrench ourselves in our own native style. Jesus' challenge is that all three colors should shine through the life of every believer.

The second part: Love your neighbor

After having spoken about our love for God, Jesus commands us to love our neighbor. While this command doesn't take the place of the first one, it is the inevitable consequence of our love for God. We cannot keep the first command without keeping the second command as well; love for God and charity complement one another.

Love for God is vertical and love for your neighbor is horizontal. As I mentioned in the introduction (page 8), loving your neighbor is of such importance that I have devoted a whole book of the *NCD Discipleship Resources* series to that theme: *The 3 Colors of Love.*

How do the spiritual styles relate to the "Jesus rule?"

The nine spiritual styles are not meant to be an exegesis of the "Jesus rule." Rather, Jesus' teaching, summed up in the "Jesus rule," is the foundation of the central idea behind the Trinitarian Compass (i.e. radically balanced spirituality).

The "Jesus rule" makes it impossible for us to simply choose our favorite style—or our favorite color—and to stay there for the rest of our lives. However, this has become common practice in Christianity. I have repeatedly heard people say, "The most important thing is to love God with your heart. Head knowledge doesn't lead us anywhere." Or, "The most important thing is one's will (or one's mind)." These well-meaning statements must be called unbiblical. They are not just questionable, they have serious practical consequences as well.

"All by itself" principle:

Key principle of Natural Church Development that comes out of the parable of the growing seed (Mark 4:26-29). Our task is not to "make" growth happen, but rather to remove man-made obstacles to growth. Then, the church is able to grow "all by itself." On a practical level, in NCD this principle is expressed by the "six growth forces:" interdependence, multiplication, energy transformation, sustainability, symbiosis, and fruitfulness.

Practical consequences

Some time ago I heard about a woman whom I will call Anna. Anna was one of those people who claimed to love God "with all her heart." She even spoke about the will and the mind with a certain amount of disdain. Tragically, Anna got cancer. She underwent medical therapy and was making good progress. The prognosis was promising. At the same time, she attended a Christian group that was just as one-sidedly "blue" as she was herself. They prayed for Anna's supernatural healing, and the leader declared her "healed." He instructed her to discontinue her medical treatment immediately. Anna did so—and soon after she was dead, which is not difficult to explain medically.

I don't doubt that Anna—along with the caring group who prayed for her—loved God "with all their heart." We shouldn't blame them for that. They put their faith in God's supernatural healing power. That was not a mistake, but a wonderful expression of their love for God. Unfortunately, they refused to love God with "all their mind" and "all their will." It's not simply that they didn't "think enough," but they didn't *love* God enough. It was their love deficit—i.e. their partial love for God—that finally killed Anna. The Jesus rule of radical balance is more than an abstract principle; it can literally become an issue of life or death.

Spiritual styles and spiritual traditions

Spiritual styles—as described in this book—must not be confused with spiritual traditions. It is possible to be part of a specific spiritual tradition that focuses on one or more of the spiritual styles, without representing those styles yourself. This distinction is of utmost importance. People who conclude that because they belong to a Pentecostal church they must have the "enthusiastic style," have completely misunderstood the point of our spiritual style typology.

The goal of the Spiritual Style Test (page 64) is not to identify the "tradition" to which you belong, but rather your *personal* antenna to God. This may be shaped by your spiritual tradition, but it is not exclusively determined by it. It can be demonstrated that within all of the spiritual traditions, just as in all denominations, there are a range of believers representing each of the nine spiritual styles (more details in the box on page 42).

Spiritual tradition:

"Spiritual tradition" must not be confused with "spiritual style." Most Christians have been shaped by a particular spiritual tradition, many of which are linked to a specific denomination, while others are interdenominational in nature. Most of these spiritual traditions favor one or more of the nine spiritual styles. However, the fact that a believer has been influenced by a specific tradition doesn't mean that he or she has automatically adopted it as his or her native style. In most cases, this doesn't apply.

Denominations and spiritual styles

In the graphic I have taken the risk of assigning different denominational traditions to different spiritual styles. This is a bit dangerous, since, without explanation, it could convey the idea that the traditions mentioned are exclusively associated with the corresponding spiritual styles. However, the fact is that while the styles associated with each of the denominational traditions are stronger within those traditions, they are by no means the exclusive focus, either theologically or practically. We are talking about *tendencies*, not about putting churches in static boxes. The result of our research would indicate that the *majority* of the members of a specific denomination do *not* have the style that characterizes that denomination as a whole. How's that for an interesting empirical observation with dramatic, far-reaching consequences?

While speaking about this graphic to church leaders I made an interesting observation. Most church leaders don't like to place their churches onto a diagram such as this. They claim that their church represents "the whole," which is true, to a certain degree. However, it is so natural for a church to prioritize one or more styles that they no longer even notice they are doing it. Obviously, all of us tend to regard those elements that shape our identity as a Christian, not as something that should be considered as one of many "spiritual styles," but as a central feature of Christianity. This simply reflects the self-perception of people in general.

Take a closer look at the diagram. Notice, for instance, that it allocates Orthodox churches (together with Roman Catholic churches) to the blue-green style family which is characterized by a special appreciation for the sacramental life. Word-orientation (which is typical for the color red) is not absent in these churches. Every Orthodox or Roman Catholic will affirm the importance of "the Word" within their church. However, *compared to other traditions*, for

This graphic describes the tendencies of different traditions: Orthodox and Roman Catholic churches tend to focus on the sacramental (blue-green) dimension; protestant and fundamentalist churches usually focus on doctrine (green-red); evangelicals and Pentecostals are characterized by a high appreciation for the holiness movement (red-blue).

instance Protestant churches, this dimension is given lower priority. As long as our thinking is limited by our own tradition, these nuances may not even present themselves in our minds. We are only able to identify them once we take a step backwards and begin to evaluate our church tradition within the context of all Christian traditions.

The bonding power of styles

It is easy to describe the spirituality of individual Christians according to the unifying and distinguishing features of the denomination to which they belong. For instance, Baptists have certain things in common that distinguish them from Pentecostals and from Roman Catholics. However, we can identify the unifying and separating factors according to spiritual styles just as easily, so that the classification transcends the denominational borderlines. According to this perspective, all Christians with a mystical style (whether they are Baptists, Pentecostals, or Catholics) form one group; Christians with a rational style (regardless of their church membership), a second group, and so on.

Sometimes the unifying power of the spiritual styles is more easily perceived than the distinguishing factors of the denominational identity. The Baptist with a mystical style may identify more with the Pentecostal or Catholic who shares that same style than, say, with a fellow Baptist who has the rational style.

At interdenominational conferences, I like to make extensive use of these dynamics in order to demonstrate, as graphically as possible, how the body of Christ functions. When we work in groups, I put the Lutheran bishop with a rational style in the same group as the Pentecostal youth leader who also has a rational style; the Methodist pastor with an enthusiastic style is in the same group as the Catholic priest who also has an enthusiastic style, etc. Of course, the way each one expresses his or her individual style may differ considerably

How are the styles distributed?

For the preparation of this book our Institute conducted extensive research on spirituality. A survey encompassing 133 different items was filled out by 3602 people from 62 countries and 71 different denominations. The scientific evaluation of this data revealed empirically verifiable realities that had previously met with varying, even contradicting opinions in Christian literature.

Now we are, for the first time, able to answer questions like these: Are spiritual styles distributed differently among women and men? Among different cultures? Within different church traditions? Is there a relationship between age and spiritual styles? Between maturity and spiritual styles? How are the spiritual styles distributed amongst evangelical, charismatic, and liberal churches? What is the distribution of the styles in every single denomination?

In an attempt to reduce the net result of this research to the most significant points, I have come up with the following four observations:

First, in every denomination researched (and also in every movement shaped by a specific tradition) we identified all nine spiritual styles, without exception. Among Pentecostals, just as among Baptists and Catholics, we can find all nine styles. All nine styles can be found both among "charismatics" and "noncharismatics." In order to learn from other styles, we don't have to search beyond our own movement: We can find all nine options within our own tradition.

Second, as might be expected, the distribution of the nine styles differs within various denominations. For instance,

> **Among Pentecostals, just as among Baptists and Catholics, we can find all nine styles.**

within the Roman Catholic Church, 23% of the active members have a sacramental style; among the Assemblies of God, 29% have an enthusiastic style; within The Salvation Army, 20% have an ascetic style (in each case significantly higher than the average of 11.1%). Clearly the styles favored by the various traditions have greater representation.

Third, while this observation is true for denominations as a whole, it does not necessarily apply to the individual churches that are a part of these denominations. There are, for instance, Pentecostal churches in which styles other than the enthusiastic style are most strongly represented. It is also true that the sacramental style is not necessarily the most represented style within every Roman Catholic parish.

Fourth, and most significant, even if the style that is theologically favored in a given church is more strongly represented, the majority of believers within that church have a different style. For instance, if, on average, 29% of the members of Pentecostal churches have the enthusiastic style (which is a very high percentage), the overwhelming majority of Pentecostals (71%) do not have that native style. In the same way, if you meet a Roman Catholic, you shouldn't assume that he or she has the sacramental style, since 77% of all Catholics (more than three quarters!) have other styles. This insight can prevent an ideological interpretation of the results.

If you are interested in some more research details, please visit the following web site:

www.3colorsofyourspirituality.org.

from denomination to denomination. The Lutheran expresses his rational style differently than the Pentecostal; the Methodist, her enthusiastic style differently from the Catholic.

Factors contributing to the formation of a spiritual style

A spiritual style is a God-given antenna for the divine; however, it does not appear in a vacuum. There are various factors that contribute to the formation of a spiritual style. The most important ones are the following:

- *Your denomination:* Even if every denomination encompasses nine styles, the fact that certain styles are emphasized more than others shapes the spirituality of every member. You grow up with certain styles that you tend to regard as more "natural" than others.

- *A specific tradition/movement:* Often movements or traditions within denominations are more influential than the denominations themselves. People who feel at home in these movements, don't necessarily represent the featured styles, but they feel comfortable in the midst of people who have those styles. That in turn shapes their spirituality.

- *Your theological persuasion:* Even though theological positions should not be confused with spiritual styles, we can clearly see how theological persuasion does influence the way in which we express our relationship with God. Conversely, the theological persuasion that tends to appeal most to us depends, to a certain degree, on the spiritual style we prefer.

- **The style of the church that initially helped you become a believer:** The spiritual family who helped you get started on your Christian journey often has a formative influence on you. This applies to your physical family as well. These influences are even greater if the relationships have included deliberate discipleship processes.

- *Your geographical location:* Even though all nine spiritual styles can be found in all cultures, our initial research indicates that some cultures have a greater tendency to certain styles than others.

- *Your mentality and gender:* Without a doubt, innate characteristics of mentality and gender influence the way we express our spirituality, but they should not be overestimated. For example, people who are extremely "sensory" in almost all areas of their lives, may not display the sensory style when it comes to their relationship with God.

Interdenominational:

Natural Church Development is interdenominational, i.e. members of very different denominations can get involved with NCD without compromising their own traditions. This is due to the fact that NCD doesn't feature the specifics of a certain tradition, but universal principles that define what all healthy churches have in common. However, the fact that NCD can be utilized cross-denominationally does not mean that every believer should be "interdenominational" (as I consider myself to be). Rather, our goal should be to implement the principles of Natural Church Development within the framework of our own denomination or movement.

The role of theology

There are many examples of authors developing theological teachings to defend their own spiritual style. I believe that theology shouldn't be used like that. Rather than justifying our own style—which always includes our own one-sidedness—theology should offer critical corrections. It should never justify our own imbalance, but help us and others achieve greater balance. The personal spiritual style that all theological authors have should never tempt them to place that style at the theological center.

Level A and Level B growth

It is quite probable that many, if not most readers will regard the discovery of their own spiritual style as the "real message" of this book. For me as the author this is a bit frustrating, as my goal goes far beyond that. My goal is to launch a spiritual growth process that would see believers discover "unity in the faith and in the knowledge of the Son of God and become mature, attaining to the whole measure of the fullness of Christ" (Eph. 4:13).

Level A growth:

The phase within the spiritual growth process that leads, metaphorically speaking, from "childhood" to "adolescence." In this phase, we discover our spiritual home, our mother tongue, our identity. This is an indispensable prerequisite for "Level B growth." The problem for many believers is either that they never get to Level A (i.e. according to our metaphor, they remain in the condition of dependent infants) or, if they do reach Level A, they remain in that stage for the rest of their lives. People who have reached Level A have made considerable progress, but have not yet reached the goal of spiritual development.

The business of spiritual entertainment

I know even now—long before this book will be on the shelves—that we will be receiving many e-mails each week asking why the Spiritual Style Test (page 64) isn't sold separately, presumably without the "cumbersome addendum" of this book. What people are really looking for is not a continual spiritual growth process, but rather a nice, entertaining session (albeit, on a lofty, intellectual and spiritual level!) for next Tuesday evening. And it is certainly possible to use the test for such a purpose.

The reason we don't offer the test separately is that we maintain the conviction that while such events may appear "eye opening" at a superficial level, i.e. most of the participants will go home with extremely positive feelings, the sustainable effects come close to zero. And as soon as the positive feelings of the initial discovery have faded, everyone will be looking for yet another emotional high. Maybe this time a Spiritual Gift Test?

Different levels of maturity

Throughout this book, I distinguish two levels of maturity, which, for the sake of simplicity, I refer to as *Level A growth* and *Level B growth*. These two levels are contrasted with each other in the graphic. Both of these levels have certain characteristics that appear to be in opposition, but are in reality complementary:

- Level A focuses on our **maximum factor.** We identify and develop our strengths. Level B, on the other hand, focuses on our **minimum factors**; it deals with our weaknesses, our dark side, our sin.

- Level A is characterized by a **spirituality of dwelling**. Reaching this level creates feelings of security, stability, and groundedness. You feel like you have "come home." In contrast, Level B is all about a **spirituality of seeking**: You take risks, you question the things that are familiar to you, you make yourself vulnerable. You feel like you are traveling into a foreign country.

- Level A focuses on the **"I"**: You discover your own identity, you build spiritual self-esteem, you look out for people who function as you do. In contrast, Level B has a **"we"** focus: You view yourself from the perspective of another person, you sense how much you are in need of being complemented by others, you seek out people who function entirely different than you do.

- Level A **defines your comfort zone**: Usually it is fun to reach this level. Here you feel at ease, you feel close to God, you feel secure. In contrast,

The relationship between Level A and Level B growth: According to this graphic, the goal is not to abandon Level A (i.e. your spiritual dwelling) in order to live exclusively at Level B (i.e. interacting with opposite styles). Rather, as you experiment with other styles, you increase your ability to live out your native style with greater effectiveness and maturity. Thus, Levels A and B are in constant interrelation with each other.

Level B is targeted on **stretching your comfort zone**. This only works if you are willing to move into areas of discomfort, which you might even sense as threatening.

- Level A can be defined as **spiritual formation**: Your spiritual experiences are intensified, you become more of what you have already been. In contrast, Level B deals with **spiritual transformation**: The focus is not on the intensification of the familiar, but on integration of what is still strange to you. In the course of this process, you will literally become a different person.

- On Level A **you are the center** of attention, which can be a helpful perspective at times. Your own spiritual style is placed at the center of your spiritual universe. In contrast, Level B changes this perspective dramatically: Here, not you, but **God is the center**, and you realize that you are just one among a multitude of people who approach God in different ways.

Goal: a matured Level A

The arrows that connect the two levels (see diagram above) indicate that the goal is not to leave Level A completely (your spiritual dwelling), but rather to mature in your own spiritual style. For example, if your own style is the enthusiastic style and you are working on the rational style as your opposite style in Level B, then the desired outcome of the process is not that you experience God in exactly the same way as representatives of the rational style. Rather, you will be integrating those elements of the rational style into your enthusiastic style, which counterbalance deficits in your current relationship with God.

In my work across many different traditions and styles I have experienced that the approaches to spirituality that are furthest away from your experiences always remind you of what is underdeveloped in your own faith. The challenge, then, is not simply to take over this aspect from the other spiritual style (including its theology and all the other elements in that "package"), but to re-invent it in the categories of your natural spiritual language. That is what Level B learning is all about.

This kind of learning should not be confused with a relativistic approach that may result in taking neither one's own spiritual style nor the opposite spiritual style seriously. These people may philosophize eloquently about integration and wholeness, but their own life is no longer characterized by passion. They pick up what is popular from both poles, and lay aside that which seems to be cumbersome. Thus, they mix their personal theology cocktail, a privatized religion of arbitrariness, a pseudo-ecumenical syncretism. The following pages will make it overly clear that this is definitely not our goal.

Childhood, adolescence, maturity

Take a look at the graphic. Once again we see the two levels of spiritual growth, Level A and Level B. Reducing the graphic to these two levels could convey the wrong idea that every believer is already on Level A and that the goal is simply to initiate the appropriate interplay between Level A and B. The truth is, however, that most Christians are nowhere near Level A. For them it would be counterproductive to pursue Level B growth right away. Before you can meaningfully interact with other styles, you must know and be secure in your own style.

Level B growth:

The stage of the spiritual growth process that can only take place when a believer has already reached Level A. In this phase Christians are led from "adolescence" in Level A to adulthood. This can only be reached by leaving one's spiritual comfort zone time and again. Inevitably, Level B growth implies some kind of pain, which is necessary to reach maturity. This is the phase in which you must interact with those styles that are opposite your native style. The reason that "spiritual resilience" is rarely seen in Christianity is that only a minority of believers have reached this stage (Level B) of spiritual growth.

The diagram therefore distinguishes three levels: Level 0 (childhood), Level A (adolescence), and Level B (maturity). Every level requires completely different actions in order to reach the next stage. If someone is on Level 0 and this book helps him or her proceed to Level A, this is real and important spiritual progress. People who have already reached Level B should never speak condescendingly about Level A. Reaching Level A is an absolutely necessary stage of the spiritual journey.

No one questions it when children (Level 0) define who they are primarily or even exclusively through their parents. It would be wrong to expect anything different. But nobody should stay on that level for the rest of their lives. At some point, we need to look critically at our parental heritage and ask ourselves: Who am I? That is the predominant question of adolescence. It is a good, correct, and absolutely necessary question.

However, we must not stay at that level our whole life. There are countless believers who have reached Level A and never moved on from there. That is similar to a person who never leaves puberty. If we stay on Level A our whole life, we may be convinced that we are becoming increasingly more spiritual, while in fact we are simply becoming increasingly self-pleasing and judgmental—what Mark Twain called "a good man in the worst sense of the word."

Why most Christians never reach Level B

It's really not overly difficult to reach Level A. Properly done, a single weekend can be sufficient to catapult your spiritual growth from Level 0 to Level A. With Level B, it's a different story. It is a process that requires a lot of time. Strictly speaking, it is a life-long, never ending process.

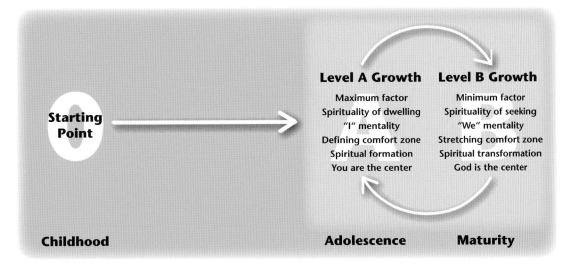

The starting point of many believers is neither Level A nor Level B, but rather what is proposed in this graphic as Level 0: They haven't discovered their own spiritual style or they have taken over their "parents'" style without ever asking if it fits them. For these people it would be disastrous to "jump" immediately into Level B. To get started, they must first discover their native style and feel secure in it.

Why are relatively few Christians willing to get involved in Level B growth? The answer is not difficult. While reaching Level A is fun and accompanied by positive feelings, progressing toward spiritual maturity (what we call Level B) does not necessarily correspond with "spiritual well-being," as the psychologist Steven S. Sandage has discovered. He writes, "Gains in spiritual maturity often fail to provide the immediate gratification or dramatically increased well-being that are more common with initial conversions... The slower and harder work for maturity may also yield gains in well-being, but the effects can often be more subtle and come with tolerating greater complexity and ambiguity. This also suggests that, for many people, spiritual maturity may not become a goal until their level of intensification reaches critical mass and the anxiety of a growth cycle becomes preferable to maintaining an unsatisfactory status quo."

The obstacle of "positive thinking"

Hardly anything has had a more counterproductive effect on Level B growth—and thus on spiritual maturity—than the ideology of "positive thinking." To be sure, if we could only choose between always seeing the positive and always seeing the negative, the positive approach is, of course, far more healthy. However, they are not alternative options. In most areas of life—including spirituality—it is important to deal with both our positive and our negative sides. The primary focus should certainly be on the positive, but the negative must never be ignored.

In Scripture we don't find one-sided "positive thinking." The biblical image of humanity portrays both dimensions—the positive *and* the negative. People who exclusively see the positive are in danger of suppressing their own shadows. When we are speaking about our spirituality—and this word is meant to imply more than just a superficial wellness strategy—we have no choice other than to face up to what Scripture calls "sin."

Three possibilities for approaching the opposite pole

As I will describe in more detail in part 3 of this book, the core of Level B growth is interaction with the spiritual style that is positioned directly opposite your native style—the style that is most remote from your natural way of experiencing God.

As we do this, we should never forget that interaction with the opposite pole is merely a means to an end. The real goal is to move closer to the "center" (i.e., closer to God). The function of the opposite pole is simply to give us a road map to the center.

Expressed in the symbolic language of the Trinitarian Compass, there are basically three possibilities for getting closer to the center:

The first option is a direct, head-on interaction with the respective counter pole (i.e. opposite styles). The strength of this approach is that it is always the direct counter pole that sheds light on the shadows of our own spirituality. As people deal with their opposite style they automatically deal with their dark side, with their sin.

This approach may be too direct, or perhaps too hasty for some Christians. They are thoroughly willing to interact with spiritual styles somewhat different to their own, but thinking of their opposite pole may be too frightening for them in the beginning. In this case, I would recommend the second option, which is to interact with one of your two "neighbor styles." Although they are relatively close to your own spiritual experience, they are different enough to provide you with sufficient challenges for spiritual growth. Once you have done this, you may wish to focus on the neighbor style of your neighbor style. Applying this procedure, you can gradually work your way over time through to your opposite style.

Although this option takes considerably more time than the first one, it will gradually bring you to your destination: closer to the center. This option is not explicitly featured in this book; however, if you should decide to follow this path, you can simply apply all of the instructions regarding interaction with your opposite style, to your neighbor style.

I would like to mention a third option, which at present is really a dream for the future, but may be a realistic possibility when enough Christians are familiar with the Trinitarian Compass. Interaction with one's opposite style is based on dialogue, which is a real improvement over the monologue of staying in your own spiritual style. But there is a third dimension that could enhance the process even more.

For the future I envision what I would like to call "trialogues of learning." Starting from your own spiritual style on the Trinitarian Compass, you would draw an equilateral triangle with each point three styles away from the other. Then you would proceed to interact with those two opposing styles simultaneously.

This kind of trialogue helps us avoid the danger of lumping together everything that is outside of our own style ("us-versus-them" mentality), by experiencing that the differences between the styles outside my comfort zone are as wide as the differences between my world and the world of the others.

> **The function of the opposite pole is simply to give us a road map to the center.**

The perils of each spiritual style

Our native spiritual style and our dark side are two sides of the same coin. The strength that is expressed through every style is, at the same time, the point at which we are most tempted to sin. One of the most important things we have to learn is that these perils differ from style to style and from person to person:

- The peril of the *sensory style* is **hedonism**. Your own positive feelings—experienced through your senses—become so important for you that you have difficulty experiencing God outside of what you consider "beautiful."
- The peril of the *rational style* is **intellectualism**. Only those aspects of God that have successfully passed through the filter of your own logical system of explanation, are approved as valid.
- The peril of the *doctrinal style* is **dogmatism**. Faith is largely reduced to your assent to certain doctrines, while personal encounter with God is moved to the background.
- The peril of the *Scripture-driven style* is **biblicism**. The written Word is virtually considered God's only means of communication; the "book" can almost take the place of God.
- The peril of the *sharing style* is **iconoclasm**. Material expressions of faith found in the Christian tradition are exclusively seen as obstacles, rather than aids to faith.
- The peril of the *ascetic style* is **escapism**. Since the world is primarily viewed as negative, the tendency is to equate "less world" with a deeper experience of God.
- The peril of the *enthusiastic style* is **emotionalism**. There is the danger that openness to the trans-rational dimension of our encounter with God slides into the irrational.
- The peril of the *mystical style* is **spiritualism**. What people perceive as "inner voices" can be equated with the "voice of God" without any critical evaluation.
- The peril of the *sacramental style* is **ritualism**. The appreciation of physical expressions of spiritual reality can tempt us to mechanically practice outer forms, without inner involvement.

What is sin?

When thinking of sin, for many people the first image that comes to mind is a married man looking at an attractive woman, or sneaking into a pub around the corner. This reveals a rather superficial understanding of sin. It seems to me that most of us could tackle this dimension of sin with some of our own self-discipline. It is much more difficult, however, to deal with those sins that are directly linked to the strengths of our spiritual styles.

Many people regard sin as the sum of individual deeds that result from disobedience to God. That is certainly an important aspect of sin, but biblical teaching goes far beyond that. In Scripture, sin is described as that which separates us humans from God and, as a consequence, from other human beings, and finally from ourselves. This concept of sin is at the heart of the Trinitarian Compass. Sin basically describes an obstruction in our relationship with God, which can result in many individual sins (not touched on in this book).

At the deepest level, sin means withdrawal from God, possibly even while expressing our spirituality. As we have seen, this danger of running away from God shows itself differently for every spiritual style. However, in every single case it is connected to a separation from fellow Christians—those who express their faith differently than we do. Sin is the opposite of community. It is separation, isolation, an autistic focus on ourselves, and a breakdown of our openness to God and to meaningful relationships to other human beings.

Different definitions of sin

Every spiritual style—when studied in real-life situations and not in the abstraction of a theological typology—is a mixture of right and wrong, divine and human, faith and superstition, holiness and sinfulness, light and darkness. It cannot be any other way since the representatives of the spiritual styles are human beings. Consequently, our daily challenge is to allow the positive elements to shine more and more so that the darkness is gradually expelled.

This implies each of us should deal primarily with his or her own perils: representatives of the sensory style, with hedonism; representatives of the rational style, with intellectualism; representatives of the doctrinal style, with dogmatism, etc. In reality, however, this doesn't happen. Our tendency is to grossly underestimate the dangers of our own style and to highlight the dangers of the other styles, almost to the exclusion of seeing anything positive in them. This is the reverse of how it should be. As far as our *own* style is concerned, we should sharpen our focus on the perils; as far as the other styles are concerned, we should primarily seek out the positive elements, without being blind to the dangers.

Opposite pole:

The styles furthest away from your native style are referred to as the opposite pole. Every style has a specific position within the Trinitarian Compass. It is important to keep this position in mind in order to determine one's opposite styles. Interaction with the opposite pole is at the center of Level B learning. The opposite pole always points to those aspects that are suppressed or neglected in your own spiritual style. Therefore, interaction with the opposite pole is the key to spiritual maturity.

The beam in our own eye

Take a look at the graphic. In it, I point out the perils of the three color zones: green tends to relativism; red, to legalism; and blue, to subjectivism. However, if you listen to representatives of each color, they will usually emphasize the dangers outside of their own color zone. For example, representatives of green spirituality will point out the legalism of the conservatives (red) or the subjectivism of the charismatics (blue). They are not all wrong, as these *are* real dangers. However, it would be more productive for them personally to deal primarily with the danger of *their* color zone, relativism.

The same thing occurs in the other color zones. Why is it that red representatives speak so frequently against relativism and subjectivism? These are real dangers, but they are definitely not the dangers of the red color zone. It would be more productive for them to deal with the danger of legalism with that same sense of relentlessness.

Rather than facing our own sin, as humans we prefer to speak about those sins that don't really apply to us—the sins of others. In this game, we are all right in what we call "sin." However, we are speaking either to the wrong audience or at the wrong time. According to the Bible, we should be doing the following:

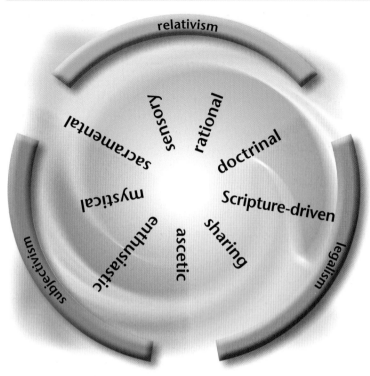

This graphic highlights the perils of the three color zones and consequently of the spiritual styles that are assigned to them. Each of the three terms mentioned (legalism, subjectivism, relativism) becomes a danger for the respective color segment when that is one's exclusive focus. The best way to avoid these perils is to integrate the virtues of the other colors into your own approach to God.

First, we work on improving ourselves—beginning with our strengths (Level A), followed by our weaknesses (Level B). Then, once we have done this, once we have identified the "beam" in our own eye, we can cautiously start to help others discover the "speck" in their eyes (Mt. 7:3). Spiritual maturity implies the ability to face *our* sin, and address it first.

Why we tend to repress our dark sides

People who play down their own sin will become increasingly less critical of themselves. They become self-pleasing, self-satisfied, and self-righteous, which usually leads them to be hyper-critical, harsh, and unloving toward others—toward "sinners." The fact that we don't recognize our own sin results in splitting it off and suppressing it.

Everything we have suppressed scares us. Therefore, fear of our opposite pole can be explained largely by the fact that the opposite style sheds light on our own sin. That's painful, and provokes fear. Naturally, we tend to avoid what we fear. Therefore, we avoid our opposite pole. We feel far more comfortable amongst the like-minded. So, we apply our strengths exclusively, and they become sin to us. It's two sides of the same coin.

How the opposite pole addresses your danger zones

In the table on page 52, I have identified two strengths (column 2) that are the reverse side of two perils (column 3) for each of the nine spiritual styles (column 1). These dangers are the result of neglecting specific aspects of balanced spirituality (column 4). It is quite striking to see how the respective opposite styles

The light metaphor:

The biblical image that describes God as "light" (1 John 1:5), and that which is distant from God as "darkness," is central to the symbolic language of the Trinitarian Compass. Green, red, and blue are nothing other than the three colors of light. The clearer the shade of green, red, and blue, the brighter the light. This understanding has practical implications for the way we deal with "darkness" (e.g. heresy or sin). Darkness has no power of its own. It is simply the absence of light. How can we fight darkness? By letting the light shine. If the light shines brightly, darkness will disappear "all by itself."

Name of style	Strengths	Perils	Neglect	Opposite styles
sensory	• appreciating beauty • enjoying God's creation	• preoccupation with aesthetics • dependency on external things	• service • inner values	• sharing • ascetic
rational	• striving for explanations • utilizing science	• intellectual pride • rationalism	• sacrifical living • the trans-rational dimension	• ascetic • enthusiastic
doctrinal	• emphasizing sound doctrine • relating to dogmatic systems	• faith confused with doctrine • dry abstractness	• personal experiences • nurturing the inner life	• enthusiastic • mystical
Scripture-driven	• faithfulness to the Bible • proclaiming God's Word	• reducing God's Word to Scripture • exaggerated view of the verbal	• listening to your inner voice • physical expressions	• mystical • sacramental
sharing	• focusing on outsiders • evangelizing people	• overlooking the needs of insiders • reducing faith to "soul winning"	• church traditions • God's creation	• sacramental • sensory
ascetic	• freedom from worldly things • sacrificial living	• negative view of the world • irrational suffering	• enjoying God's creation • common sense	• sensory • rational
enthusiastic	• openness to the supernatural • striving to see God's power	• negative view of the natural • accepting unbiblical practices	• scientific reasoning • sound doctrine	• rational • doctrinal
mystical	• cultivating the mysterious • focus on the inner person	• exaggerated view of the mysterious • confusing feelings with God	• logic and systems • Biblical standards	• doctrinal • Scripture-driven
sacramental	• expressing faith physically • appreciating traditions and rites	• magic view of sacraments • insensitivity toward outsiders	• the verbal dimension • the needs of the unchurched	• Scripture-driven • sharing

The table (left) lists the strengths and perils of each style and reveals how interaction with the opposite styles can help counterbalance your own danger zones.

correspond *exactly* to these neglects and perils (column 5). Take time to study this table in more detail.

Dangers cannot be avoided

It is not only unrealistic, but also counterproductive, to avoid the dangers mentioned at all costs. They are inevitable; to a certain degree, they are part of the make-up of the individual spiritual styles. The goal of the growth process is "radical balance" (see page 16), not a reduction of the passion through which we express our respective style. The motto should never be: "Be less radical." In practicing your spiritual style you cannot be radical enough! However, the more radical you are, the more you should strive to integrate the valuable concerns of your opposite style.

Spiritual growth works like a pendulum. Sometimes it swings too strongly to the left, and later on, too strongly to the right. The position in the "middle" is not a mathematically defined standpoint where we could abide without any motion. Rather, it's a theoretical reference point that can help us perceive our unavoidable swings to the right and to the left.

People who are constantly afraid of swinging too far to the right or to the left, won't grow in their faith. Since they focus primarily on the "weeds," which inevitably grow together with the wheat, they tend to pull up the wheat with the weeds (Mt. 13:24-43). We need to identify wheat as wheat and weeds as weeds, consciously acknowledging the weeds as weeds in our own field, without trying to eliminate them right away.

Light and shadow

We have to learn to perceive ourselves with both our light and dark sides. The light shining from our strength cannot illuminate our shaded areas, since this shadow is on the flip side of the coin and cannot be reached by our own light. This dark side can only be illuminated by the light shining from the opposite pole.

The sins connected with our own style should be taken seriously. Above all, we must perceive them in ourselves: I am the person who *has* these feelings, but I *am* not these feelings. This is one of the reasons why I am so vehemently opposed to treating spiritual styles as unchangeable personality traits (page 32). I *have* a style, but I *am* not the style. I may speak a sacramental language, but I am not a sacramentalist. My identity consists of much more than my corresponding thoughts and feelings. In particular, it includes the wonderful opportunity to integrate the strengths of my opposite pole. Then that becomes my identity, my new, transformed identity.

Spiritual pendulum:
Though the goal of spiritual maturity is balance, this doesn't imply that balance is a state that can be statically defined like the "happy medium" between two extremes. In real-life growth processes, it is not only normal, but necessary, that an overemphasis on one side is counter-balanced by an overemphasis on the other side. Of course, both extremes aren't without their dangers; but only through this constantly moving pendulum can we finally expect to achieve spiritual balance.

People who recognize their shadows are not so quick to condemn other people. The sin of the other person reminds us of the complementary sin in ourselves. As long as I try to hide my weaknesses, I am restricted to a relatively superficial kind of communication. Acknowledging my own sin, however, enables me to become transparent and honest in my encounters with others.

The power of purple alligators

"Please, don't think about a purple alligator," I asked the seminar participants. All of them looked at me as if to say, "Why on earth would we think about purple alligators?" I continued, "Now, shut your eyes. Don't think about anything, in particular don't think about purple alligators." Then, I told them to open their eyes. "What did you see when you closed your eyes?"

Each time I have conducted this small exercise, the results have been the same: There was hardly anyone who did not see a purple alligator!

This phenomenon is due to easily explained psychological dynamics. If we intently try to avoid something, we will automatically be attracted to the very thing that we want to avoid. The consequences of this insight are far-reaching: If we want to abstain from sweets, we must not think continually about abstaining from sweets, since this would pre-program our mind to think constantly about sweets and consequently develop the corresponding appetite. Instead, we should say: "I love fruit and vegetables; I would like more fruit, I cannot get enough vegetables." The more we try to fight certain tendencies, the stronger the counter forces.

The same holds true for our handling of sin. If we focus on getting rid of sin, we only increase its power. Our sin becomes a purple alligator, whose inner image follows us everywhere. Rather, our goal should be to perceive the sin on the one hand, but then to focus on the contrary positive attitudes or actions.

Take another look at the table on page 52. For every "peril" (sin) of the respective styles, you will find the name of the opposite style. Let's assume you have the

> **If we focus on getting rid of sin, we only increase its power. Our sin becomes a purple alligator.**

sensory style. If you were to constantly tell yourself, "No hedonism, that's not allowed," hedonism would become your purple alligator. Rather you should focus on one of your opposite styles, for instance, the ascetic style. You could ask yourself, "In what way can I experience God through my senses as part of an ascetic exercise?"

Or, let's assume you tend to the enthusiastic style. It would be counterproductive to constantly say, "No emotionalism, refuse any of those feelings." Rather, you could focus on one of the opposite styles—e.g. the doctrinal style—and ask, "Which image of God does the biblical doctrine portray? What can I learn from this doctrine about God's power, about his will for my life?" This is the way to deal with the opposite pole that is at the heart of what we have called Level B learning. This is the way to deal with the dark side of our native style.

The fact that Scripture connects sin to "darkness" points us in the same direction. We can only "expel" darkness (our own sin) by letting the "light" shine (in this case the positive aspects of the opposite pole). The light that has such a transforming influence on our life, is none other than God's presence. "God is light," says the New Testament, "in him there is no darkness at all" (1 John 1,5).

The presence of light has another important consequence. The more light shines in us, the more likely other people will be able to see God's presence in us. As Richard Foster says, "Our little light (which is not the source of light but only a reflection of the Light—and often a distorted and faint reflection at that) might lead others all the more fully to see Jesus, the Light of the world."

Three spiritual value systems

The process of spiritual growth, as outlined in this book, is certainly not easy. Why should we get involved in it? Because we human beings—all human beings—have been created such that it is not enough for us to have our superficial needs met. Because all of us have the built-in desire to transcend our current state. Because all of us are programmed for spiritual growth. When this does not happen, we become dissatisfied, we may even get sick.

Abraham Maslow has become famous for his hierarchy of human needs, in which he distinguished so-called *basic needs* (among them, security, power, and self-esteem) from each other. Less known is that Maslow also spoke of so-called *meta-needs*, which he also called *B-needs* (for being). These meta-needs include the desire for the True, the Good, and the Beautiful. If these meta-needs are not met, human beings will get just as sick as if their basic needs remain unfulfilled. Maslow calls these diseases "meta pathologies" and defines them as a consequence of the "deprivation of B-values."

Different motivations

When seeking God, some people are driven by their desire for Truth; others, by the desire for what is Good; still others, by the desire for Beauty. Not everyone has the same degree of receptiveness for each of the three dimensions, but everyone is at least receptive toward one of them:

> **Spiritual desires:**
>
> *Different people are motivated by different desires, even in their approach to God. For every believer it is helpful to know the primary desires that motivate us, and those desires that motivate other people. These desires have a close relationship to the nine spiritual styles. Seeking what is "True" is usually connected to the rational, doctrinal, or Scripture-driven style; seeking what is "Good," with the sharing, ascetic, or enthusiastic style; and seeking what is "Beautiful," with the mystical, sacramental, or sensory style.*

- People with a primary orientation toward the **True** are most satisfied if they are given reasons. They are neither overly interested in investing themselves in an implementation process, nor do they appreciate the work of those who do. For them this is pure "pragmatism." In their eyes, striving for the Beautiful—even if they may have an aesthetic antenna—has little to do with knowing the truth. I refer to this orientation as the *dogmatic value system.*

- People with a primary orientation toward the **Good** function differently. They may be bored to death by abstract principles. They tend to view empirical research as "purely academic." They would never even imagine an encounter with God in the midst of it. Moreover, many of them have no antenna for aesthetics. According to their standards, doing the will of God and living a transformed life is what counts. I refer to this orientation as the *ethical value system.*

- People with a primary orientation toward the **Beautiful** also function differently. They can be deeply moved by Bach and Beethoven, by the splendid and noble in the arts, in literature, in religion. It's not only that they feel moved; they experience God in the midst of it. At the same time, they are tempted to downplay all Christian activities that do not meet their sophisticated aesthetical standards. I refer to this orientation as the *aesthetic value system.*

People are looking for meaning

Human beings are created with a longing for the True, Good, and Beautiful. It's rather shallow to assume that people are motivated exclusively by self-interest. When leaders honor us with opportunities to see what is really occurring in the world and support us as we explore the deeper meaning of events, we instinctively reach out to them. When leaders simply appeal to our self-interest, we despise them in the end. As Victor Fankl says, our greatest motivation in life "is not to gain pleasure or to avoid pain, but rather, to see a meaning."

Three kinds of knowledge

All three value systems are concerned with "knowledge," but with different approaches to knowledge. Not only science and theology, but also the arts and action can reveal truth. All three systems are looking for truth. Those who explicitly strive for the True, define truth in a specific, abstract, verbally transmitted manner that appeals primarily to rational knowledge.

All three orientations indwell one another. Aesthetic knowledge can be intensified by rational, scientific knowledge, and both can be deepened by ethical knowledge. We can observe this in musicology. Analytical, scientific knowledge has the goal of supporting knowledge through the senses. As musicologist Hans Heinrich Eggebrecht expresses it, "Rational knowledge enriches the aesthetic play of the senses through reflecting play: It makes the musical soul intelligent." However, both rational and aesthetic knowledge are still restricted to the consumption of music. It is only when we perform music ourselves (in our terms: the ethical dimension) that both the rational and the aesthetic knowledge reach their deepest dimension.

Desiring the True

The dogmatic value system stresses that truth is more than what we experience; truth is truth even if we experience nothing at all. Because of that, representatives of this value system have an instinctive distrust of the subjective. They fear that subjectivism may lead to a self-invented faith, and finally to a self-invented God. They stress the importance of external authority, since a purely internal authority lacks any means of verification.

Dogmatic style family:

The family of styles that is motivated by a search for what is "True" (usually in written and spoken form). This family is made up of the rational, doctrinal and Scripture-driven styles. It is positioned on the interface between the green and the red color zones and thus opposite the blue color zone. Due to that position, there is frequent tension with the blue color zone.

Representatives of this value system appreciate precise terminology much more than rhetorical verve or vivid communication, as those are purely aesthetic criteria. Within this system—depending on whether it leans more to green or to red—scientific or theological proofs are of utmost importance. For these people it is very important that the foundation of the faith is reliable, and that it should be purified from all sentimentality. Terms like "infallible" are typical for this value system. It may stress the infallibility of Scripture or the infallibility of the Pope, but in either case, it is motivated by the desire to create a secure foundation.

Sometimes this orientation appears "negative" to outsiders, as it, more than either of the other value systems, deals with demarcations. These boundaries are, however, nothing other than the necessary consequence of striving for what is True: In order to highlight the truth, we also have to expose that which is not true.

Desiring the Good

Desiring what is Good leads to a primarily ethical orientation. This is evident when we examine the three spiritual styles that are related to this value system.

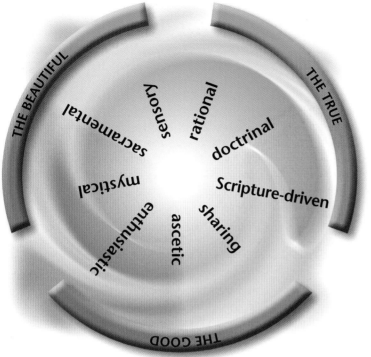

The three major motivators: Seeking the True (green-red), the Good (red-blue), and the Beautiful (blue-green). In this diagram the three desires are the fixed points, the three colors are the spaces in between.

All three styles lean toward purity (and some toward puritanism as well) more than the other styles, as all of them are positioned opposite the green area: the ascetic style (a certain level of detachment from the sensual, material world is at its very heart); the enthusiastic style (acting above and beyond the established rules); and the sharing style (concerned with seeing the effects of transformed lives). The historic holiness movements have their roots in this value system.

Christians with this orientation rightly stress that according to Scripture we have to "do the truth" (John 3:21). Our deeds have to reflect the goodness of God. This kind of "goodness," which implies orientation toward the high standards that God has set, should not be confused with being "merciful," as tends to happen in ordinary language.

Within this value system the ultimate criteria for a Christian is not theory, but practice. How people act in their daily lives is the decisive matter, not what they think about a certain doctrine. The focal point of this system is the visible transformation of life.

Ethical style family:

The family of styles that is motivated by a search for what is "Good" (in the sense of doing what is good). This family is made up of the sharing, ascetic, and enthusiastic styles. It is positioned on the interface between the red and the blue color zones and thus opposite the green color zone. Due to that position, there is frequent tension with the green color zone.

Desiring the Beautiful

While in Protestant circles striving for the True and Good are relatively undisputed value systems, many Protestants, and especially Evangelicals, have difficulty with the third category: striving for the Beautiful. For historical reasons, all that is pictorial, symbolic, ritual, and sacramental has been banned from many churches, since their founders had only seen excessive abuse in these areas. Thus, the whole aesthetic value system is suspected of being "heretical." As if humans only have ears and no eyes, as if there is no need to address the

The three value systems in NCD

We have worked hard to include all three value systems in the Natural Church Development tools.

The **dogmatic value system**, with its focus on truth, is reflected in our tools in two ways: First, through the strong emphasis on empirically verifiable truth. We only call those features "principles" that can be clearly proven by empirical research to be universally applicable. Regardless of how popular they may be, church models have no place in NCD unless there is clear proof that we aren't just speaking about the favorite idea of a successful pastor, but about universally applicable principles. The use of abstract language, when it comes to universal principles, is not a weakness of the system, but a necessity: Principles are nothing other than abstractions. We have to find terms that cover a plethora of extremely different expressions.

However, it is important to understand that the empirical research of NCD serves as descriptive criteria of truth ("This is what we find in growing churches"), not prescriptive criteria ("It should be like this"). All of the empirical data is evaluated in light of biblical, theological standards. Only those elements that have passed the theological truth check are included in the NCD tools. The Trinitarian Compass plays a central role in ensuring we always strive to consider the whole of Scripture, rather than just eclectically picking out our favorite Bible verses.

The **ethical value system** with its practical orientation is demonstrated in NCD by the fact that the question of implementation always plays a decisive role. In a book like this you won't find a single chapter that doesn't have practical relevance for our lives. In other words, the NCD tools are not concerned merely with knowledge and definitely not with spiritual entertainment. The criteria of life transformation—and the transformation of whole churches—is a central criteria of success. By means of empirical research we constantly evaluate whether such a change process is actually achieving growth, and how sustainable it has proven to be.

The **aesthetic value system** introduces criteria such as symmetry, proportion, wholeness, and harmony. This is the background of communicating by means of images. The many graphics in the major NCD books are not, as some people erroneously say, "illustrations" of what has been expressed in words; rather, they are central expressions of the message itself. To a certain degree, the words merely describe the truth that has been expressed in the graphics; what can be seen at a glance, by viewing the pictures, is translated into the linear logic of the verbal.

Since my own spiritual style belongs to the aesthetic style family, it's not hard for me to express myself in this way. When writing a book like this one, the first things I produce are all of the graphics, which I place in their final positions within the empty book layout. Much later, only a few weeks before printing starts, I complement the book with my words. As far as I am concerned (I say this as a representative of the aesthetic style family) we could just as well do without these words. For me, they are not overly important. However, since I communicate to people with other value systems, I communicate verbally as well, but without feeling restricted to it.

> **In our NCD tools we have tried hard to give credit to all three value systems.**

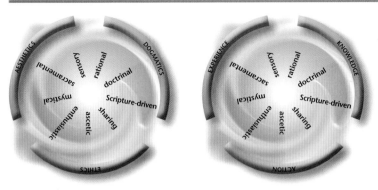

Description of the three style families, which derive from their orientation toward the True, the Good, and the Beautiful. The focus of the dogmatic style family is knowledge; the focus of the ethical style family, action; the focus of the aesthetic style family, experience.

imagination, the emotions, and the senses as well! In its justified quest of correcting errors, the Reformation has been guilty of throwing out the baby with the bath water. For that reason, in some Protestant churches, believers with a primarily aesthetic value system have a hard time finding an approach to spirituality that suits them. In contrast, the Eastern theological tradition has a long history of emphasizing the significance of aesthetic desire for spiritual transformation. In Protestant churches as a whole, this dimension is not absent, but it is usually less developed.

Striving for the Beautiful is not primarily expressed through the activity of the mind in the form of words, conclusions, and judgments, but first of all through our senses. In Greek, *aisthesis* means sensory perception. There is a form of knowledge that doesn't come through words and their rational connection, but directly via the senses.

In this value system, criteria such as symmetry, proportion, wholeness, and harmony play an important role. People who have difficulty with these criteria should be reminded that in the sciences, particularly in physics, beauty is considered a powerful pointer to the truth of a theory. The "elegance" of an equation (expressed by symmetry, proportion, wholeness, and harmony) is often greater evidence of its truth than an experiment would be.

The interrelationship of the three

Take a look at the two graphics above. It is characteristic of Christian understanding that the True, the Good, and the Beautiful form a unified whole. All of them reflect essential attributes of God (see page 25). Though all three systems appeal to human needs, we cannot ignore the fact that we may have to invest considerable energy to access these dimensions:

Aesthetic style family:

The family of styles that is motivated by a search for what is "Beautiful," which is understood as a manifestation of truth. This family is made up of the mystical, sacramental, and sensory styles. It is positioned on the interface between the blue and the green color zones and thus opposite the red color zone. Due to that position, there is frequent tension with the red color zone.

- The dogmatic value system, with its verbal and logical orientation, demands primarily mental work, including a certain degree of abstraction.

- The ethical value system, with its practical orientation targeted on purity, demands the willingness to be self-disciplined, austere, and sacrificial.

- The aesthetic value system demands a continuous development of our aesthetic sense. Aesthetic expressions such as symbols, liturgy, icons, and architecture are not necessarily easily accessible. Without a certain effort to understand these traditions, we won't be able to appreciate the aesthetic approach.

My nine spiritual mentors

There is a simple and effective way to learn about a spiritual style: encounter people who have this style. By this, I don't mean reading books by authors whom we suspect represent this style. Neither do I mean attending churches that are supposedly marked by a specific style.

What I do suggest is that you find an opportunity where there is direct communication between two people, one who represents style A; the other one, style B. In the third part of this book, under the heading of Mutual Mentoring, I will deal with this kind of learning in more detail, showing how fruitful these dialogues can be if performed on the basis of the Trinitarian Compass (page 182).

Mentoring as a lifestyle

My work automatically connects me with Christians from all kinds of spiritual backgrounds. With many of them I have intense, sometimes very personal, communication. I am frequently contacted by people who would like to learn from me, in some way or other. My standard response is, "If time allows, I am more than happy to teach you everything that I know and can, if you are also willing to teach me everything that you know and can." Applying this procedure over the years, a lot of my "students" have become my "teachers." As a result, I have been placed in the midst of a sizzling environment of continual learning, including spiritual learning.

When I began to work on this book I sought out one spiritual mentor for each of the spiritual styles portrayed in this book, in an effort to better understand the essence of each style. In the beginning, I worked with mentors from my immediate circle of friends: people who, while representing the respective styles, displayed them in a way that I could easily relate to. This was a good and "gentle" introduction.

Spiritual mentors:

Almost all spiritual traditions are familiar with the idea of "spiritual mentoring," that is described by different terms, such as spiritual director, discipler, spiritual father, etc. In NCD the term has a narrower, more clearly defined meaning. Spiritual mentoring is always related to spiritual growth processes that are based on the Trinitarian Compass. These mentoring processes are generally less hierarchical in nature and always have an affinity to "mutual learning."

How I selected my mentors

However, before long I sensed that this was not enough. I started to look for more extreme representatives of the individual styles, for expressions of spirituality that were beyond my comfort zone. In the second part of this book I will talk a lot about my mentors. I have placed pictures of them on the graphic. Some readers will be able to identify these people despite the fact that I usually only refer to them by their first name. However, I want to avoid the impression that I am using their names and credibility to somehow "prove" my own thesis. My purpose in referring to them and to my conversations with them is to report on my *own* learning processes, and to portray the respective styles in a narrative way.

When you look at the graphic, you will notice that my mentors are members of nine different denominations, but this is purely coincidental. My goal was not political correctness in terms of denominational representation. I could have learned the essence of the nine spiritual styles equally well from nine Lutherans, nine Baptists, nine Pentecostals, or nine Catholics. Of course, as we have previously seen (page 40), our groundedness in a given church tradition does influence the way we express our styles. However, these differences should not be overestimated. My goal was not

Jack • U.S.A.
Methodist

Thomas • Germany
United

Jonathan • U.S.A.
Orthodox

Gene • U.S.A.
Baptist

sacramental

sensory

rational

doctrinal

Ole • Denmark
Lutheran

mystical

Scripture-driven

Ian • Australia
Anglican

enthusiastic

ascetic

sharing

Olli • Germany
Vineyard

Victor • Asia
Independent

Henrik • England
Salvation Army

For each of the spiritual styles I have selected a mentor who helped me understand the respective style. In my work with these spiritual mentors, I learned that it is not advisable to try to bridge several significant gaps simultaneously (i.e. differences in spiritual styles plus differences in culture, in gender, etc.). For this reason, most of my mentors are Westerners and male, like me, which enabled me to focus 100 percent on the differences in spiritual style.

to learn from the *traditions* that are featured within the different churches, but from the styles of individual people.

Growing in nine different directions—simultaneously

The work with my nine spiritual mentors happened in the context of preparing this book, but not *for* this book. First and foremost, I wanted to learn for myself as a Christian and a human being, not primarily as an author or the leader of NCD International. I wanted to experience first-hand how it feels to move far outside of my comfort zone, not in order to be part of "polite" theological conversations, but to open my heart, to make myself vulnerable, to explore my own shadows. I wanted to learn how it feels to grow in nine different directions simultaneously and, through that very process, to become more "Christlike" (as nothing less than this is the goal of the whole endeavor).

As I refer to my learning process with all nine mentors, my intention is not to motivate you to find nine mentors for yourself. I would actually advise against that. Look for one mentor in the area of your native style, and as soon as you are secure enough in that area, find a mentor in the area of your opposite style. That will give you plenty to do. However, for me, because of my ministry, it wouldn't have been enough. I literally had to immerse myself in each of the nine spiritual styles.

The nature of our communication

I had a series of meetings with each mentor. In most cases, they were live, face-to-face encounters; in other cases, we met through video conferencing. All of our conversations were recorded on video, just by switching on the in-built camera of my laptop—whether we were sitting in a sidewalk café, the subway, a lecture hall, an office, or sipping a late night cup of coffee in the kitchen.

My own style and the message of this book

My theology is, at least I hope, quite balanced. However, I am not. Since I constantly speak about spiritual balance, some fellow Christians have the impression that in my own life all three colors, and thus all nine spiritual styles, are in perfect balance. But my own spirituality is as imbalanced as everybody else's. In contrast to many others though, I am aware of this imbalance. And I make painstaking efforts not to portray my style as the best of all styles nor to build a whole theology around it.

As I mentioned earlier, my native style is the sacramental style, which is located on the borderline between green and blue. Therefore it is only natural that physical expressions (green) of spiritual reality (blue), which are characteristic of this style, speak to me. It explains why I am less responsive to words (red) than to images. It also explains why I, in my own ministry, use primarily visual forms of communication.

Without a doubt, my style helps me to make spiritual realities visible, palpable, and perceptible; in this way it does influence my work. But, never fear, I wouldn't allow myself to place my own spiritual style at the center of my teaching. I want to teach the biblical truth of balance, rather than make my own imbalance the theme of my book (an obsession with one's style is nothing other than that). I definitely don't want to sell you the sacramental style as the best of all styles, but want to help you find your own antenna to God.

When dealing with the theme of spirituality, I have discovered, however, that many authors—maybe even most—don't have a well-developed ability to discriminate in this area. They do exactly what I, for good reasons, hope never to do myself: They build a theology around their own style. Rather than seeing the function of theology as communicating the whole of the biblical message, so that our own one-sidedness is critically questioned, they follow the paradigm that "theology" justifies their one-sidedness, which blinds them to their own shadows, thus making any spiritual correction virtually impossible. Most people do this with the most noble intentions and aren't even aware of the fact that they have become the victims of circular reasoning.

For leaders and teachers, I would consider this procedure unacceptable. Theology should never fulfill the function of justifying our own one-sidedness and then teaching this one-sidedness to others, so that they become more like us. I know that my style is not what everyone needs. For 11 percent of Christians, it is exactly the right thing; for that reason I am going to describe this style in detail in the second part of the book. But 89 percent have a different style and need something different. Therefore, 89 percent of what I write about spiritual styles deals with styles other than the sacramental one.

Of course, all of us are tempted to view the very things that are at the center of our style as being central to the Christian faith. Our style functions as a lens through which we study the Bible. However, I would expect Christian leaders to be continually aware of this trap. It's not the task of teachers to propagate their own favorite ideas. That would be like being a medical doctor who prescribes the same medicine to everyone of his patients because he or she has found it personally helpful.

> **My theology is, at least I hope, quite balanced. However, I am not.**

Later, when I watched the videos again and again, what struck me even more than the words that we exchanged was the look in each mentor's eyes, the gestures they made, what made them smile, cry, or become angry. Asking a person, "What makes you angry?", and listening to their well-articulated answer as to what *should* make them angry, according to their theological paradigm, is completely different to what I saw *really* made my mentors angry, pensive, sad, or upbeat. In this way, I experienced the practical relevance of what Desmond Tutu expresses in the following words: "We bear witness more by what we are than by what we say and even do."

Focus: not theology, but spirituality

Six of my nine mentors have authored books. I had some of these books on hand, I even read a little bit in them, but this was not my main interest. I wanted to learn from each individual the very things that cannot be learned from books. I didn't want to discuss theology with them, I wanted to talk about their personal antenna to God. While this cannot be completely separated from theological convictions, my focus was not theology, but personal experience of God.

Qualitative research:

In psychology and sociology there is a distinction between "quantitative" and "qualitative" research. Quantitative research is a category that encompasses, for instance, the scientific normation of the Spiritual Style Test (page 64). All of the essential observations can be expressed in precise numerical values. Qualitative research, on the other hand, is carried out through conversations, role plays, and observations. My work with the nine spiritual mentors as described in this chapter, is an example of this. The results cannot be strictly quantified, but they are valid nonetheless. At least they help to form a working hypothesis, on the basis of which our quantitative research has been done.

After reviewing my mentoring videos, I repeatedly had to change the content of that which I had written in the seclusion of my theological study. Minutes before, I had been so proud of the precise and sharp distinctions that I had drawn in my text. But when I looked into real faces, perceived real concerns, observed real passion for Jesus, real hurts, real sadness, I had to completely rewrite my text. Looking into the eyes of people who have meant a lot to me, influenced my writing of this book at every turn.

Occasionally, I would have intense communication with two different mentors on the same day—with both my rational and enthusiastic style mentors, or with my mystical and my sharing mentors. Sometimes after these conversations, I would lay wide awake in bed until the break of dawn, feeling initially more confused than enriched. In most cases, the overwhelming sense of blessing from this kind of communication emerged considerably later.

The whole Christ and different aspects of Christ

Every single mentor tended to a certain one-sidedness—some more, some less. When listening to some of their pointed remarks, it was sometimes hard for me to sense Jesus' message. Many things sounded quite extreme. In most cases, our conversations revolved around the same favorite topics that, of course, differed from mentor to mentor. However, when viewing all of the videos simultaneously (I have made a compilation of the nine videos in which the sound is turned down, but the body language communicates very clearly) I can sense the message of Jesus indeed: nine ambassadors of Jesus, expressing different aspects of his message. Meanwhile, I sense their different voices as a part of a great symphony (*sym-phony* means "sounding together"). When "listening" to their voices in this way, the message is considerably stronger than listening to each voice in isolation.

The Spiritual Style Test

The Dutch theologian Geert Groote (1340-1384) made the following wise statement: "Nothing is so dangerous as to preach about God and perfection, and not to point out the way that leads to perfection." It is not enough for Christian teachers to describe the destination of life, they must also help people identify their starting point. On the basis of these two pieces of information (starting point and destination), the challenge is to work out a growth plan that will help you get from your starting point to your destination.

For that reason, we have developed the Spiritual Style Test. Identifying your starting point (native style) automatically helps you discover what you have to do in order to experience further growth in your faith.

The Spiritual Style Test hasn't been developed as a personality test. It doesn't define your character. Rather, it describes the way you currently and most naturally connect with God. The test result is neither "good" nor "bad," since no style is better or worse than the others. However, the result would definitely be "bad" if it does not lead you to pursue greater spiritual growth. A profile should be regarded as "good" only if it motivates you to get involved in a concrete growth plan.

Spiritual Style Test:

Since most Christians tend to confuse spiritual tradition with personal spiritual style, it is important to have an instrument that helps us identify our native style with precision. In 2009, to develop such a test, the Institute for Natural Church Development conducted research in 62 countries and 71 denominations. On the basis of this research, it was possible to develop a survey that enables every Christian to identify his or her spiritual style. At the same time, the survey can be used—if repeatedly taken—to highlight progress in the growth process.

How to complete the test

1 Read through the following **72 statements** and, using a pencil so you can repeat the test in the future, place an "X" on the answer that is *most applicable* to you. Answer as spontaneously as possible, thinking primarily of your most recent experiences. Be honest with yourself. Only then will you get helpful results.

2 Once you have answered all of the questions, follow the **instructions on pages 69-70**. The results will reveal how strongly each of the nine spiritual styles is presently developed in your life.

3 Page 71 gives you five **evaluation questions**. Once you have answered these questions, you will know (a) your native style, (b) the wing of your native style, (c) your style family, (d) your opposite style, (e) the predominant style of your church.

4 This is all the information for **individualizing the remaining pages** of this book for your personal needs. At the same time, this is all the information needed for starting a "training program" (both in the area of your strengths and your weaknesses) that is based on your actual needs.

5 In order to monitor the success of your growth, you are advised to **repeat the Spiritual Style Test** periodically. As you do this, you can monitor your progress in the area of the style you have focused on, as well as discover if another style has become your most natural style.

And now—enjoy the exercise!

The following statement applies to me:

	not at all	slightly	moderately	to a large extent	very much	
1						My spiritual life is very much influenced by artistic or natural beauty.
2						In my view, the study of science can be a wonderful way to learn more about God.
3						A theological system that reflects God's truth helps me in my spiritual life.
4						Scripture is a filter through which I assess all of my opinions.
5						I strongly sense God's presence whenever I pass on the grace of God to others.
6						The "desert" as a place to gain spiritual experience is appealing to me.
7						For me, being excited about God is an important aspect of the Christian faith.
8						My faith is very receptive to personal revelations from God.
9						For me it is important that faith is expressed in visible, physical forms.
10						Others would say that I am very perceptive to what is happening around me.
11						People would say that I love the Lord with my mind.
12						I believe that wrong teachings are one of the greatest dangers to the church.
13						I am constantly asking how the Word of God applies to my daily life.
14						My prayer life is characterized by intercession for people who have not yet experienced God's love.
15						For me, freedom from worldly things is an important sign of spiritual maturity.
16						I seek to experience more and more of God's power in my life.
17						The mysteries of the Christian faith are very appealing to me.
18						I am very receptive to symbols and liturgy.
	1	2	3	4	5	

The following statement applies to me:

	not at all	slightly	moderately	to a large extent	very much	
19						For me, growth in faith includes growing in my ability to enjoy God's creation more fully.
20						I am curious to find truth wherever it may appear.
21						The accuracy of our stated beliefs is of utmost importance to me.
22						When God's Word is proclaimed I feel very close to him.
23						It saddens me when church traditions create a barrier to those outside the church.
24						I believe that a Christian's life should be sacrificial.
25						I believe that whenever Christians come together for worship, the presence of God should be strongly felt.
26						The goal of my Christian pilgrimage can be described as increasing unity with God.
27						Traditions and ceremonies are very helpful for my spiritual development.
28						For me, physical pleasure can be a great way to experience God's love.
29						Intellectually learning something new about God is a deep spiritual experience for me.
30						I would prefer to be seen as somewhat "judgmental" than as someone who compromises the truth.
31						My personal Bible study is focused on personal life transformation.
32						It is of utmost importance to me that people outside the church are a major focus of Christian activity.
33						Purity and holiness are important values for me.
34						It is very important to me to experience God's supernatural acts.
35						Sometimes the Spirit speaks to me directly, without mediation of other people or the Bible.
36						Visual forms of presenting God's truth are very appealing to me.
	1	2	3	4	5	

The following statement applies to me:

	not at all	slightly	moderately	to a large extent	very much	
37						Many things that have a high spiritual impact on me, are viewed by other believers as "worldly."
38						I consider it positive to have a critical mindset toward spiritual questions.
39						It is important for me to keep the biblical message pure.
40						For me, the Bible is a great way to connect with Christ.
41						I am deeply moved if unchurched people are touched by Jesus' love.
42						It is important for me that Christians don't conform to the world.
43						I would rather be called a "fanatic" for my trust in God's power than be seen as boring.
44						I am convinced that without deep personal experiences faith cannot be fully expressed.
45						I experience Christian rituals as life-altering encounters with God.
46						I frequently perceive God's presence in the "everyday" aspects of life where other people see nothing spiritual.
47						I am skeptical toward a faith that constantly offers "easy solutions."
48						It is important to me that my faith does not depend on momentary feelings.
49						Throughout the day, Scripture verses often come to my mind.
50						One of my greatest desires is to respond to the hurts and needs of unchurched people.
51						I enjoy worshiping God in an environment without decor.
52						For me it is important to feel the presence of God.
53						Silence is very helpful to me in seeking the face of God.
54						Rhythm and repetition in life help me to grow in my understanding of God.
	1	2	3	4	5	

The following statement applies to me:

	not at all	slightly	moderately	to a large extent	very much	
55						I like to use all of my senses (touch, smell, taste, sight, hearing) to encounter God.
56						It is important for my faith that my mind is regularly stimulated.
57						I feel close to God when I sense that God's truth is being communicated in an uncompromising manner.
58						I strongly sense God's presence when applying his Word.
59						I believe that the Christian faith comes alive primarily in giving away what you have received.
60						As part of my Christian testimony, I deliberately try to adopt a simple lifestyle.
61						It is important for me to get direct guidance from the Lord.
62						I feel very close to God whenever he quietly touches my heart.
63						For me, pre-written prayers are very appealing.
64						I enjoy being surrounded by physical objects that have a spiritual meaning.
65						Hardly anything nurtures my faith more than several hours of uninterrupted study or reflection time.
66						Feeling secure in my beliefs is very important to me.
67						My daily decisions are strongly influenced by biblical concepts.
68						I enjoy caring for people outside of the church.
69						In order to be available to God, I try to abstain from worldly things.
70						Prayers for supernatural healing are appealing to me.
71						It is important for me to feel God's presence within me.
72						Places of worship that radiate awe and majesty are very appealing to me.
	1	2	3	4	5	

How to evaluate the Spiritual Style Test

Having answered all of the questions, you can now begin the evaluation. It is quite simple if you follow the four steps explained below:

Step 1: Collect the raw data

Using the following scoring grid, enter the numbers (1-5) that correspond to your answers on the questionnaire (pages 65-68). These numbers are found at the bottom of each column.

Now add up the eight numbers in each row of the table below. Write the result for each row in the *Total* field. This will give you a "raw value" for each style.

								Total	**Name of style**
1	10	19	28	37	46	55	64		**Sensory**
2	11	20	29	38	47	56	65		**Rational**
3	12	21	30	39	48	57	66		**Doctrinal**
4	13	22	31	40	49	58	67		**Scripture-driven**
5	14	23	32	41	50	59	68		**Sharing**
6	15	24	33	42	51	60	69		**Ascetic**
7	16	25	34	43	52	61	70		**Enthusiastic**
8	17	26	35	44	53	62	71		**Mystical**
9	18	27	36	45	54	63	72		**Sacramental**

Note that these values do not represent the results of the *Spiritual Style Test*. To find out which style is most strongly developed in your life—and which one is the least—you need to transfer the raw data calculated above into the "normation table" found on page 70. The scientific normation has been developed by our Institute on the basis of inter-denominational sample groups in 62 countries.

In order to do the normation, please turn to the next page.

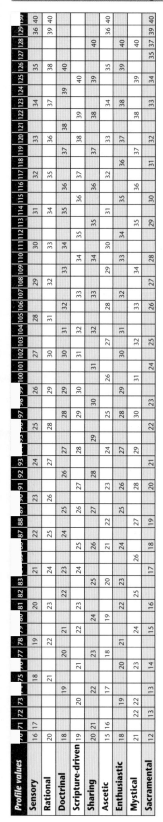

Profile values row (black header, left table). Style rows: Sensory, Rational, Doctrinal, Scripture-driven, Sharing, Ascetic, Enthusiastic, Mystical, Sacramental.

How to evaluate the *Spiritual Style Test* (continued)

Step 2: Transfer the raw data to the normation table

After completing the scoring grid (step 1), transfer the totals for each style onto the normation table on the left. For each item, mark the number yielded by the scoring grid. For example, if the scoring grid shows a total of 27 for *Rational,* you should mark the number 27 in the normation table for the row labeled *Rational.* If the corresponding number does not appear, simply mark the next highest number.

Step 3: View the results

The normation table now shows you which style has the highest profile value, and which has the lowest (the *profile values* are the numbers in the black row at the top of the normation table). Write the name of each style into the table below, starting with the one that has the highest profile value, and ending with the one that has the lowest. Write the profile value of each one into the right column of the table.

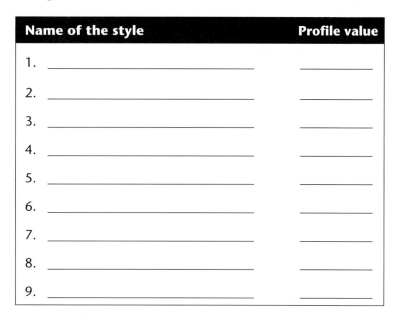

Name of the style	Profile value
1.	
2.	
3.	
4.	
5.	
6.	
7.	
8.	
9.	

Step 4: Answer the evaluation questions and fill in the table on page 73

Now move on to page 71 and respond to the five evaluation questions. That will enable you to fill in the table on page 73.

Five evaluation questions

Evaluation Question 1: What is your native style?

Every Christian has *one* predominant style, which I refer to as their native style. Even when all nine styles have achieved relatively close values, there is always one style that is more strongly developed than the other eight. If you have more than one style with identical highest values, do the following to each. Add to it the values of its two neighboring styles. Your native style is then the one that has the highest total.

For example, if the sacramental and the Scripture-driven styles have the same profile values, for the sacramental style you would add together the values of the two neighbor styles, "mystical" and "sensory." For the Scripture-driven style, you would add up the values of the two neighbor styles, "doctrinal" and "sharing." This will indicate whether the sacramental or the Scripture-driven style—in spite of identical values—is your native style.

Evaluation Question 2: In which direction does your native style lean?

There is no pure style; every style has a certain tendency toward one of its neighbor styles. Based on the test results, it is easy to find out the direction in which your native style leans: Simply identify which of the two neighbor styles has the higher value. Let's assume your native style is the sacramental style, and the sensory style has a higher value than the mystical style. In this case the exact description of your native style would be this: the sensory wing of the sacramental style. This fine-tuning is important in order to later choose the exact opposite style (step 4).

Evaluation Question 3: What is your style family?

In some situations it is helpful to focus not so much on one's individual style, but on the style family as a whole.

- If the *sensory* or *rational* style is your native style, you are part of the **green** style family (which also encompasses, to a lesser extent, the *sacramental* and the *doctrinal* styles).

- If the *Scripture-driven* or *sharing* style is your native style, you are part of the **red** style family (which also encompasses, to a lesser extent, the *doctrinal* and the *ascetic* styles).

- If the *mystical* or *enthusiastic* style is your native style, you are part of the **blue** style family (which also encompasses, to a lesser extent, the *ascetic* and the *sacramental* styles).

- If the *sacramental* style is your native style, you are part of the **aesthetic** style family (which also encompasses, to a lesser extent, the *mystical* and the *sensory* styles).

- If the *doctrinal* style is your native style, you are part of the **dogmatic** style family (which also encompasses, to a lesser extent, the *rational* and the *Scripture-driven* styles).

- If the *ascetic* style is your native style, you are part of the **ethical** style family (which also encompasses, to a lesser extent, the *sharing* and the *enthusiastic* styles).

Test normation:

Every book in the NCD Discipleship Resources series contains one major test which helps you identify your starting point in the area of the respective theme (i.e. a "Three-Color Gift Test" in the book, "The 3 Colors of Ministry," the "Fruit of the Spirit Test" in the book, "The 3 Colors of Love"). All of these tests are based on a scientific normation derived from comprehensive international samples. Exact results are only available by way of such a normation. "Tests" that do not have a normation or that are conducted on the basis of inadequate data (e.g. based on samples that are too small or too homogeneous), should not be used. Most Christians take the test results very seriously, some even allow them to determine plans for their life. Because of this, wrong or imprecise results present an ethical problem, comparable to doctrinal heresies.

In other words, your style can be assigned to more than one style family, as the families overlap. Depending on the context (group discussion, mentoring, interdenominational encounters, etc.), it will be helpful to sometimes focus on one style family, at another time on another style family. For instance, if you have the sensory style, it may be comforting for some people to know that you are part of the green style family as they are, but it might be challenging to another group that you are part of the aesthetic style family.

Evaluation Question 4: What is your opposite style?

When it comes to Level B growth, you need to focus on the style that is located opposite your native style. Since your native style has two opposite styles, it is important to know, in which direction your native style leans (see Evaluation Question 2). Let's assume you have the mystical style. Then your two opposite styles are the doctrinal and the Scripture-driven styles. Which one should you focus on? If your mystical style leans more to the sacramental style, then your opposite pole is the Scripture-driven style; if it leans more to the enthusiastic style, your opposite style would be the doctrinal style.

Don't forget that the goal of Level B growth is *not* to focus on your weakest style, but on the style opposite your native style. That makes a huge difference. While in some cases, your opposite style may be identical to your weakest style, it could also be your second most developed style. The closeness of your native and opposite style is a strong indicator of your progress in spiritual maturity.

Evaluation Question 5: What is the style of your church?

As explained in the box on page 74, it is helpful to conduct a Spiritual Style Profile for a whole church. By doing so you can easily identify the most strongly developed style of your church, which usually shapes the climate of the church. If you have this information on hand, fill in your church's predominant style in the table on page 73.

Comparing your native style with the predominant style of your church can help you know how to interact with your church environment in order to experience further growth. If your church's predominant style matches your native style, you will have to follow a different path than if your native style is different. You'll find more on this topic on page 176.

This is not a personality profile

Always remember that the Spiritual Style Test doesn't test your personality type, but simply describes how you encounter God. One's personality type and spiritual style type are not necessarily identical. There are people who are markedly rational in most areas of their life, but in their approach to God they don't display the rational style, but maybe the mystical or enthusiastic style. Though personality type and spiritual style can be close to each other, you shouldn't take this for granted.

There is another difference. In contrast to a personality test (in which the results are often seen as unchangeable), the results of the Spiritual Style Test can change relatively quickly, especially if you deliberately work on your opposite style. You will see the effects of this change process if you do the test repeatedly. The present result simply describes your current *starting point*. One to two years from now your starting point might be altogether different.

NCD Coach:

Presently, there are NCD National Partners in about 70 countries. Most of them have established a network of NCD Coaches who have the task of supporting local churches in the practical implementation of Natural Church Development. In contrast to spiritual mentors who, in the context of the NCD network, help individual Christians in their spiritual growth process, NCD Coaches usually deal with whole churches or leaders of these churches. Several studies have demonstrated that utilizing a coach significantly increases the potential of success.

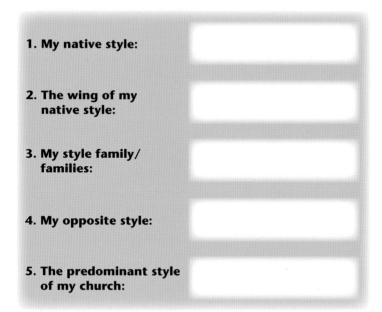

In order to interpret the data it is not only important to know which style is strongest and which is weakest, but also to understand the relationship that the individual styles have to one another within the Trinitarian Compass. Therefore, write the numbers 1-9 into the white circles (1 for your most strongly developed style, 2 for the second strongest, etc.). Take the data from the table on page 70, as it indicates the exact sequence.

1. My native style:

2. The wing of my native style:

3. My style family/ families:

4. My opposite style:

5. The predominant style of my church:

Once you have answered the Evaluation Questions (pages 71-72), you will be able to fill in the table to the left.

Remember that, according to your preference, you can include one or more style families in answer to question 3.

In order to answer question 5 ("the predominant style of my church") you will need the results of the Spiritual Style Test on the level of your whole church. If that hasn't been done yet, simply leave the field next to question 5 blank.

For this reason I avoid speaking about mystics, sacramentalists, enthusiasts, etc. You may *have* a sacramental style, but you *are* not a sacramentalist (see page 32). It would be helpful for you to stick to this language as well. People who ignore this distinction communicate that they treat the typology of spiritual styles as a more or less static concept, rather than seeing the test results as an indication of a starting point for change and spiritual growth.

The benefits of a corporate evaluation

What is the spiritual style of a church? It is not necessarily the style that is favored by the tradition that has shaped the respective church, nor is it the personal style of the church leaders. Both are mere clichés that often have little in common with empirical reality.

Can we take it for granted, for instance, that the spiritual style of a Pentecostal church is the "enthusiastic style?" By no means. In some Pentecostal churches, the red or green styles are more strongly represented than the blue ones. And even in a church where all the pastors have a sacramental style, we cannot take it for granted that this is also the style of the church. It may be that only a tiny minority of the members have a sacramental style, while the leaders are absolutely sure that this is the "church's style."

The spiritual style of a church is the very style that is most frequently represented among the members. The only way to identify the church's style is to have as many members as possible—at least 50%—complete the Spiritual Style Test. On the web site that accompanies this book you will find assistance for using this data to derive a Spiritual Style Profile of your whole church. Such a profile helps you see at a glance, how strongly each of the nine styles is represented in your church (www.3colorsofyourspirituality.org).

These results are highly relevant for church leaders. They will give them answers to the following questions. While some of these answers will be directly supplied by the data, some have to be found out in the process of interpretation:

- What is the most developed style within our church, i.e. the church's style?

What percentage of the members display this style? Is this a new discovery or something we expected? Do our church programs address people with this style? Do members with this style experience continuous growth in their faith?

- What is the style family of our church? Are we primarily green, red, or blue? Is a dogmatic, ethical, or aesthetic orientation predominant? Does this tendency reflect our theological persuasion, or is there a tension between empirical data and theology?

- To what degree are the opposite styles developed? Are we rather one-sided or are we integrated? How are we dealing with members who have a different style than our predominant style? Can they live out their style within our church? Are we helping them to grow in their styles? Do we want them to grow in their styles? Or do we expect them to adapt to the predominant style of our church?

- How does the church's style compare to the personal style of the leaders? Could it be that the church programs are developed more around the spiritual needs of the leaders than around the members' needs?

All of these questions are highly relevant for church leaders. We can't expect a church to minister to the spiritual needs of its members, if the leaders don't even know their members' styles.

However, knowing your church's style is also helpful for those members who don't have any leadership position within the church. This piece of information enables them to compare their own style with the church's style and thus gain a better understanding of what their future growth processes should look like.

> **The spiritual style of a church is by no means identical with the spiritual style of the church leaders.**

Part 2

Level A growth: Discover your spiritual style

The Spiritual Style Test has helped you identify your native style. It's possible the result has just confirmed what you have known for a long time; or maybe you have made a new discovery and you sense that you really haven't started to live out your native style. Level A growth is targeted on deepening this discovery. It is the point where you really can say "I am," rather than "I'm expected to be;" where you say, "I want," rather than, "I should;" where you say, "I enjoy," rather than,"It's my duty."

The essence of Level A growth

Take a look at the graphic. Level A growth describes the process that takes place as you move from *Level 0* (you don't know your spiritual style or you are living in contradiction to that style) to *Level A* (you are living and growing within your style). Once you are secure in your spiritual style, the growth process continues toward *Level B* (you are interacting with your opposite style); but this can and should only happen once you are sure that living on Level A has become natural for you.

Especially for believers who have lived in the "wrong" spiritual style all of their lives, reaching Level A can be an overwhelming experience. They may even interpret it as "transformation;" however, on closer observation, it isn't. They have merely discovered what has always been within them, but what they could not live out—for whatever reasons. Level A is better understood as an experience of "intensification" rather than of transformation.

Your God-given uniqueness

Reaching Level A is so important because it reveals your God-given uniqueness. It is realizing that you have a special contribution to make in this world, that there is something that can only be expressed by you and that can only be made available to others by you. The spiritual identity that you discover in Level A is something you will never abandon. Even if later on, in Level B, you will be stretched beyond Level A, you will always hold on to the discovery of your uniqueness.

In my experience, Level B is the really exciting part of spiritual growth, but for many people it has to be put on hold for a period of time. They are still bogged down by the hurts that stem from having lived according to the "wrong style" for too long. Spiritual hurts, in the majority of cases, are rooted in not being respected as a unique human being. John Bradshaw, who has dealt a lot with spiritual abuse and hurts, expresses it in the following manner: "Spiritual hurts are to blame more than everything else if we develop into dependent, shameful adult children."

Difficulties in reaching Level A

I would love to invest one hundred percent of my energy in Level B learning. If the whole world already functioned according to Level A, that would be possible. But we are not there yet, so it makes sense to discuss the implications of Level A first.

It is possible to think that reaching Level A is the easiest thing on planet earth. I, for one, am convinced that it doesn't have to be an excessively difficult endeavor. If I have the chance to work with a group of Christians for one weekend, I can help every participant to identify their native style within a relatively short period of time. This process may take two hours, fifteen hours, or in some cases even a little bit longer, but it definitely doesn't take a lifetime. If you don't know your spiritual style, it is not because it is so incredibly difficult to discover, but exclusively because nobody has ever taken you through this process. You may even be part of a community that views such an attempt rather skeptically, one that

Dwelling and seeking:

Two important dimensions of spiritual development, in which dwelling is related to Level A growth; and seeking, to Level B growth. Knowing your spiritual identity and displaying a certain security in expressing this identity are indispensable prerequisites for launching a process of spiritual inquiry (Level B). Only from the security of your own home can you explore new territory without fear. Conversely, your home should never be the destination of your journey, but the starting point for courageous spiritual excursions, from which you always return home.

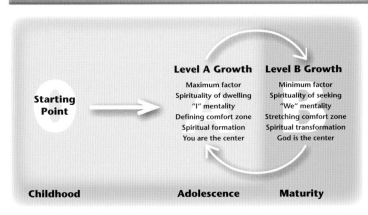

The focus of Level A growth is on the growth process represented by the left arrow: from Level 0 (childhood) to Level A (adolescence). That is a precondition for Level B growth, which is represented in the cycle between boxes A and B.

favors one particular style as the real, the right, or even the only possible one. Difficulties in reaching Level A are, in every single case, artificially created by human beings.

Why Level A is the precondition for Level B

Level B growth is an entirely different matter. At this level, we are confronted with difficulties that are part of the very nature of the process. As you interact with your opposite pole, you will encounter your own shadows. That is neither fun nor easy, making it all the more important to have built up strength on Level A that you will badly need on Level B. You can only handle looking into the eyes of somebody who is spiritually different from you if you are stable yourself, if you have a healthy spiritual self-esteem. In other words, you have to be somebody (Level A) before you can afford to let go of yourself (Level B).

The fact that many Christians see interaction with their opposite style (Level B growth) skeptically or even anxiously is often due to a lack of security within their own native style. Insecurity prevents us from being curious, from questioning who we are. Level A growth gives us the confidence that we need in order to get involved with Level B learning.

The need for training your native style

Ask yourself, "At what point did I feel most alive this past week?" You will find that the answers that you give are almost exactly the same as if you had asked, "At what point did I experience God practically this past week?" In both cases, if aware of your native style, you will inevitably refer back to experiences that have an affinity with it. Your native style describes that which comes naturally to you, that which is enjoyable for you. However, this experience of "easiness" shouldn't stop you from permanently training your native style. Consciously look for new ways to challenge yourself in this area. Connect with people who share your native style but have more experience than you do, or who have the same style as you (i.e. who speak the same spiritual language), but express themselves in a different "dialect."

When I discovered that I have the sacramental style, I noticed that I am not especially trained in this style. All of my life I have belonged to churches that haven't provided an awful lot of stimuli for spiritual growth in terms of this specific style. Therefore, I consciously sought to get close to people who are more experienced than I am (e.g. Christians from an Orthodox or Catholic tradition). When doing this, my goal was not to become like them. Rather, it was to leave my comfort zone, even in my native style in order to grow in that style.

Misusing the style typology

This book offers a typology that helps you grow in your faith. Such a framework can become quite powerful in your life as it gives you labels for your experiences and ways to understand and express what you have encountered. However, it can also become a hindrance, limiting your ability to recognize only those features that you can name. Erik Erikson, himself a great theory maker, once said, "We must take our theories with a serious playfulness and a playful seriousness."

A typology like the one presented in this book is like a map, not like the actual landscape. It is designed to be a meaningful, yet deliberately simplified, image of reality. Every typology answers certain questions especially well, but you must not expect it to answer questions that it was never intended to address. A typology always has a specific purpose that comes with its own strengths and weaknesses. No typology is comprehensive; none is identical to reality, just as studying a map can never be a substitute for studying the landscape.

All typologies have the disadvantage of neglecting the uniqueness, originality, and distinctiveness of the individual. On the other hand, compared to the widespread tendency to project a certain "standard style" on all believers, the breakdown into nine different styles (18 styles if we include the respective wings, see page 71, Evaluation Question 2) is much more fine-tuned. But of course, it is still a gross generalization to reduce spiritual expressions to such a limited number. You can expect that the description of your native style given in this book will apply to you with precision in some aspects, while in other aspects it will not. Strictly speaking, there are as many "styles" as there are Christians on this planet.

A typology of nine spiritual styles is neither true nor false, but only useful or not useful. Just as you cannot see both sides of a coin simultaneously, this typology of spiritual styles places a shadow on countless aspects of reality in order to highlight other aspects with even greater clarity. To see one thing always means you will not see other things. To speak about some things always means to be silent about other things.

Incidentally, the same applies to all scientific theories. Even electrons and photons cannot be empirically verified. Rather, they give us different ways of understanding reality, and it is up to us to choose among them. However, we always need to make scientific knowledge graphical. As long as a symbolic representation of scientific knowledge is missing, it is difficult to deal with it in practical terms. We need a window that will allow us to look into the depth of space. This applies even more when we are dealing with areas that we can only approach indirectly through our senses—both electrons and God belong to this category.

In this book the individual styles are presented in a relatively one-sided way in order to distinguish them from one another. If we tried to extend the individual terms in order to encompass the whole issue of spirituality, they would lose all their distinctiveness. This would make them entirely useless in terms of a typology. According to Aristotelian logic, the broadest terms have the least content. Nevertheless, a narrow understanding of the individual styles should not lead us to project every detail of a specific style on every representative of that style whom we encounter in reality.

> *This typology is neither true nor false, but only useful or not useful.*

What all styles have in common

The different spiritual styles encompass both overlapping and non-overlapping areas of concern. I tried to communicate this reality in the diagram on page 81. In this graphic I have reduced the representation to just three styles. If we charted all nine styles into this diagram, we would see that the intersections among the individual styles differ in size. Neighboring styles have a relatively large overlap with one another; opposite styles only overlap in a very small area.

The point of this graphic is to demonstrate that the very things that are perceived as "central" (i.e. as indispensably important), are always outside of any overlap with other styles. From the viewpoint of the individual styles—and the spiritual traditions that are based on them—it is not true that the differences between styles take place at the periphery, and the similarities are found "at the center."

It is just the other way around. The differences are at the center of each given style, and the overlaps are found at the periphery. This is due to the fact that what is regarded as "central" is not positioned in the middle of the compass (and thus possibly outside of one's own comfort zone), but in the middle of one's own spirituality. However, most people are honestly convinced that *their* center is "the center of the Christian faith." This dynamic is important to understand for any interaction between spiritual styles.

Why the usual approach to ecumenism doesn't work

If we regard the things that are at the center of our style as the center of faith, then the other styles are not really faith or at least defective faith, simply because they have different centers. However, if we realize that our own spiritual style is not at the center of the Trinitarian Compass, but that God is at the center, what we previously saw as our "center" moves closer to the fringe along with the "centers" of all the spiritual styles. You and your spirituality (and possibly your theology) would no longer represent the center—God would. On page 158 I will explore in more detail the different conclusions that can be drawn from a "God-centered" versus "style-centered" approach.

We could claim that there are central elements that are shared by (almost) all Christians. These include the Bible, some central doctrines, and generally accepted practices such as worship and prayer, etc. After all, aren't these the elements that are at the center and thus unite us?

Unity:

Almost all church traditions regard Jesus' prayer for the unity of his disciples (John 17) as the major teaching on the theme of "unity." Opinions differ, however, about how this unity should be achieved. While in some church traditions unity has to express itself institutionally and legally in order to be regarded as "valid" (i.e. others have to join your own church tradition), other traditions claim that believers can be united "in Christ," even if they are part of different church institutions and may differ in many convictions.

This is only true when we view things superficially. In reality, it's exactly those things that are interpreted differently by representatives of every style—and even more so by the different spiritual traditions. Approaches to the Bible differ among the various groups as much as the interpretations of doctrine and the practices of worship and prayer. The identity of the respective groups manifests itself in exactly these differences! As I will demonstrate in the box on page 82, this is the major reason why the usual approach to ecumenism doesn't work.

Does Christ unite us?

Of course it is correct to say that it is God himself who unites us. This is the message of the Trinitarian Compass. However, the *images* of God—along with the images of Christ featured by the individual styles and the traditions based on them—are so different that the teaching that "God unites us," in and of itself, is of little help. Every tradition places different aspects of God at the center while considering other aspects as secondary. For as long as we hold to the image of God and Christ featured by our own spiritual tradition when we speak of "God" and "Christ," such references are more likely to be divisive than unifying.

We are dealing with nine different images of God and with nine different images of Jesus. We could try to regard these different emphases as something on the fringe, but that wouldn't do justice to the underlying images of God. Representatives of the different spiritual traditions regard their specific emphases not as peripheral, but as essential.

How is cooperation possible?

I do not mean to imply that every style is okay just as it is. What I do wish to communicate is that while the center of every style expresses something important, every style needs to be complemented by the other styles. The same applies to spiritual traditions in which the differences effect theology and church structure. I will explore in more detail the practical consequences of this approach at the end of part 2 (page 147).

It is my experience that cooperation is possible on the basis of the Trinitarian Compass without having to agree on our core values. We must agree, however, that every believer may have certain values that differ from other believers. This is what characterizes values. They are subjective. They describe what we, personally, regard as valuable. Principles, on the other hand, are objective. They apply regardless of our values. Representatives of different value systems can agree on principles, since these don't question their values at all.

What principles create unity? Within Natural Church Development we find the following: The concerns behind all three color zones. The concept of the opposite pole. The eight quality characteristics. The six growth forces. The minimum factor approach. All of these principles apply independent of whether you have an enthusiastic, sensory, or ascetic style. You can apply them if you are a Catholic, a Pentecostal, or an Anglican. The very things that we call "NCD principles" have demonstrated an immensely unifying power.

Misunderstandings of the spiritual styles

I have repeatedly encountered a gross misunderstanding of the concept of spiritual styles. According to this misunderstanding the very elements that are essential characteristics of any form of Christian faith, are assigned to the individual styles. One style is characterized by prayer and worship; another, by Bible study; another, by dealing with sin and forgiveness; another, by humility; yet another, by spiritual passion, etc. However, all of these dimensions are not features of one specific style, but central elements of *every* spiritual style.

Every style is concerned with the Christian faith, but depending on the style family (see graphic), faith is expressed differently. Within the dogmatic style family, the focus is on sound doctrine; within the ethical style family, on life transformation; and in the aesthetic style family, on incarnational faith.

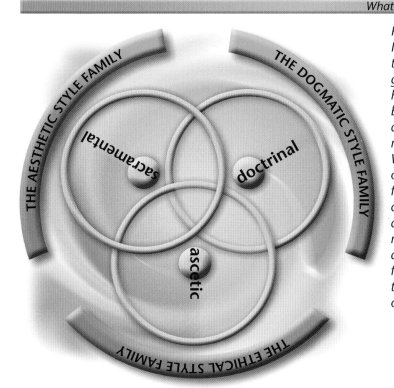

For the sake of visual clarity, I have displayed only three of the nine spiritual styles. This graphic reveals that all styles have certain areas of overlap, but that the areas of overlap don't include the centers of the respective styles (yellow dots). When we are at the center of a style, we feel separated from the others. There is only common ground in areas that are located at the edges of our respective paradigms. This is an extremely important insight for interacting with other spiritual styles, spiritual traditions, or denominations.

What are the elements that are fundamental for every spiritual style as well as every spiritual tradition? The following is an overview of the most important factors:

Common ingredient 1: Prayer and worship

If you look at the different style families, you will observe huge differences in the practices of worship and prayer. Within the dogmatic style family there is a preference for prayers that describe the nature of God (in an extreme case even the Apostles' Creed, which is not a prayer, can be experienced as a "prayer"); within the ethical style family, prayer is focused on life transformation (be it healing, strength in your everyday life, or steadfastness in temptation); in traditions related to the aesthetic style family, there is a preference for liturgical prayers (set prayers taken from Christian tradition). However—and this is my point—not a single style can do without prayer. For Christians, prayer is like breathing, and nobody would imagine breathing as the hobby of only those people who sense a certain appreciation for air.

Common ingredient 2: Learning from Scripture

The way people deal with Scripture also differs considerably from one style family to another. People in the dogmatic style family prefer rational approaches to Bible study that sometimes focus on the historical and linguistic background, and other times focus on extracting principles for our time. The ethical style family sees in Scripture, standards for holiness that must not be watered down. Traditions related to the aesthetic style family appreciate the public reading of Scripture within a liturgical setting.

One of the nine styles—the Scripture-driven style—has the term "Scripture" included in its name. This doesn't mean, of course, that it is the only style that takes the Bible seriously. However, in the Scripture-driven style the Bible is more

The "Become like us!" approach

There is an unrecognized problem within Christianity that I have regularly dealt with in my interdenominational work. Most Christians are sincerely concerned with "unity." They are also aware that unity is not the result of being in agreement with everyone about every last detail. Therefore, people tend to say, "We must be united at the center of our faith; on that basis, we can have different forms, which no longer separate us."

This sounds reasonable: Unity "at the center," not at the periphery. That seems to be in full accord with the Trinitarian Compass. However, the unrecognized problem is that every spiritual tradition defines this center differently. This is demonstrated in the graphic on page 81. Thus, the well-sounding appeal to meet "at the center," turns out to be nothing more than an invitation for other people to move closer to my own center. The invitation to unity becomes identical to the demand of becoming "more like us."

If unity is sought "at the center" of what a given tradition defines as the center, the consequence is an understanding of unity that demands other people to move into our terrain. In this sense a Roman Catholic is no different from a Pentecostal or a Baptist. Stretching out one's hand to unity means, "Please, become like us. Of course, not in every detail, but at least adopt my center as your center."

For that reason it seems counterproductive to me to regard those aspects of our faith that are especially important to us as "unity-building." The inevitable result is placing "our" core values at the center, since we honestly believe that these are the core values of Christianity. That is the major reason why the usual approach to ecumenism, despite all sincere and energy-consuming endeavors, cannot work. The mistake is in seeking unity "at the center" without realizing that, depending on our spiritual traditions, we are speaking of extremely different "centers."

Rather than seeing your own core values as "unity-building," it would be much more helpful to regard them as merely "identity-building." They express who you are, what you believe, what your convictions are, and what your image of God is. Precisely because these things are incredibly important to you, you will never be willing to sacrifice them on the altar of ecumenism.

Therefore, it can be easily understood why discussions on unity that stress the "center" must come to a dead end. It is characteristic of different traditions to display different sets of "highest values." It would be a gross misunderstanding to downplay these differences as if they were merely concerned with variations in prayer or worship styles (e.g. arms up or head down). Even beneath these external forms there are different values that derive from different images of God.

Values are identity-building. Though they may be regarded by like-minded people as unity-building, they definitely are not. On the other hand, principles—such as the dynamics expressed by the Trinitarian Compass—are unity-building. They create a platform on which believers displaying different value systems can cooperate with one another in order to become more effective in their own ministry.

> *Values stress what distinguishes us; principles stress what we have in common.*

at the core of expressing faith than it is in the other eight styles. We should not glean from this that the Bible is less important for representatives of other styles. They simply have a different approach to the Bible than representatives of the Scripture-driven style.

Common ingredient 3: Addressing sin and forgiveness

It is interesting to note which aspects of sin (and consequently, of forgiveness) are placed at the center of each style and the respective traditions. In traditions that have an affinity to the dogmatic style family, heresy can be seen as the epitome of sin. Within the ethical style family the focus is more on moral sin—on the failure to lead a holy life. Within the sacramental-aesthetic family, sin is often understood institutionally—failure to attend the worship service or leaving one's own church to join another denomination can be viewed as a form of sin. The ways people experience forgiveness are just as diverse as these respective concepts of sin.

The representatives of each tradition agree that sin is, at the deepest level, separation from God. Therefore, it would be helpful for each tradition to focus on *their own* group's aspects of sin, where this separation is most likely to occur, rather than focusing on the sins of the *other* groups. We have already spoken about these dangers in the chapter on the perils of each spiritual style (page 49).

Common ingredient 4: Humility

Thomas a Kempis wrote, "The measure of our spiritual growth is our humility. The higher we are in the spirit, the more humble we will be." However, depending on the respective style families, the word "humility" will be interpreted differently. Within the dogmatic style family, it manifests itself essentially by living "under the Word." Within the ethical style family, it is often expressed by a simple lifestyle abstaining from worldly pleasure. The aesthetic style family stresses integration into tradition: "You are part of a larger entity."

The acknowledgement of our own imperfection and the need to be complemented by others, as is characteristic of Level B growth, is the soil on which authentic humility can grow. The opposite of humility is arrogance, pride, and the presumption of seeing ourselves as complete, which positions us in the place of God. Since this conceit is the opposite of the Christian faith, humility is a central value.

Common ingredient 5: Growing in passion

Though there is a widespread notion that passion is primarily expressed in the "blue" styles, it must be maintained that all style families depend on passion and teach passion. Within the dogmatic style family, there is the passion for God's Word and truth; within the ethical style family, there is passion for a holy life that doesn't conform to the world; within the aesthetic style family, passion for the values found in the church's tradition takes a prominent place.

Ecumenism:

The term can have two fundamentally different meanings. In one case, unity is sought primarily through institutional means (e.g. through joint decrees or the merger of churches). In the other case, diversity of churches is seen more positively than negatively. Here the activities focus on more effective cooperation, while maintaining diversity, or even increasing it. The goal is a cross-fertilization of the various approaches that makes every single one more effective.

Hardly anything blocks spiritual passion more than the feeling of self-satisfaction. The opposite of spiritual passion is a consumer spirituality that really shouldn't be labeled "spirituality." Consumer Christianity is not a spiritual style; it is the opposite of authentic spirituality.

The sensory style: Enjoying the works of God

The first time I met Jack was at one of my conferences, when I was video-recording a group exercise. All of the participants had identified their color profiles and were supposed to share their results. Jack had a markedly green profile that tended more toward blue than red. My camera recorded his words, "Yes, that's right. I am quite imbalanced." One of the group members contradicted, "No, Jack, the result can't be true, you are more balanced than that." Jack corrected her, "I don't believe you are right. My weakest area is definitely red. I still have to learn a lot in this area, and I depend on your help."

Jack, my mentor for the sensory style

Jack is the pastor of a relatively large church in Florida. It's not difficult for him to speak about his strengths and weaknesses. In his own church, both his strengths and his growth areas are commonly known. I heard from some church members, for instance, that Jack's sermons are "not biblical enough." I asked him to comment on this. "Yes," he said, "that is a correct observation. In this area I have to grow and I want to grow."

Jack is the archetype of sensory spirituality. Everything that he experiences with God or that he shares about these experiences, is expressed in concrete, visible, palpable symbols. Jack has strongly developed brainpower and is able to think very abstractly, but his approach to God is not marked by these abstractions. His spirituality is rather down-to-earth. It is grounded; it doesn't happen outside creation, but in the midst of it. I visited Jack in diverse contexts in order to learn from him. I observed him in worship, in prayer, in discussions with church members, with critics, with waiters in a restaurant, with people on the street. It is certainly valuable to listen to Jack, but only by watching him in real-life situations was I able to access the core of his spirituality.

Sensory style:

On the one hand, the sensory style belongs to the green style family; on the other hand, to the aesthetic style family. Depending on its leaning toward one of its two neighbor styles, it can manifest itself in a more sacramental or more rational variety. For Christians with a sensory style, it is most natural to express their spirituality through their five senses. The strength of this style is its well-developed perceptual capacity, including its ability to enjoy God's creation; its peril is a dependency on what is sensually perceived as beautiful (hedonism).

Jack's worldly appearance

In the eyes of other Christians, Jack may appear "worldly." The same things he regards as being of great spiritual relevance, may be seen by others as dull daily routine. Conversely, he can make fun, tell jokes, or laugh in the midst of times that other Christians (with a stronger red or blue background) observe as a somber moment of God at work. Jack doesn't regard this as "unspiritual," but as an expression of being "natural."

A typical symbol of Jack's value system is a picture of Jesus that he has in his office. I have seen pictures of Jesus in the offices of many pastors. That is not unusual. But Jack's Jesus is unusual. Jack's Jesus laughs. Of the many Jesus pictures that I have seen, rarely is Jesus portrayed laughing. I asked Jack about this. It's no accident that he opted for a laughing Jesus above his desk. He said, "If Jesus isn't laughing, he isn't fully human." In Jack's spirituality, Jesus is not reduced to being human, but the human side of Jesus—the full, real man—definitely plays a special role in Jack's life. His image of Jesus is not that of

Graphical representation of the sensory style: It is essential to understand the positioning of this style within the Trinitarian Compass. Christians with a sensory style should take into special consideration the two opposite styles (sharing and ascetic) as these throw light on the dark side of the sensory style.

a "bony ascetic." Jack reminded me that Jesus was called a "drunkard." "Since I know that these accusations don't come completely out of the blue, this makes me feel even more love for my Boss and Savior," he said.

Three-Color architecture

You can be sure that everything that is important to Jack is expressed in symbols, in stories, in categories that can be approached through the senses. He likes to take items into his hand, hold them up, point out things that he currently sees. This consistently sensory approach has even shaped the architecture of his church. At present, there are two large worship halls which are connected by a communication area. The first hall, which Jack himself refers to as "green," is a classical church building. High steeple. Italian pipe organ. Stained-glass windows. The scent of wood polish. Symbols. The worship service celebrated here corresponds to the environment: A 100-voice robed choir. High quality orchestral music. A bell choir. Everything grand, dignified, majestic.

Opposite this sanctuary is the "blue worship hall." An almost virtual environment. An ultra-modern sound system. A platform with space for a band that significantly calls itself "Channel Blue." A technically sophisticated lighting system. The worship service in this sanctuary also corresponds to its environment: Informally-dressed attenders. Interactive sermon. Video clips and interviews that interrupt the preached word. Some raise their hands, others kneel down, some laugh, some have tears in their eyes.

Expressing your beliefs physically

"And here," said Jack, pointing out a piece of grassland, "we will have our red worship hall. Here the focus will be on the application of the Word of God: Bible study, spiritual growth groups, accountability groups for a life that is morally strong, guided by Scripture. We are not strong enough in these areas yet." Jack's concern is that spiritual insights become palpable. The architecture symbolizes what the church believes, including its present shortcomings and its eagerness to grow.

When I was asked to preach in Jack's church I was curious to see which worship hall they would assign to me. Significantly enough, it was the "green hall." And I must admit that I felt perfectly comfortable there. What a feeling to preach in this majestic setting! As soon as I had said my "Amen," about 100 singers solemnly dressed in robes stood up behind me and sang the "Hallelujah Chorus" from Handel's *Messiah*. I perceived it as a very fitting response to my sermon.

The Quilt Ministry

The best symbol for the sensory expression of spirituality in Jack's church is the "Quilt Ministry." This doesn't describe a crafting group, but a lively prayer ministry. I experienced the Quilt Ministry in action when speaking at a conference that was hosted by Jack's church. During the conference one of the participants, Michelle, was informed that her son, Tim, had fallen life-threateningly ill, so that she had to fly home. Jack reacted as probably anyone else would have reacted. He asked the conference participants to pray for little Tim. In most places people would have folded their hands, bowed their heads, and prayed a spontaneous or a pre-defined prayer.

But not in Jack's church. Everyone who wanted to pray for Tim, drew near to a specially prepared quilt and tied a knot. People remained at a respectful distance until it was their turn to pray their prayers and to tie their knots. After countless people had prayed, the quilt was handed over to Michelle. On her flight home, she wrapped herself in the quilt. When arriving at the hospital, she wrapped Tim in the quilt. Both of them could sense the healing power of the prayers. Michelle was comforted, and Tim was healed.

I asked Jack if he believes there is magic power in the quilt. "Absolutely not," was his immediate and strong response. "The quilts are simply meant to represent prayer in a tangible way. The knots represent every prayer a person has made. It is not a miracle quilt. It is a symbol of our prayers. People are literally wrapped in our prayers. We want people to notice, 'Look how many believers are praying for me.'"

The core of the sensory style: Expressing faith through the senses

Of course, any kind of spirituality is, in some way or other, shaped by our sensory perception, but for the sensory style this perception is a central feature. In this spirituality, the senses are not one thing, and faith something different. Faith is experienced and expressed through the senses. For those who have this style, it is usually easier to pray when they are holding something in their hands. In both the Roman Catholic and the Orthodox traditions, use of the rosary is widespread and, as such, not necessarily an indication of the sensory style. However, when I encounter people within Protestant circles who make use of comparable haptic prayer aids, I can be sure that they have either the sensory or the sacramental style.

What fascinates me most about Jack

Jack sees spiritual significance where others merely see "the world." Jack perceives where others don't perceive anything at all. And that which he perceives, he would like others to perceive. I had dinner with Jack in a restaurant, the food was excellent (which is important for Jack), the waiter was exceptionally friendly. Jack paid her compliments the entire time, commending her for her work, for her appearance, for her apparently warmhearted character. When receiving the check, he asked her for her name and wrote it on his paper napkin: "Danielle." Then he went to the restaurant manager and said, in a way that could be well overheard, "I have never been served as excellently as by Danielle. She is an incredible woman. You can be proud of having her as an employee." Jack beamed with joy, the manager beamed with joy—and Danielle, who watched us from a distance, beamed even more. This was "her day." Today a beam of God's light had reached her life.

Christians with a sensory style perceive God through their five senses. Enjoying his wonderful creation is an essential part of their experience with God.

People with a sensory style prefer worship experiences that address all five senses, if possible: taste, touch, smell, sound, and sight. Usually these people like the Apostle John's letters, which document the fight against a "heavy-headed" faith. Throughout his letters, John stresses the following: "Stop making God abstract. Don't think of him only in sophisticated, doctrinal terms. We have dined, laughed, sweated, wept, celebrated with Jesus." Or, expressed in the original words of John: "That which was from the beginning, which we have heard, which we have seen with our eyes, which we have looked at and our hands have touched—this we proclaim concerning the Word of life" (1 John 1:1).

Representatives of the sensory style are particularly receptive to sensory methods of Bible study. They can virtually move into a biblical setting and attend to the sights, sounds, and smells of a story. They like to ask questions such as: How did the arms of the old father feel when he put them around the prodigal son? What did the fish and bread that Jesus multiplied to feed the five thousand taste like? What did Mary feel in her heart when standing at the foot of Jesus' cross? Doctrinal purists, who would never imagine asking such questions, may be horrified by this method, but by applying this approach the readers of a biblical narrative literally become part of the story themselves.

A bodily spirituality

Jack's example shows us that there are people who regard the sensory style as quite "worldly." For sensory-perceptive people, this worldliness is not unspiritual. They experience God in the midst of it. In his writings, the German pastor and resistance fighter Dietrich Bonhoeffer repeatedly draws our attention to this interrelationship. His concern was that we experience God as the transcendent in the midst of the profane. His ideal for Christians was this: "Their worldliness doesn't separate them from Christ, and their Christlikeness doesn't separate them from the world. Wholly committed to Christ they stand, at the same time, wholly in this world." The body and spirituality, according to Bonhoeffer, are inextricably linked to each other. He spoke repeatedly about the "right to experience bodily pleasure." Sensory spirituality is a bodily spirituality.

The two wings of the sensory style

The sensory style appears—depending which neighbor style it leans toward—in two varieties. If it tends toward blue, it bears more resemblance to the sacramental

To those approaching the sensory style from the opposite side

You are thinking about exploring the sensory style, and your own spiritual style is either the sharing or the ascetic style—the first one stressing ministry, commitment, and self-forgetfulness; the second one stressing voluntary renouncement of worldly pleasures. The way you have experienced God may make it difficult for you to see anything "spiritual" within the sensory style. You may point to the fact that behind the sensory style there lurks the danger of hedonism. And, you have hit the nail right on the head. That is clearly the peril of the sensory style, and your experiences in your own spiritual style have sharpened your eyes to that peril. Your worries are absolutely justified.

However, right now we aren't speaking about Christians representing the sensory style, but about you. Since you are so strongly rooted in the sharing or ascetic style, you don't have to be overly concerned about these dangers for yourself. You're right, hedonism is a danger, but it is not your danger, at least not your primary danger. The foundation that has been laid in your life is too strong for you to worry about deteriorating into a hedonistic "feel-good" faith.

Your starting point: either the ascetic or the sharing style

Your goal should definitely not be to become like Christians with a sensory style. Rather, as you interact with your opposite style, you will begin to see your own perils. Could it be that one of the reasons you are so critical about the sensory style is that it reveals your own shadows? You are grounded in Scripture enough to know that—contrary to Greek thinking—the body (and not just the soul) is the creation of a good God. After each act of creation, the Creator stepped back to admire his handiwork: "And God saw that it was good." From its origins, Christianity has been an embodied spirituality, insisting on the goodness of body as well as soul. God created our senses. "Enjoyment through the senses was his idea, not Satan's," as Gary Thomas puts it.

Could it be that your own spirituality is shaped by a primarily negative view of the body, or even of "the world" as a whole? If so, interaction with the sensory style can help you correct this one-sidedness. In the end you will not abandon your native style, but you will become more effective, more joyful, more contagious, and more mature in your own style. Your spiritual style brings so many needed things into the body of Christ. If you could come to grips with your shadow areas, it would be an enormous step ahead in becoming the very person that God had in mind when he created you.

style. Just like the sensory style, the sacramental style is concerned with the physical expression of spiritual reality; however, in sacramental understanding, the significance of physical expression goes beyond symbolic meaning. The sensory style may also lean toward the rational style. In that case, it is positioned almost exactly at the center of the green color zone. Sense (rational style) and senses (sensory style) don't only belong together from a language perspective. Perceiving through the senses is an integral part of understanding spiritual experiences.

Both wings enjoy expressing themselves through gestures: open hands, the kiss of the altar, the Bible, or an icon. Within the sacramental wing this is simply interpreted a little bit differently than within the rational wing. People leaning toward the sacramental style probably wouldn't talk about "enjoying gestures" but would regard them more as a spiritually significant ritual. However, the preferred expressions are, in spite of the different interpretations, exactly the same. In groups that have been strongly shaped by the sensory style, you will never hear the following: "The only thing that counts is your inner life." The sensory style is concerned with the connection between the external and the internal, and the external expressions are seen as essential.

The strengths of the sensory style

Christians with a sensory style not only appreciate beauty, but are able to see God's handwriting in it—whether it be the beauty of nature or beauty created by human beings, the arts. Representatives of this style can be extremely creative. If God is primarily seen as Creator, the highest dignity of human beings is to be creative, to be artists, craftspeople, poets, musicians. People with this antenna to God usually don't find it difficult to come up with many ways to celebrate God's beauty. They have a strong sensitivity for the atmosphere of a meeting. Some people might even see this as a "sixth sense," since people with a sensory style perceive things that others wouldn't even notice. However, it has nothing to do with a sixth sense. It is simply the involvement of all five senses, which have been trained over many years.

Representatives of the sensory style are able to enjoy God's creation. In areas where other believers (for instance, those with an ascetic style) primarily see dangers or preach abstinence, they see God at work. For them it would be ungrateful—and consequently sin—not to enjoy wholeheartedly what God has given us. Sensory spirituality is a strongly creation-oriented kind of spirituality.

The perils of the sensory style

The dangers of the sensory style are found on the other side of their strength. Their appreciation of the beautiful can lead to a preoccupation with the beautiful; the ability to enjoy God's creation can result in a dependency on the external. Gary Thomas describes this peril as follows: "Unfortunately we can mistakenly slip from using our senses to worship God, to using our senses to worship worship." There is the danger of confusing the aesthetic experience with God himself. An idolatrous view of the arts or of natural beauty can emerge.

The sensory style may be tempted more strongly than other styles to worship creation rather than the Creator. However, as with other styles, this is just a peril, not an unavoidable condition. It is simply important to keep this temptation constantly in mind. The dangers of the sensory style are real; they should not be played down. However, it can be demonstrated that these dangers can be dramatically reduced if representatives of the sensory style would learn from their two opposite styles: the sharing and the ascetic style.

Spirituality from below

In my work on spirituality, I encountered two different approaches that the Benedictine monk Anselm Grün refers to as "spirituality from above" and "spirituality from below." While spirituality from above experiences God primarily, if not exclusively, in the spiritual ideals that we strive to achieve, spirituality from below is characterized by the ability to relentlessly perceive our own reality, which may be far away from those ideals. In this very process, spirituality from below is able to sense God's voice.

In and of itself, the topic "spirituality from above" and "spirituality from below" has nothing to do with one of the nine spiritual styles. However, since the sensory style places one's own perception (which includes a sharpened self-perception) at the center of its approach to God, it has a higher sensitivity toward a spirituality from below than can be expected of the other styles.

Especially in the beginning of our faith, spirituality from above plays a crucial role in our development. It largely corresponds to that which we have labeled Level A growth. In this process, we discover spiritual ideals that we can identify with. However, the more we proceed to grow, spirituality from above has to be complemented by a spirituality from below, which brings us in contact with our own shadows. This largely corresponds to what we have called Level B growth.

Spirituality from above and spirituality from below should not be seen as either/or, but as both/and. Spiritual ideals are important. They only stunt our growth if they make us blind to our own reality. In order to keep up our ideals, we may ignore our shadows, but harshly criticize the shadows of others. Often it is our ideal to be like the heroes of our own spiritual style. Any emotions that contradict that ideal are then suppressed. But it is precisely these uncomfortable feelings that could bring us in touch with what God would like to communicate to us, but which is masked by our own ideals. Then we may meet the fate of Icarus, the famous high-flyer, who finally had to crash since his wings were made only of wax.

Spirituality from below opens the door to a deeply somatic approach to God that includes our drives and our emotions, both the positive and the negative ones. It opens the door to our shadow areas. We no longer perceive God's voice exclusively through spiritual ideals, but also through our interaction with our own thoughts and feelings, our wounds and our alleged weaknesses. Why am I the way I am? What are the fears that drive me? What may God want to communicate to me through all of this? Why am I more prone to this specific kind of sin than others? Only when we perceive these feelings can we utilize them as a source of learning.

> **Spirituality from below opens the door to a deeply somatic approach to God.**

According to C.G. Jung, humility is "the courage to face one's own shadow." Anselm Grün writes, "Often enough, proud people who have identified themselves with idealistic images, can only be healed if they have fallen flat on their face."

Christians with a sensory style have a far more unbiased relationship to a spirituality from below. Sensory spirituality is a bodily, a somatic spirituality. People who don't have the sensory style usually have to invest much more energy before they can open up to a spirituality from below. However, if they succeed to do so, they will have an experience that may prompt them to say, along with Anselm Grün: "It's not my virtues which open me up to God, but my weakness, my helplessness, even my sin."

The rational style: Understanding the nature of God

It was one of those regular music evenings of the early forties in Berlin. As usual, uncle Dietrich was sitting at the piano, playing Mozart, or at times one of his own compositions. Father Klaus accompanied him with the cello; mother Emmi, with the violin. Thomas, at that time 11 or 12 years of age, already prepared for bed, washed, and in his nightgown, was allowed to stay awake for a while despite the late hour. His task was to turn the pages for Dietrich, his godfather.

What sounds like untroubled childhood memories, had a deadly serious background. The music evenings in the house of the Bonhoeffers were primarily camouflage. If a representative of the Gestapo, the secret police of the Nazis, patrolled in front of the house, he was supposed to think: "Yeah, Mozart. How boring. I might as well go home." Inside the house, later in the evening, things happened that Thomas wasn't aware of: Conspiratorial meetings of people who were preparing a deed for which they were willing to give their lives—the assassination of Adolf Hitler.

Thomas, my mentor for the rational style

Many years later I asked this same Thomas to become my mentor for the rational style. Thomas is now in his seventies and has spent all of his life at the interface between theology and science. We discussed this scene in his parents' house. In ethics textbooks, the conspiracy being plotted in his home—called "tyrannicide"— is usually treated as one of prime ethical conflict. Without a doubt, this conspiracy was of inconceivably agonizing scope for those involved. After all, the murder of the democratically-elected chancellor of Germany was being prepared. Such a decision would have to result in hundreds of subsequent actions: Not just being prepared to kill somebody, but being ready to consistently speak untruth, in order to protect one's family and others.

I switched off the camera with which I recorded my mentoring sessions. Thomas was weeping. "Before he was executed, my father was in jail for a longer time. We children didn't know that, nobody ever told us." One day Klaus said good-bye to Thomas, knowing that he would never see his son again in this life. Could he not, at least at that moment, have told him the truth? No, he couldn't. Those were formative moments for young Thomas, and important moments for my mentor Thomas as well.

What fascinates me most about Thomas

There are many things that I admire about Thomas, not least of which is his sharp mind. However, what really impresses me is not so much his intellect, but his modesty. His latest book has the revealing title: "About God's Modesty." And this modesty is reflected by Thomas as well, which isn't necessarily typical of representatives of the rational style. In most of the 80 e-mails that we have exchanged over the past months, there is a remarkable sense of self-mockery, the attitude that he doesn't take himself too seriously. Thomas can take a distanced perspective on himself. He not only questions my positions through his constant "but," but he questions his own positions as well. Barely have I summarized one of his statements in my own words, when he again reacts with a "but." He relativizes me, he relativizes himself. What he doesn't relativize, it seems to me, is truth itself.

"You shall not kill, you shall not lie..." The Bonhoeffer family tried to be obedient to God, and precisely because of that pursuit, they have broken these and other commands. "Just believe and everything will turn out right," many Christians flippantly say, but those words sound like mockery in Thomas' ears.

Thomas doesn't quickly enter into rapture, but rather begins to brood when he is confronted with the same realities as my mentors in the blue zone, for instance.

Rationality as a family heritage

For me, Thomas is the archetype of the rational style. Interestingly enough, he doesn't share my point of view. "I really wouldn't say that I am that rational," he said. It seems to me that this is due to the incredibly high standards that Thomas applies to a term like "rationality," something that is directly linked to his family heritage: His great-great-grandfather was Justus von Liebig, probably the most distinguished German chemist of all ages, whose discoveries ("minimum-oriented fertilization") resulted in an agricultural revolution. His great-uncle was Adolf von Harnack, probably the most famous German theologian of his time. An uncle from his mother's side was the Nobel laureate Max Delbrück, companion of Niels Bohr, the most important friend and opponent of Albert Einstein. Theodor Heuss, his mother's cousin, was elected the first president of the newly created Federal Republic of Germany. I could indefinitely continue with this "ancestral portrait gallery." It highlights the environment in which Thomas was raised. The possibility of developing a parochial faith, a hostile attitude toward scientific reasoning, a "spirituality of inwardness" reduced to pious feelings, was—I could almost say—a genetic impossibility for Thomas.

Loving the abstract

Thomas' writing style is "lean." His language is stylistically clear—every word is well-reflected—but extremely tight, and thus not easily accessible. This love for the abstract has shaped his relationship with God as well. In one of his e-mails, he wrote to me: "I have the impression that I don't have to say a lot about God. However, the few things that I have to say, I try to express as precisely as possible—no more, no less. Since I live very much in the abstract, the things that I can share about my life with God, are highly abstract as well. I believe that we experience God from morning to morning, but usually we understand it differently."

Rational style:

On the one hand, the rational style belongs to the green style family; on the other hand, to the dogmatic style family. Depending on its leaning toward one of its two neighbor styles, it can manifest itself in a more sensory or doctrinal variety. For Christians with a rational style, it is most natural to express their spirituality through mental activity. The strength of this style is its reflective ability; the peril is its tendency to overstress the rational component (intellectualism).

Thomas' spirituality is not primarily concerned with "assurance." He likes to call things into question. "Scripture is unsurpassingly puzzling," he said and quoted Genesis 28:17: "How dreadful is this place!" This is "blessed, dreadful, fruitful, volcanic soil; here temples are standing and shaking." Thomas doesn't shy away from this "shaking," rather, he seems to be attracted by it. He criticizes Bible study groups that aren't characterized by a "spirit of exploration." "All too often, the discussions are confined to a playpen," he said, "and the Spirit of God can only cooperate in the form of disturbing thoughts." Well, Thomas himself formulates these kind of disturbing thoughts almost continually. Again and again I have let them sink into me and have benefitted immensely from that exercise. Indeed, this is how the Holy Spirit works, at least it is *one way* in which he works. "Spiritually, I am constantly thirsty," Thomas wrote me some time ago, "but stale water nauseates me."

A distrust of simplistic answers

Thomas displays a deep-rooted mistrust toward simple answers. When he commented on one of my books, he said, "What you are writing, sounds so easy."

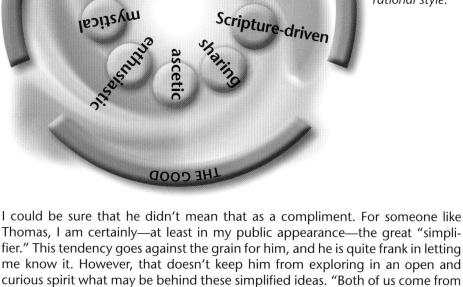

Graphical representation of the rational style: It is essential to understand the positioning of this style within the Trinitarian Compass. Christians with a rational style should take into special consideration the two opposite styles (ascetic and enthusiastic) as these throw light on the dark side of the rational style.

I could be sure that he didn't mean that as a compliment. For someone like Thomas, I am certainly—at least in my public appearance—the great "simplifier." This tendency goes against the grain for him, and he is quite frank in letting me know it. However, that doesn't keep him from exploring in an open and curious spirit what may be behind these simplified ideas. "Both of us come from very different camps, but this could make our exchange of ideas all the more fruitful. In good conversations, both parties learn," he wrote to me. That was exactly the kind of dialogue that I was looking for in my mentoring relationships!

Whenever Thomas encounters solutions that appear too smooth to him, he begins asking questions. In the end nothing remains "smooth," but more realistic, more honest, certainly for him, more "biblical," more "spiritual." Consider the Ten Commandments ("You shall not kill, you shall not lie," etc.) and the way his father and uncle dealt with these standards. Smooth answers? Certainly not. Intellectually difficult answers? Sometimes, yes. However, what made them really difficult was the fact that they had to be given with one's whole life.

A life of unanswered questions

After World War II, Thomas' mother gained certain recognition—after all, she was among those few Germans who saved the honor of their country at a rock-bottom moment of its history. On the other hand, her husband was seen by many Germans as a "traitor"—what today we would probably call a "terrorist." Folk hero or terrorist? Both interpretations are possible, depending on the value system applied. Thomas' life was permanently locked between these two different patterns of interpretation.

I was deeply moved by a journal entry made by Thomas' mother in which she described how she traveled—after she had been informed about her husband's execution—to meet her blissfully ignorant kids who were hiding in the

To those approaching the rational style from the opposite side

If your own starting point is the ascetic or the enthusiastic style, it could be that you have considerable difficulty warming up to the rational style. Isn't it purely "head faith?" Is it faith at all? Isn't it more important to believe with your heart (enthusiastic style)? And isn't it more important to demonstrate with your whole life that the message of the gospel has fallen on fertile ground (ascetic style)? You are right. These are essential, and there is no question that there are representatives of the rational style who have greatly neglected these two dimensions.

However, you shouldn't forget that Jesus never said, "The most important thing is to believe with your heart. Your mind isn't that important." Sure, he commanded you, unmistakably, to love God "with all your heart" and "with all your will"—but he also commanded you to love him "with all your mind." Could it be that you need to grow in that specific area of your love for God? And could it be that in this area you could learn an awful lot from representatives of the rational style?

Your starting point: either the enthusiastic or the ascetic style

When you think about representatives of the rational style, the image of one who continually criticizes, rarely experiences God (and gives all Christians who do a guilty conscience), may come to mind. Maybe you can no longer hear their criticism, since you sense that it is not just directed against sentimental superstition, but against any kind of dynamic faith. Consequently, you close your ears whenever you face such criticism. If this is true, you are in danger of not hearing a message that could be most helpful for you. You should never forget that an uncritical faith is not necessarily a sign of a strong faith; sometimes it is simply a sign of poor thinking. To translate this into Jesus' terminology: Poor thinking could be an indication that your "love for God" is deficient, that you don't love God with "all your mind." Could the lack of a critical mindset be an indication of a lack of love for God? You should at least think about this possibility.

Your goal should not be to reduce your enthusiasm for God, your anticipation of the supernatural work of the Holy Spirit, or your commitment to Christ—not even in the slightest way. On the contrary, these are your strengths, and it is important to continue growing in this area. However, it would be profitable for you to give the rational component of your spirituality higher value. The result would be to experience God deeper, better, more holistically, and especially in a more crisis-proof way. The fire of doubt that is linked to the rational style, can become an experience through which your own faith gains power and depth.

For Christians with a rational style, thinking has a prominent place in their approach to God. Science and logic are not seen as opposing faith, but play an important part in their spirituality.

Schleswig-Holstein countryside. "I can still picture myself coming down the street, when the cottage appeared around the corner," she wrote, "looking through the small window and seeing my three healthy kids sitting around the table. Then they asked me, 'Where is daddy?' That was the terrifying moment that I had feared more than anything else. I answered, 'Daddy is far ahead of us...'"

A man of humility

It would have been easy for Thomas' father to hide himself in the countryside. He could have avoided imprisonment. He didn't want that, as he feared that others could be taken hostage. After he was sentenced to death, he swiftly wrote a letter to his children that revealed what moved him: "I won't live much longer and want to take leave of you," his hand-written lines began. "This is extremely hard for me, since I love every single one of you so much and you have always been the joy of my life. I am not going to see how you grow up... Therefore I want to tell you some things that are important for your lives... Be demanding of yourselves and your friends. Don't strive for recognition, as it enslaves you. Take the people you encounter just as they are. Don't be afraid of things that are strange or unfamiliar to you... Don't become a victim of your pious sentiments. Don't remain in semidarkness, but strive for clarity, without hurting the tender and desecrating the inaccessible. Inhabit the Bible and take possession of the world in which only those things are valid that you have experienced yourself and have acquired in ultimate honesty."

Every time I sit across from Thomas, to speak with him about spirituality and the Bible, God and Jesus, I have the impression that the seed of this letter has borne fruit in his heart.

The core of the rational style: Applying logic in your approach to God

Christians with a rational style don't see faith and thinking as opposites (see box on page 96). In all of us a considerable part of our faith is performed through the act of thinking; for representatives of the rational style, this "considerable part" is simply considerably larger. This doesn't imply that emotions and practical actions go completely by the wayside. If their spirituality is integrated, these two dimensions also play an important role. However, for representatives of the rational style this must never be achieved at the expense of logical thinking.

Thinking and believing are not opposites

What is more important—thinking, or believing? Put like this, for most Christians there is no doubt what our preference should be. The teaching of both the Old and New Testaments on the centrality of faith are overtly clear.

But we must ask if the question has been formulated correctly. It implies that thinking and believing are two opposite, maybe even contradicting, dimensions that are in an either/or relationship with each other. People who hold this view overlook the fact that faith itself is expressed—at least to a considerable degree—through the act of thinking. Just try believing for five minutes without doing any thinking. Have fun! The result would have nothing to do with what Scripture calls faith.

To pray, to thank, to praise—all are expressed in thought processes. Although faith cannot be reduced to thinking, without thinking faith is virtually impossible. Hans Küng expresses this in the following words: "What we know and what we believe cannot be adequately separated. You think in your faith and you believe in your thinking!"

The peril of the rational style is to confuse thinking about God with encountering God. In other words, it is tempted to confuse theology (thinking about God) with spirituality (encounters with God). Both dimensions are important, and interdependent, but they are not the same.

How does spirituality work, and how does theology work? Faith says, "The Lord is my God." Or even more precisely, "You, Lord, are my God." Theology then picks out one of these words—for instance, the word "God"—and asks what that word means. It moves God from the "you" perspective into the more distanced "he" per-

Just try believing for five minutes without doing any thinking. Have fun!

spective. It doesn't speak to God and it is not addressed by God, but it makes God the object of our reflection. That is absolutely legitimate; in fact, it is necessary. But it is theology—thinking about faith. It is not spirituality—the practice of faith.

The Swiss theologian Emil Brunner has given us a formula for the ideal way in which faith and theological reflection can complement each other. He compares both dimensions with different fields of force, one tangential and the other centripetal. "The purely rational element of thought, logic, has the tendency to go straight forward from each given point; but faith continually prevents this straightforward movement by its pull towards the center. So instead of a movement in a straight line there arises a circular movement around the center." For Brunner this is a description of how spirituality and theology can cross-fertilize each other.

Dallas Willard writes, "The prospering of God's cause on earth depends upon his people thinking well. Today we are apt to downplay the importance of good thinking in favor of strong faith, and some, disastrously, even regard thinking as opposed to faith."

Growth in faith demands thinking. Level B growth, especially, is based on a considerable amount of mental performance. We have to learn to process our experiences, to view ourselves "from the outside," to mentally take the role of others, to distinguish between our comfort zone and the presence of God. All of that will only work if we are willing to invest time in reflection. To put it differently, all of that is only possible if we allow the Holy Spirit to transform our thinking, if we learn to love God "with all our mind."

The rational style does not necessarily imply a high IQ. People don't need an above-average IQ in order to love God "with all their mind." Conversely, extremely intelligent people can have a completely different style.

The rational style can be found in all camps of theology, among liberals as well as in the midst of Pentecostal or Baptist churches. It can go hand in hand with a markedly conservative theology. However, especially in these cases, the questioning mindset displayed by the rational style often confuses people.

The two wings of the rational style

Christians with the rational style feel close to God (even if they may avoid this terminology, since both the terms "close" and "feel" give rise to hundreds of questions), when they have really understood something. The rational style doesn't exist in "pure" form; either it tends more to the left (the sensory style) or to the right (the doctrinal style). In the first case, that which can be empirically perceived plays a more prominent role; in the second case, striving for "sound doctrine" is the focal point of one's rational endeavors. This second version, in particular, may appear extremely "dry" to outsiders. It doesn't only appear dry, it *is* dry. But it is exactly this dry soil from which people with this variety of the rational style gain their spiritual energy.

The strengths of the rational style

The rational style doesn't take things for granted. Rather, it strives for explanations. Only when these explanations are sufficient, does faith have a solid ground. The rational style displays an unprejudiced relationship to science. While some spiritual styles have the tendency to feel threatened by scientific knowledge, the rational style integrates science into its approach to God. Faith based on illusions is not seen as biblical faith, but as superstition. If science helps us to unmask superstition, representatives of the rational style can sing their "Hallelujah" (even if in reality they may prefer a less enthusiastic expression).

The perils of the rational style

The perils of the rational style are obvious. There is the danger of only accepting as "authentic experiences with God" those things that have successfully passed the filter of our own rationality. Ultimately, this implies telling God how he has to work. Should he decide to act in a way that transcends our rationality, we know from the outset that it is an invalid experience of God. The trans-rational dimension is excluded by definition. The experiences with God characteristic of the enthusiastic style are seen as pure sentimentality, if not something worse. This form of rationalism can take an almost fundamentalist vigor. The question of Hans Küng points in the right direction: "Couldn't it be that a dogmatic hubris of reason, which may finally be irrationally founded, can make us in a questionable way self-secure and blind toward the whole of reality?"

A second peril of the rational style is intellectual pride. My mentoring experiences with Thomas are very pleasant, as he constantly displays the very opposite mindset. Intellectual pride is not typical of the rational style in itself, but it is the result of withdrawing from the dimension of sacrificial living found at the center of the ascetic style. A representative of the rational style who has gone through these personal lowlands will be able to interact with his or her opposite styles differently than someone for whom faith is actually a purely intellectual category.

The doctrinal style: Thinking correctly about God

After having been in e-mail contact for awhile, we were now meeting face-to-face for the first time, at the entrance of his church. I had asked Gene to become my mentor for the doctrinal style. Shortly before the worship services started, he greeted me: "That's a good fit, Christian. I am going to preach this morning on the virgin birth. That is certainly the right message for you." While saying this, he was all smiles, and I was not sure whether this was simply a friendly greeting or if there might have been a little touch of irony in his words, as Gene probably views me as a German "liberal," who certainly has difficulty with the doctrine of the virgin birth.

Gene, my mentor for the doctrinal style

When visiting Gene's church I repeatedly sensed that people take it for granted that I do not agree with some of the doctrines that are so important for Christians like Gene. However, I don't have these difficulties at all. For me personally, the classical doctrine of the virgin birth makes an awful lot of sense, both logically and theologically. However, in my own spirituality—i.e. the way I experience God—this and other doctrines don't really speak to me. Together with Gene, I deem many doctrines as theologically important. But in contrast to Gene, I am not significantly touched by them. They shape my life, but only to a small degree. That's the reason why I visited Gene and his church: to grow in this area of my faith.

In our typology, the doctrinal style doesn't relate to the specific contents of doctrine. It describes the way doctrinal content is approached. As I mentioned before, my chief interest within the mentoring project was not to discuss theological content, but to learn about ways of experiencing God. It seems to me that people with a doctrinal style misunderstand this approach more frequently than others. Maybe they have to misunderstand it, as it is characteristic of their style to speak almost exclusively about content (the objective) rather than experiences (the subjective).

Doctrinal style:

On the one hand, the doctrinal style lies exactly on the interface between the green and the red style families; on the other hand, it is at the very center of the dogmatic style family. Depending on its leaning toward one of its two neighbor styles, it can manifest itself in a more rational (green) or more Scripture-driven variety (red). For Christians with a doctrinal style, it is most natural to express their spirituality through a clear demarcation of truth and heresy. The strength of this style is its focus on sound doctrine; the peril is its tendency toward a static concept of truth (dogmatism).

A man of strong convictions

I couldn't have selected a better mentor for the doctrinal style than Gene. He seems to love confrontation. For him it is an expression of strong conviction. "Most politicians feel the wind," he said, and moistened his right forefinger in his mouth in order to subsequently stretch it into the air, "and they go with it." Gene's face took an almost disdainful expression, "And unfortunately even Christian leaders start to go with it." This is exactly what he cannot bear—an opportunistic "going with the wind." An adoption of truth to the spirit of the time. A sacrifice of your own convictions on the altar of recognition, comfort, or commerce.

Gene can accept that other believers have different opinions than he has, but hiding one's own convictions would be downright dishonest in his view. That's not surprising, as the doctrinal style is at the center of the dogmatic style family which knows no value higher than truth.

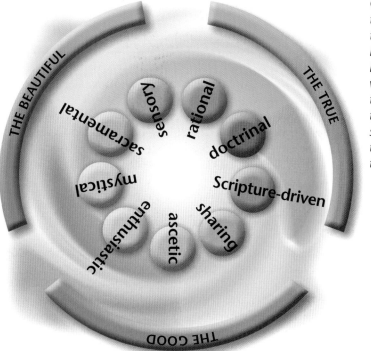

Graphical representation of the doctrinal style: It is essential to understand the positioning of this style within the Trinitarian Compass. Christians with a doctrinal style should take into special consideration the two opposite styles (enthusiastic and mystical) as these throw light on the dark side of the doctrinal style.

"I am passionate about truth," Gene said. "Truth is the only thing we should become passionate about—not styles and methodology. They can be changed. Truth can't." And since he knew that my main interest in our conversations was the "passion factor" within spirituality, he added, "How could I become passionate about something if I can't be sure it is true?"

Gene told me how important it is for him to set boundaries. "I clearly say, here are the boundaries; once you pass them, it is error, it is heresy." I wanted to know if he thinks that people whose convictions are outside those boundaries are not part of the body of Christ. "No, that is not what I am saying. They may be part of the body, but they are wrong." While vocalizing with emphasis the one-syllable word "wrong," he smiled. But without a doubt, he meant it very seriously. And he made it clear that for him this belief is much more than just an expression of a spiritual style: "We are dealing with the accuracy and final authority of the Word of God."

"Chapter and verse"

Whenever I tried to explain my views to Gene, he would take the Bible, which was constantly within his grasp, hold it directly in front of my face and say, "Christian, please, chapter and verse. Tell me what verse we are talking about, then we can intelligently speak about it. Then we can see if this is just your opinion, or if the Word of God teaches it. When people talk about doctrine, I want to know where they found it in the text, in its grammatical and historical context."

This approach has shaped Gene's whole church. It is taken for granted that everyone attending the worship service has a Bible in hand. Important points of Gene's sermon are projected in PowerPoint on a screen. But the most important points, the biblical texts, are *not* projected. Gene wants everybody to open their own Bibles and to look up the texts. He wants to empower people to argue with the Bible as their chief weapon, the same way he does it.

A systematic approach

This stress on the Bible may give the impression that we are dealing with the Scripture-driven style, and certainly there is an overlap of the two styles. However, there is one important nuance which separates them. The primary focus of the doctrinal style is not an existential understanding of Scripture—Gene immediately corrected me when I used the term "existential"—but rather, the doctrine that has been revealed through the Bible as a whole. "I don't subscribe to just a biblical theology," Gene said. "Theology should be systematized, coherent, pulled together. I see a system from Genesis to Revelation. I want to speak about this system." This systematic approach is at the heart of the doctrinal style.

The fear of subjectivism

Outsiders sometimes perceive the doctrinal style's focus on setting boundaries as a bit awkward. However, this is the other necessary side of its strength—striving for truth. If you name the truth, you must name the opposite of truth as well. The doctrinal style is characterized by a deep skepticism toward everything subjective. Representatives of this style fear that human beings may create their own private faith. This also explains their skepticism toward both of the opposite (blue) styles, as each of them have a much more positive view of the subjective side than is characteristic of the doctrinal style.

Believers whose spiritual style is rooted in the blue zone, have repeatedly told Gene, "Your problem is that you have a different Trinity, the father, the son, and the Holy Scripture." Gene told me that he understands exactly what they mean. But he is convinced that "the Holy Spirit doesn't reveal apart from Scripture." Thus, it is not just a caricature to say that in the psychology of this approach the Holy Scripture and the Holy Spirit are perceived almost as identical entities.

The role of feelings

In the course of our mentoring sessions, I have asked each of my mentors about situations in which they have felt especially close to God. I was curious to hear how Gene would answer this question. "Feelings come and feelings go, and feelings are deceiving," he said, "my trust is in the Word of God. It is the only thing worth believing." He didn't seem to be overly interested in delving into the topic of my question. I remained persistent: "But I have asked you about your feelings. *When* do they come and *when* do they go?" Gene paused for a moment. "I am a pretty emotional person," he finally said, "but I am not driven by emotion. Regardless of how I feel, if something is true, we will go there. How I feel shouldn't make any difference. Do I have positive feelings when I share the gospel? Sometimes yes, sometimes no, because I may be tired. But I know it is my mission to share Christ. Do I get frustrated? Yes, sometimes I do. But it doesn't matter."

It is obvious that the theme of "feelings" is not Gene's favorite topic. I tried to build a bridge in this area by moving onto the terrain that Gene feels comfortable with. "If you, in your Bible study, discover truth, I would guess this has a

---

What fascinates me most about Gene

Gene calls himself "a fundamentalist in doctrine, an evangelical in attitude, and a liberal when it comes to methods." Gene the liberal? That sounds like a combination to puzzle the mind. He gives an example. There was a professor from Talbot Seminary who visited him once and attended all three of his Sunday services. The first one was a traditional worship service, with hymn books, choir, robes, and Gene in a suit and tie. The second service was contemporary, with guitar and synthesizer, and Gene in a polo shirt and blue jeans. The third service was even more informal, Gene just wore pants. The professor commented, "I am so glad that Gene doesn't have four worship services." For Gene, all of these expressions, while not being arbitrary, are changeable. However, the content of the gospel is not.

For Christians with a doctrinal style the truth revealed in Scripture plays the decisive role in their spirituality. The focal point of this spirituality is that of constantly deepening our understanding of the objective standards that God has set.

positive correlation to your emotions, right?" I could immediately detect a sparkle in his eyes. "Absolutely true. In these situations my sense is, 'Wow, God, I discovered you today. I discovered you through your Word, you revealed yourself to me through your love letter called the Bible, and I met you today.' That's a deeply moving experience for me." At this point he actually used the two terms that don't seem to be an important part of his vocabulary: "experience" and "deeply moving." He is by no means opposed to moving experiences. For him the question is what triggers these experiences. And after his almost enthusiastic emotional outburst, he added—in order to avoid any misunderstandings— "But regardless of how I feel, it does not change what is true."

The core of the doctrinal style: Avoiding a self-created faith

People with a doctrinal style certainly don't want to appear judgmental, but they view this as less dangerous than compromising the truth. They want to have as much to do with heretics as the apostle John had with the heretic Cerinth. John skittered away when he heard that Cerinth was in the same public bath house. He supposedly exclaimed: "Let us flee! We have to fear that the whole bath will collapse since Cerinth, the enemy of truth, is in it."

People with the doctrinal style have feelings just like anyone else. However, they assign them a far lower significance than others. This is one of the reasons why representatives of the doctrinal style can be suspicious of signs and wonders. There are some who deny miracles as a matter of principle. But the majority don't really have difficulty with miracles in and of themselves, but with a "miracle addiction," an inner attitude that is dependent on supernatural experiences. Their concern is that people should believe in Jesus' words even without miraculous proof.

The two wings of the doctrinal style

The doctrinal style comes in different varieties. In almost all Protestant versions, "doctrine" is strongly interpreted as "biblical doctrine," which creates a significant overlap with the Scripture-driven style. In non-Protestant traditions, Scripture is also emphasized, but it is not as strongly—at least not as exclusively—in focus as in Protestant groups. The content of what we believe can differ from tradition to tradition. The way this content is approached is exactly the same.

To those approaching the doctrinal style from the opposite side

If you have one of the two blue styles (enthusiastic or mystical), you may regard it as a "setback" to deal with the doctrinal style. Isn't that exactly that sort of "dead orthodoxy" that almost all renewal movements have attacked?

You sense that faith enlivens your emotions. You expect God to work supernaturally. You experience how the Holy Spirit literally works within you. Those are your strengths. You should never abandon them. However, if you play off these experiences against the relevance of doctrine, you are in danger of leaving the ground of biblical faith. Very likely you are not among those people who flatly reject the central teachings of Christianity or even question them. You probably wouldn't speak in any disrespectful way about Scripture. But, when in doubt, isn't it true that an inner image, a prophetic word, a meaningful dream, a trans-rational experience becomes more relevant to you than the standards of Scripture or the teachings of the church?

Your starting point: either the mystical or the enthusiastic style

Christian doctrine is supposed to prevent us from viewing God and the world through falsified lenses. The church has always reacted with dogmas when wrong interpretations of our salvation in Christ were promoted. The dogmas created boundaries and hindered arbitrary interpretations. That is their function. Take, for instance, the dogma of the Trinity. It teaches us, among other things, that the Spirit whom we experience in us, isn't just a gift of God, but God himself; that through the Spirit we are immersed in God. In different ways, the dogmas encapsulate the fact that we have been redeemed through the death and resurrection of Christ. We can look into the dogmas as into a mirror. By doing so, we recognize ourselves better and more clearly than by just looking at ourselves. Even the early church expressed its faith in concrete statements. The central statement was: "Christ has died for us, and he has risen." There has never been a Christianity devoid of dogma—and where it has been attempted, the results have not been encouraging, to put it mildly.

You have experienced God speaking directly to you. You have learned to listen to God's voice within you. That is incredibly valuable. However, the problem with purely internal authority is that it lacks any means of verification. There is the danger of confusing your feelings with God's voice. Therefore you need external authority. You need doctrine. And this doctrine needs not only to reach your ears, but also your heart. You should approach it with the same inner attitude of receptivity with which you anticipate God's supernatural work in your life.

When the doctrinal style leans more toward green, it has a lot in common with the rational style. In this variety the process of thinking, especially systematic thinking, is emphasized. If the doctrinal style tends toward red, it becomes more like the Scripture-driven style. In this variety, the focus is still on the dogmatic system, but the doctrinal content of this system has the same roots as the Scripture-driven style (see the box on page 110).

The strengths of the doctrinal style

The greatest strength of the doctrinal style is its emphasis on the objective, which remains true regardless of our human experiences. The doctrinal style seeks to purify the Christian faith of all blending with human sentimentality and thrives on saving it from any kind of syncretism. On pages 22-23 we have already addressed the fact that faith can be understood on the one hand as "standing and understanding," and on the other hand, as "moving and being moved." The doctrinal style clearly has its focus on "standing and understanding," whereas "moving and being moved" is more characteristic of the blue styles.

The doctrinal style doesn't treat Scripture as a quarry, from which we can select those verses that are most fitting, while our own subjectivity decides what we deem important. The focus is rather on biblical doctrine as a whole.

The perils of the doctrinal style

The greatest peril of the doctrinal style is the reduction of faith to the acceptance of certain teachings—the idea that "if your attitude toward doctrine is correct, you are a Christian." Throughout church history, this kind of spirituality has often been characterized by a noticeable lack of love. There are Christians whose biblical knowledge is ten times greater than others' knowledge of the Bible. But are they ten times more loving than others? It is very significant that, according to NCD research, the quality characteristic "loving relationships" is the most frequent minimum factor of churches that favor the doctrinal style.

Even if representatives of the doctrinal style may proclaim with John that "the Word became flesh" (John 1:14), they sometimes give the impression that their real motto is: "The Word became book." It is not the emphasis on Scripture that is the problem (that is the strength of this style), but the general skepticism toward the dynamic component of the Christian faith. If faith is exclusively understood as "standing and understanding," all attempts focused on "moving and being moved" are suspected of being heretical. In many doctrinal style groups, faith is characterized by a dry abstractness.

The fact that I felt so comfortable in Gene's church, was probably because he is very different from many representatives of the doctrinal style. It is "fun" (I deliberately use this subjective, emotional term) to listen to his sermons. Though even Gene knows that his teaching style is the exception, not the rule. Many preachers who display the doctrinal style, are dogmatically "correct" when they preach, but at the same time frighteningly lifeless, detached, and boring.

It may seem impossible for some representatives of the doctrinal style to learn from the two blue styles (enthusiastic and mystical). However, these are precisely the styles that address the deficits of the doctrinal style: the neglect of personal experience and the tendency to a dry abstractness. In this growth process, representatives of the doctrinal style are not supposed to give up their strengths. However, they should be humble enough to acknowledge that their own approach has its perils just like every other style.

The contents of faith and the act of faith

Early church father, Augustine, has taught us the distinction between fides qua creditur (the act of faith through which we believe) and fides quae creditur (the contents of faith, which is believed). Both are important, there is no fides qua without fides quae, and the other way around. However, you must not confuse the two. By agreeing to a certain doctrine (fides quae) it is by no means guaranteed that your relationship with God is intact and your life is transformed.

In English, a proper understanding of these two categories is complicated by the fact that, although we have the two nouns "faith" and "belief" (where faith corresponds to the fides qua, and belief, to the fides quae), there is only one verb, which is "to believe." There is no "to faith." This linguistic detail has contributed to the widespread misunderstanding of seeing assent to the content of faith as the central expression of the act of faith. There can be people who have a number of strong religious beliefs but little faith in God.

The relevance of this distinction can be clearly seen if we look at the Apostles' Creed. It summarizes the central contents of the Christian faith (fides quae), but it doesn't say anything about the relevance of faith in the life of those who recite this creed. In the Apostles' Creed, we neither address God personally, nor do we express that Christ's sacrifice happened "for me." It does not even mention the most important word in Christianity: love. It neither speaks about love for God nor love for other people; it consistently avoids personal categories.

This is by no means a criticism of the Apostles' Creed. It is fides quae, not fides qua. Difficulties only occur when fides qua and fides quae are confused with each other, and the Apostles' Creed is actually viewed as a "prayer." But that is definitely not its nature. We don't say the things that are summarized in the Creed to God, but we say them to ourselves and to other believers. Communication with God demands a different kind of language and different content than the ones recited in the Apostles' Creed.

Assent to the contents that the Creed summarizes, is only one part of faith, it is fides quae creditur. If this is not complemented by fides qua creditur—through the act of faith, through personal commitment—then the ultimate cause of the Christian faith has not yet been reached. To state it another way, an act of faith (fides qua) that is not interested in the content of faith (fides quae) is no longer on biblical ground. The two dimensions belong together; they complement each other.

It is quite simple—just as "simple" as the Trinitarian Compass with the opposite poles that complement each other.

Faith cannot be reduced to an act of one's mind, to agreeing that biblical or doctrinal statements are "true." That would be a dogmatic misunderstanding. Neither should faith be reduced to accepting God's moral standards, to practicing the Sermon on the Mount, to loving your neighbor. That would be an ethical misunderstanding. And finally, faith is more than becoming part of a church tradition, participating in the liturgy, and celebrating the Eucharist. That would be a sacramental misunderstanding.

> *It is quite simple—just as "simple" as the Trinitarian Compass with the opposite poles that complement each other.*

The Scripture-driven style: Applying the Word of God

Though Ian is a classical representative of the Scripture-driven style, he doesn't like the term "Scripture-driven." Throughout the course of our mentoring process, he repeatedly sent me new suggestions for supposedly "better terminology," and in the end he asked me, "What would be so wrong with calling it simply 'scriptural?'" The struggle for terminology, for formulations, for definitions, is a typical feature of a certain variety of the Scripture-driven style. After all, more than other styles, it is concerned with the "Word," and people who have this style, are especially receptive to words, and careful in their own use of words.

But back to Ian's question. Why not simply call it the "scriptural style?" Because then the distinctiveness of that style would be lost. Each of the nine styles is "scriptural," and each of them deals (admittedly in different ways) with the Bible. I had to look for terms that would describe the one-sided emphasis of the respective style (insinuating their potential perils). However, Ian himself is too balanced—or at least striving so much for balance—to identify with such one-sided terminology.

Ian, my mentor for the Scripture-driven style

When asked to describe what Scripture means to him personally, he says something like this: "Scripture is a filter through which I objectively measure the subjectivities of my opinions, the opinions of others, and life's experiences in general." Every single word is carefully chosen, and that is immensely important for Ian. What I like about his definition is the interplay between subjectivity (in Ian) and objectivity (in Scripture). This interplay is characteristic of the Scripture-driven style. It doesn't describe people who deem the Bible as "important," but those for whom Scripture is the decisive factor in their daily lives.

Ian told me extensively about the influences that have shaped his spirituality. His father is a scientist, and so it was very natural in his family—even expected—to explore new ideas and to approach them with an open mind. "I grew up in a family where reason and faith were presented in one package," Ian told me. "We were urged always to begin an argument by defining our terms. If there were different opinions about the meaning of a specific term, we used a dictionary. So I got used to this habit."

What fascinates me most about Ian

I have a downright allergy for a certain approach to the Bible—the approach where you take a specific concept (e.g. the minimum factor or the Trinitarian Compass), and consult a concordance under M like "minimum factor" or C like "compass" or T like "trinitarian" to check for biblical references. And the more references you find, the more "biblical" the concept! In contrast to other Scripture-driven people, Ian seems to share this same aversion. His concern is sober hermeneutics, the exposure of biblical principles that are then applied to life. In the development phase of our NCD tools he has repeatedly offered biblical insights which have challenged my own thinking. Whenever I get an e-mail with a "biblical thought" from Ian, I think, "Christian, you should take this very seriously. This could be, yet again, God's message for you, communicated through Scripture"—and delivered by Ian, my mentor for the Scripture-driven style.

In our conversations, I tried to make it clear that it is not so much the term chosen for a specific style that is the decisive factor, but rather the positioning of the style within the Trinitarian Compass. In other words, it is the "picture" that counts. Once we have this picture stored as an inner image, we have understood the nature of the Trinitarian Compass. Throughout the course of my mentoring processes I learned, however, that the word-centered ("red") styles are not as familiar with this visual kind of thinking as, for instance, representatives of the aesthetic style family. All that matters to them is really the word. Images may be helpful illustrations (at most), but they are not essential. Through precisely chosen words, everything of importance has already been communicated.

My own need to learn

In this area, I function entirely differently. I don't think in words, but in images. For me words are (at best) "illustrations" of what I have already expressed in images. For me personally, the criteria that the aesthetic style family applies in its search for truth (such as symmetry, proportion, wholeness, and harmony, see page 59) play a far greater role than definitions. By this I don't want to say that I function "better" than Ian, but simply differently. And in my approach, I am as one-sided and in need of being complemented as he is. That's the reason why I want to learn from him.

As far as my theological convictions are concerned, I place "the Word" on the same high level as Christians with red spiritual styles. In this area, there is no difference. But theological persuasions shouldn't be confused with spiritual styles. The written word—including the biblical Word—doesn't speak to me as strongly as visual expressions or artistic representations do. When I have to read long chapters about the "biblical foundation" of an author's teachings, "proven" by countless Bible references, I have to invest a considerable amount of energy to struggle my way through them. Or I simply scan through them without feeling like I have missed anything essential. I also have to discipline myself much more than red-style believers in order to keep on track with my personal Bible study.

I was honest with Ian about my experiences, feelings, and difficulties in this area. I asked him to give me some homework that could help me move a step forward. My goal is not to attach more importance to the Bible than I already do. In my mind, Scripture has always been of utmost importance. That's not my problem. It's just that I am not really touched by the written Word.

Scripture-driven style:

On the one hand, the Scripture-driven style belongs to the red style family; on the other hand, to the dogmatic style family. Depending on its leaning toward one of its two neighbor styles, it can manifest itself in a more doctrinal or sharing variety. For Christians with a Scripture-driven style, it is most natural to express their spirituality through the study and proclamation of the Word of God. The strength of this style is the application of biblical principles to everyday life; the peril is to appeal to Scripture in areas where it doesn't offer any teaching (biblicism).

A transformational homework

Ian agreed to think about a fitting assignment. When he sent it to me by e-mail, my first reaction was a slight disappointment. He wanted me to do a Bible study, a word study at that. What else could I have expected of a Scripture-driven person? A biblical word study, that is their standard repertoire. To me, this didn't sound overly creative. But then I got curious. I was to study the term "transformation" in its biblical context. Presumably, Ian guessed that this very word would make my heart beat faster. My whole life—both personally and in my ministry—is targeted on initiating transformation processes. My frustration with many of the long-winded "biblical proofs" is that I cannot sense any spirit of transformation among them.

I started with Romans 12:2 ("be transformed by the renewing of your mind"), studied the whole passage in Greek, and analyzed it word by word. It struck me that the decisive word is expressed in the form of a "passive imperative," i.e. neither a simple imperative ("Transform yourself!"), nor a simple passive ("You are transformed!"), but rather the "call to be transformed." Later, I studied the story of the "transfiguration of Jesus" (Matthew 17:1-13), since in Greek it

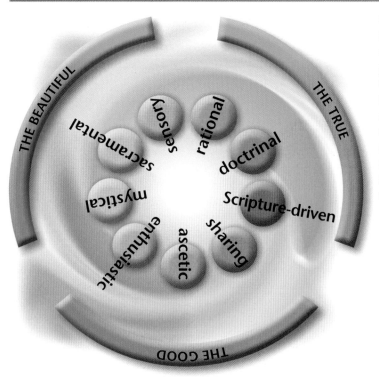

Graphical representation of the Scripture-driven style: It is essential to understand the positioning of this style within the Trinitarian Compass. Christians with a Scripture-driven style should take into special consideration the two opposite styles (mystical and sacramental) as these throw light on the dark side of the Scripture-driven style.

uses the same term that is translated "be transformed" in Romans 12:2. I was fascinated by the fact that the Greek term for "transfiguration" (which sounds so extraterrestrial) and for "transformation" is exactly the same. Are transformation and transfiguration just different descriptions of the same basic process?

I began to perceive interrelationships. What does the transformation process that Paul describes in Romans have in common with the transformation that is reported in the story of Jesus' transfiguration? My body began to produce adrenalin. I spent several hours with these texts, studying, meditating, praying, reflecting. I completely forgot the world around me. In the end, I had the impression that I not only understood more about transformation, but that I had been transformed in my spirit as well.

A dynamic understanding of Scripture

When reporting my experiences to Ian, he seemed to be satisfied with the progress that his student had made. He told me that he had given me this assignment because he had the impression that my idea of Bible study was far too "static." He wanted me to experience personally how existential such a word study can be. He had expected that this exercise would stimulate my emotions, release enthusiasm, and instill in me the desire for more.

Ian explained to me that, in his opinion, the important difference between the doctrinal and the Scripture-driven style lies exactly in this area. The Scripture-driven style is entirely focused on adopting and applying the Word of God. It draws its spiritual energy from that source. The decisive point is the relationship between the Word and the Spirit. In his Word, God promised that the Spirit would come and speak to us. I can turn to a text that I have read innumerable times, and all of a sudden discover something completely new. As Ian expressed

To those approaching the Scripture-driven style from the opposite side

If you have the mystical or the sacramental style, there is no doubt that the Word of God plays an important role in your life. Even if you have heard representatives of the red styles say that you have virtually disregarded the Word of God, you know that this isn't true. In your style, Scripture also plays an important, even essential role. However, in your daily life it plays a different role than it does for representatives of the Scripture-driven style.

As we have seen, the Scripture-driven style takes the subjective aspect of our approach to the Bible very seriously. However, within the aesthetic style family (the category that mystical and sacramental styles are part of), this subjectivity plays a far greater role. This can—especially in the case of the mystical style—go so far that Scripture is really negated as normative authority. Take a look back into church history: Have there been "mystics" who have succumbed to this danger? Yes, there have been, and more than a few. Has everyone with a mystical approach to God succumbed to this danger? Of course not. However, when thinking about the dangers of the mystical style, we should look out for this. The focus on "inwardness," the experience of "Christ in me," the feeling of "unity with God" (all such typically mystical categories) can be so strong that the Scriptures, even if they may not be questioned on a theological level, are hardly given any significance on a psychological level.

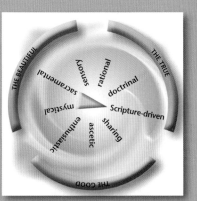

Your starting point: either the mystical or the sacramental style

In the case of the sacramental style, the perils are slightly different. Representatives of this style frequently prefer the public listening of the biblical Word, especially in the context of a worship service, or the concerted reading of Scripture passages, especially in the form of prayers (e.g. Psalms). That is a wonderful approach to the Word of God that can appeal to many people, but especially to those who display the sacramental style. Don't let anyone convince you that this is just "dead ritual." You know very well that it is far more than that.

What, then, is your danger? Precisely that your own approach to the Bible is reduced to these public settings, while at home, in your daily decisions, you only rarely open your Bible to receive guidance from the Word of God. Maybe you believe that without a theologically trained expert you cannot really understand God's Word. Or you are simply lacking practical instruction on how to do it. If this is the case, you can learn a lot from representatives of the Scripture-driven style. You need not become like them, but they can provide you with the very prompts that will help you integrate the Word of God into your daily life with greater power.

Christians with a Scripture-driven style feel closest to God when they are directly dealing with the Bible. All of their experiences are perceived through the filter of their biblical understanding.

it, the Scripture-driven style expects "the Holy Spirit to take the Word of God in a particular situation for a particular person to minister to him or her in a particular way."

Ian asked me what makes me passionate. "Certainly not Scripture, but Christ," I answered. "Exactly," Ian said, "that is what the Scripture-driven style is all about. Christ makes you passionate, and Scripture is a means. It's not that Christ has become ink and paper, it is not the ink that speaks to you. It is Christ who speaks to you when you read the Bible." This differentiation—that it is not the Bible, but Christ who is the highest authority—is of utmost importance for Ian. "The peril of the Scripture-driven style is to neglect this distinction," he said. In the end, Christ is virtually identified with the Word of the Bible, which is what we touched on earlier when describing the doctrinal style—"the Word became book."

The focus on hermeneutics

In Ian's approach to the Bible, hermeneutics plays a crucial role. In order to illustrate this, he quoted the theologian, Gordon Fee, who said, "The pastor must live between the Word and the people." The same applies to every Christian who interprets Scripture, not just for pastors. *Hermeneutics* starts where *exegesis* ends. It asks for the principles that are in Scripture. Then *homiletics*, the third step, is concerned with the presentation and application of these principles. "Far too many preachers," Ian said, "are only interested in homiletics. They would like to communicate something interesting. Consequently they are looking for a fitting text from Scripture to which they can anchor their message." With this approach, however, they shut themselves off from the kind of experiences with the Bible that are characteristic of the Scripture-driven style.

When approaching Scripture, Ian would say that it is legitimate to start an idea rather than the "text." However, he believes that when we then deal with the text, we should be open-minded enough to expect the Holy Spirit to use the text to show us things that correct, expand, or transform our original idea. Far too many Bible studies are characterized by the following scheme: Participants are given a question along with a Bible verse that contains either a direct or an indirect answer to that question. Ian is convinced that it should be exactly the other way around. We should start with the Bible verses and then ask questions that stimulate us to adopt and apply the biblical message.

Scripture-driven versus doctrinal style

Especially with reference to the doctrinal and the Scripture-driven styles, it is important to stress, yet again, that our typology of spiritual styles doesn't deal with theologies, but with a different degree of personal responsiveness to spiritual things. You may have a theology that can be described as "doctrinal" or "Scripture-driven," but at the same time display maybe the mystical or ascetic or sensory spiritual style. This would be no contradiction whatsoever. In fact, it is the norm.

Of course, it is possible to build whole theologies around your own spiritual style in order to guarantee from the outset that there is no tension between personal style and theology. However, I would view such a situation rather skeptically, since the critical function of theology—enabling me to question my own practice—is virtually suspended by this approach.

Doctrinal and Scripture-driven styles are neighbor styles. In other words, they have a considerable overlap. This particularly applies to the Scripture-driven wing of the doctrinal style and the doctrinal wing of the Scripture-driven style, which only differ in nuances. Nevertheless, we should not confuse the doctrinal and Scripture-driven styles.

Almost all Protestant variations of the doctrinal style place the Word of God at the center. However, this specific kind of theological content is not necessarily linked to the doctrinal style. In Roman Catholic and Orthodox churches we can encounter the same doctrinal style filled with slightly different content than in its Protestant counterparts. My mentor for the doctrinal style, Gene (in his case, I know it), and Pope Benedict XVI (in his case, I would guess it) have exactly the same spiritual style, even if their theologies only overlap in certain aspects.

Scripture itself offers a multi-dimensional portrait of Christ. Doctrinal people are more concerned with looking at what all of these different portraits have in common. Scripture-driven people can be quite happy to move freely into these different aspects, and apply them individually to life. Both are possible and legitimate ways of dealing with Scripture.

Scripture-driven people have no problem whatsoever with the fact that there are four gospels rather than one, and many apostolic letters rather than just one apostolic doctrine. Faith in Jesus allows various perspectives on him. Scripture-driven people are usually not pre-occupied with harmonizing these different views, they can even appreciate that kind of plurality. They know that "the Bible's witness to God's pursuit of human beings is a story of relationship, and therefore it is messy. It is not ordered by straight lines of logic," as Richard Foster puts it.

Both styles like to quote 2 Timothy 3:16-17: "All Scripture is God-breathed and is useful for teaching, rebuking, correcting and training in righteousness, so that the man of God may be thoroughly equipped for every good work." While the focus of the doctrinal style is on the expression "Scripture is God-breathed," the Scripture-driven style is concerned with the practical consequences (teaching, rebuking, correcting, training in righteousness, good works). Of course, these are just differences in tendencies. The overlap between the two styles in this area is far greater than these differences.

> **Scripture-driven people have no problem with the fact that there are many apostolic letters rather than just one apostolic doctrine.**

The core of the Scripture-driven style:
The Bible as a "living Word"

The Scripture-driven style stresses the fact that the Bible is the living Word addressed to us. It is not exclusively concerned with exegesis, but rather focused on personal application, "all the time remembering that the goal is not the mastery of the text, but the discovery of God through the text," as Richard Foster puts it. We don't treat the text as an object, but ourselves as the object of the text.

There are countless ways of approaching Scripture, and all of them have their value. You can read the Bible to study doctrinal issues, to understand historical contexts, to satisfy your hunger for knowledge. However, in the framework of the Scripture-driven style, the goal is the transformation of our lives and the desire to become more Christlike in that very process. In this style the Bible holds the key role for spirituality, as it serves as the most reliable bridge to Christ.

The two wings of the Scripture-driven style

The Scripture-driven style can lean either toward the doctrinal style, placing more stress on the objective element and becoming a bit more static, or toward the sharing style, focusing more on outsiders and relating the Biblical message to their needs. The first option places a stronger emphasis on receiving; the second, on giving. Incidentally, the Scripture-driven style isn't linked to any specific interpretation of the Bible, conservative or less conservative. The style in itself has nothing to do with how one explains the "inspiration" of Scripture. We can find representatives of this style in all kinds of theological camps.

The strengths of the Scripture-driven style

The most obvious strength of the Scripture-driven style is its faithfulness to the Bible. Christians displaying this style think Bible, speak Bible, pray Bible. Scripture speaks to them as if it hadn't been written 2,000 plus years ago, but recently, just for our time. Sometimes the historical distance between the writer then and the reader now almost vanishes. Scripture-driven people can be somewhat expressionistic. Here and there the gap between the artists and their objects is melted away by the pulsating life that is boiling behind both of them, so that artist and artwork form a unity. Richard Foster, who has written so many wonderful things about an existential approach to the Bible, expresses it like this: "Reading the Bible with human 'eyes' alone is like mentally registering the words of the text without recognizing who is speaking through them. This is why Paul speaks of 'the eyes of your heart.'"

The perils of the Scripture-driven style

The closer the Scripture-driven style leans to the doctrinal style, the greater the danger of reducing God's Word solely to the Bible. At that point, people risk no longer expecting to hear God's voice within them as they read the Bible. In order to avert this danger, interaction with the mystical style is helpful, as here the focus is on listening to God's voice "within us." The second peril of the Scripture-driven style is an exaggerated view of the verbal, which goes hand in hand with neglecting physical expressions. Interaction with the sacramental style helps to counterbalance that one-sidedness.

Richard Foster writes, "The legalism of the Pharisees is an expression of bibliolatry—a rigid adherence to the letter of the Scriptures, devoid of the presence of the Spirit, which makes a virtual idol of the Scriptures. Our God is not the Bible, but its living Author." Christianity is not, even if it has produced the most widely distributed book of all time, a "religion of the book."

The sharing style: Passing on the grace of God

Since my own spiritual style is the sensory wing of the sacramental style, my opposite pole is the sharing style. Taken superficially, this may seem a bit odd, since my whole ministry is focused on sharing, on communicating, on passing on what I have received from God. However, in my case this sharing is not an expression of my spiritual style (I couldn't say that my experience of God is especially strong in the midst of these activities), but it is the result of immense self-discipline. It is by no means "natural" for me to pass on what I have received.

Victor, my mentor for the sharing style

Victor, my mentor for the sharing style, functions altogether differently. For him, sharing is part of his spiritual DNA. It is so natural for him that he expects it of other believers as well. It has permeated his whole ministry. Both Christians who have this style, and those who have completely different styles—such as myself—can learn how to share their faith from Victor. It seems to be his spiritual style, combined with a breathtaking strategical consistency, that has made Victor one of the most successful ambassadors of Christ I have ever met. To date, about 13,000 churches (of 20-40 people each) have emerged from his ministry, most of them in the Muslim world.

Sharing style:

On the one hand, the sharing style belongs to the red style family; on the other hand, to the ethical style family. Depending on its leaning toward one of its two neighbor styles, it can manifest itself in a more Scripture-driven or ascetic variety. For Christians with a sharing style, it is most natural to express their spirituality through passing on the love of God to others. The strength of this style is its focus on people outside of the church; the peril is in not appreciating Christian traditions and symbolism (iconoclasm).

Three years ago I received an e-mail from our NCD Partners in a Muslim country in which they told me about Victor and insisted that I meet him. They had learned as much from him as from me, they wrote, and deemed it important that we get to know each other. What I didn't know was that parallel to this e-mail they had written another e-mail to Victor with exactly the same content, i.e. insisting that he meet me. And, since the two of us are people who listen to the advice of good friends, we finally found ourselves sitting together on the patio of a hotel in Copenhagen, Denmark, asking ourselves what God had in mind through our meeting. That same afternoon, I asked Victor to become my mentor for the sharing style.

"I am not a Christian"

Many of the things that Victor shared with me are outside of my comfort zone. For example, when Victor has been asked by authorities in a Muslim country if he is a Christian, in many cases he has answered "No." What? He disowns his faith in Jesus? When I heard this for the first time, I was sure I had heard another rooster crow!

But Victor took time, a lot of time, to explain his motives to me. Security reasons? Sure, that is a factor, but not the most important one. His reasoning is different. When Victor uses a word like "Christian," he hears it through the ears of those with whom he is speaking. He must apply their understanding of this word, not his own. If he tells a Muslim that he is a "Christian," the other person might possibly identify it with the "Crusades," or at least with the suspicion that he is anti-Muslim. Because of that, it would be wrong—morally wrong—to use that word. Therefore Victor says, "No, I am not a Christian." And he explains

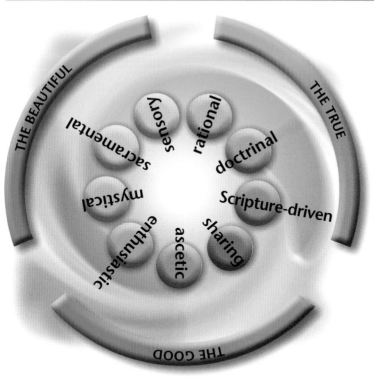

Graphical representation of the sharing style: It is essential to understand the positioning of this style within the Trinitarian Compass. Christians with a sharing style should take into special consideration the two opposite styles (sacramental and sensory) as these throw light on the dark side of the sharing style.

to the Muslim, "I believe in God. I believe in *one* God. I believe that God has created us. I believe that he has created the whole universe. That he is almighty. That he will judge us one day." No Muslim has difficulty with these statements. "I want to create curiosity, honest interest, maybe even friendship," Victor said. "We Christians have been world champions in creating unnecessary barriers. Jesus has come to break down these barriers. We should do the same."

Avoiding unnecessary barriers

In pursuing this approach, Victor can be excessive. Not everyone with a sharing style has the same excessive mindset, but they all share Victor's central concern: to do all that we can so that unchurched people are touched by the love of God. People with the sharing style aren't focused on Christian insiders. They constantly view themselves through the lenses of outsiders. Their relationship with God is shaped by this outward orientation. When unchurched people experience God's love, a believer with the sharing style feels especially close to God.

Christian symbols? If they are helpful for outsiders, why not. If they aren't helpful? Then we do without. Church buildings? Why not, if they build a bridge to outsiders. And if it is a mosque that builds this bridge? Then those people who are so reluctant in calling themselves "Christians," but who *are* very committed Christians indeed, meet in a mosque. This is one of the most extreme, but also most impressive examples of how the sharing style is expressed in Victor's life.

Ministry in the Muslim world

To date there are 47 Muslim Imams who have found Christ due to Victor's ministry. Fifteen of them are still responsible for a mosque, in some of which the Christians meet for prayer. "If people are accustomed to going to the mosque, they shouldn't immediately stop once they have found Christ. Muslims go there for prayer. Now, after meeting Christ, they have even greater cause for prayer. And there is a large segment of the community in that place—religious people whom God loves. They should take that as an opportunity to pray for the others in the mosque."

These Christians call themselves "al arafin," an Arabic term derived from the "Emmaus story" as reported in Luke 24. It means, "those whose eyes have been opened." These "al arafin" disciples have no difficulty continuing to call themselves "Muslims." They are Muslims whose eyes have been opened. "If you are born in a Muslim family, you bear that mark on your body forever," Victor stated, "you can never say, 'I am not a Muslim,' because that would mean, 'I am no longer a part of that community.' We shouldn't take away that identity, it would be like stripping people naked in public."

Not concerned with church traditions

When applying this approach it goes without saying that Victor isn't overly concerned with Christian traditions. If he should draw attention to tradition, then it is to the traditions of those he wants to win. He has often experienced that Christian traditions and doctrines have been more of a hindrance than a help to the spread of the gospel. "Do you know the difference between a Calvinist and a terrorist?", Victor asked me, smiling from ear to ear. I suspected that he was trying to teach me something in his humorous way, so to be on the safe side, I said I didn't know. "You can negotiate with a terrorist," he finally answered and burst into laughter. That my own laughter was a little bit more muffled than his, certainly has something to do with the fact that I have a different spiritual style. However, I fully understand Victor's point: Dogmatic narrowness often makes Christians inflexible and rigid. They honestly believe they are defending the truth of the gospel, but in reality they are discussing insider problems, while many people for whom Christ has died have run away without being noticed. "Many times existing churches create more barriers to outsiders than they facilitate opportunities to experience the love of God," Victor said.

In Victor's movement, a person doesn't first of all become a believer, then grow in faith, and finally, once he or she is mature enough, begin to consider (most likely in a conference room) what to do in order to share his or her faith. If that happens, Victor is convinced that it is too late. Christianity essentially expresses itself in the act of sharing one's faith, literally from the first moment.

"Jesus, Hallelujah"

Victor's favorite story is that of a criminal illiterate. Seven years ago the wife of this man was diagnosed with incurable cancer. The doctor sent her home to die. One night, her desperate husband heard the gospel on the radio. The only thing he understood was that Jesus saves and that he changes the lives of those who believe in him. Then a song was played in which the word "Hallelujah" was sung repeatedly. This man had not learned what prayer was, nor had he the slightest idea of what a "change of life" could be. Basically, he

---

What fascinates me most about Victor

Though not having the sharing style myself, I have learned a great deal from Victor—both for myself and for my work—about what it means practically to share your faith. Not just to pass on what you have received, but to share it in a way that enables others to share it. That is Victor's real point. To share something is addition. To share something in a way that the receiver shares it with someone else leads to multiplication. And perhaps the most important aspect of this perspective is that the invitation to join this multiplication process is not placed somewhere at the end of a discipleship process, but right at the outset. You can only take part if you share. Actually, your own participation is essentially expressed by the act of sharing. This is a lesson that all of us need to learn, whether we have the sharing style or not.

Christians with a sharing style don't need church buildings in order to feel close to God. They experience God most strongly when they can pass on to others what they have received from God.

remembered two words, "Jesus" and "Hallelujah." So he started to pray for his wife, "Jesus, Hallelujah, Jesus, Hallelujah." He did that for one month. His wife was healed. The doctor asked what had happened, and the man's answer was, "Jesus, Hallelujah." The doctor wanted to know more. Finally, the man who was now a *former* criminal, got in contact with Victor's group. Through his testimony and the doctor's, more than 4,000 people have found Christ.

Victor told me the story many times, especially when we were discussing "church quality." Quality doesn't mean "professionalism." It simply means to give all that you have. And if all that you have is Jesus and Hallelujah, then you give Jesus and Hallelujah. The rest, Victor said, is performed by God.

No "purely academic" questions

This is how the sharing style functions. You don't learn something first in theory in order to put it into practice later. No, the most effective way of learning is simply by doing. In the process, you will encounter problems, which give rise to questions—*real* questions, not the so-called "merely academic questions"— that stimulate us to continue our growth process. "Most churches, especially in the West, practice the very opposite," Victor said. "You can take your exam without ever having touched a human life."

When I asked Victor about the relationship between evangelism and social justice in his ministry, it seemed that he didn't really understand my question. For him, the issue is relatively simple: You give away what you have received, be it material resources or the message of God's love. "The body has a need, the soul has a need. If someone is hungry, you cannot share only the gospel." A considerable part of Victor's ministry is research. Victor wants to identify the needs of people. "If we don't know our neighbors, we won't know how to pray for them, because research leads to the items that become prayer points, and prayer points lead to the plans that serve the community." According to Victor, if Christian groups don't see the need for this kind of research, that is a sure sign that they aren't really interested in ministering to unchurched people.

The core of the sharing style:
Experiencing God by giving away

The sharing style is driven by the desire to bring the presence of God to bear in all of life, not just in a privatized "religious sphere." By doing this, representatives

To those approaching the sharing style from the opposite side

If your own spiritual style should be the sacramental or sensory style, there is a certain probability that the very things that I share in this chapter in reference to my mentor Victor, don't speak to you at all. Especially if your own spiritual style is the sacramental one, you will hardly be able to identify with Victor's experiences. You may even be saying, "That is no longer church as I understand it." However, the topic of our discussion is not getting you to join Victor's team. Instead, we are talking about your own spiritual growth in your own spiritual style exactly at the place where you have your spiritual home. The goal is for you to appreciate the strengths of your own style, while clearly recognizing the potential perils.

What is the danger of your style? The answer to this question differs depending on whether you have the sacramental or the sensory style, but in either case it could be that your spirituality is so much focused on your own experiences that you aren't even aware of the fact that countless people are unable to experience God as you do. The fact that an artistic expression of faith is appealing to you, may lead you to the conclusion that, at least with a little bit of effort, it should be appealing to everyone else. You may honestly be convinced that the doors of your spirituality are wide open to "everyone." But in reality, only very specific people find their way through those doors.

Your starting point: either the sacramental or the sensory style

Some Christians may even express forthrightly, "We don't have to adapt to the needs of the unchurched, they should adapt to the existing forms of Christianity. We don't approach other people, but expect them to approach us. We don't question ourselves, but expect others to question themselves." Countless believers are unaware that while they are experiencing their own way of worshiping God as natural and valuable, they are unconsciously creating unnecessary barriers to the Christian journey of others.

If you come from the sacramental or the sensory style, you could learn a lot from representatives of the sharing style. Consider the question they ask: "Where do we have barriers—unnecessary barriers—that may hinder an outsider from encountering God?" If only a few people become Christians, representatives of the sharing style usually don't see the problem as residing in the outsiders ("Unbelievers!", "Hostile to traditions!", "Culturally uneducated!"), rather, they begin to question themselves. In what ways are we insensitive? In what ways are we too strongly focused on our own spiritual well-being? Where do we expect others to become "Jews," metaphorically speaking, before they can become Christians?

of this style sense that they are participating in what God is doing. They can easily identify with Emil Brunner's classic statement, "The Church exists by mission as fire exists by burning." The call to mission applies to every believer, independent of our spiritual styles. However, for Christians with the sharing style, this aspect is the core of their relationship with God.

If our initial research on this theme isn't misleading, this style seems to occur more frequently in situations of persecution than in "stable" situations. While a consumer Christianity attracts primarily practicing consumers, a persecuted Christianity attracts people who are willing to share their lives with others. It is more than a linguistic accident that the New Testament word for "witness" *(martys)* can also be translated "martyr." The martyrs took their name from the fact that they witnessed to Christ by the shedding of their own blood.

The two wings of the sharing style

If the sharing style leans toward the Scripture-driven style, the way in which the gospel is shared takes on a "word-oriented" flavor. If it leans toward the ascetic style, the focus is more on the sacrificial life—witness as *martys*. However, it is characteristic of both varieties that God's love is shared holistically, not only in words, but also in deeds, in the way that the people we minister to need it most. In contrast to a widespread prejudice, Christians with a sharing style don't tend to display "imperialistic attitudes." Imperialism declares: You have to become like me. In contrast, the sharing style makes Christians creative so as to get involved in the culture and the needs of other people without fear.

The strengths of the sharing style

The first and most noticeable strength of the sharing style is the focus on the unchurched. The Word of God is seen primarily as a Word for others, it can only be received if we give it away. This makes Christians with this style creative in finding new ways of spreading Christianity, in literally inventing them. Christians with this style may have the gift of evangelism, or not (see box on page 118), but they definitely contribute, directly or indirectly, to world evangelism. This is the second strength of the sharing style.

The perils of the sharing style

As with all styles, the perils of the sharing style are the flipside of its strengths. The focus on the unchurched can go so far that church traditions are approached with hostility, as something to be avoided, maybe even fought. This can lead to an iconoclastic attitude whose motivation may be understandable, but that can do—and has done—a lot of harm. As sympathetic as representatives of the sharing style can be toward the culture of the unchurched, they can be just as unsympathetic toward the culture of other Christians. Nothing would be more effective in preventing iconoclastic consequences as interaction with the sacramental style.

The second strength of the sharing style—its focus on evangelism—also has a peril. There is the danger of reducing the whole Christian life to "soul-winning." Countless other aspects of the Christian faith (for instance everything that is represented by the color green), if perceived at all, will be seen exclusively as a means to the end of evangelism. The whole Christian faith is understood as service, and exclusively as service. Enjoying God's creation, which is characteristic of the sensory style, has no place. It is in this area that Christians with the sharing style can learn from representatives of the sensory style about the very things they need for their spiritual growth.

The sharing style and evangelism

Our research on spiritual gifts confirmed the famous thesis of C. Peter Wagner that exactly 10 percent of all Christians have the "gift of evangelism." And exactly 11 percent of Christians have the spiritual style of sharing. Without a doubt, both dimensions—spiritual styles and spiritual gifts—have an affinity to each other, but they are not identical. Not every Christian with the sharing style has the gift of evangelism, and not everyone with an evangelistic gifting has the sharing style. What is the difference?

The question relates to the general difference between spiritual gifts and spiritual styles, which applies in a similar manner to other gift/style combinations as well: for instance, the gift of voluntary poverty and the ascetic style; the gift of artistic creativity and the sensory style; the gift of knowledge and the rational style; the gift of teaching and the doctrinal style, etc. In all of these cases, it is true that gifting and style can coincide with each other, but they don't have to coincide. However, if both "related" dimensions are paired—for instance, the gift of evangelism and the sharing style—the result is an exceptional "power package." The spiritual style provides the spiritual energy, which is released and made available to others through the respective spiritual gift. Regrettably, in the past these dynamics have not been considered in Christian literature. It seems to me that a lot could be discovered about this reality that could dramatically enhance the efficiency of future Christian ministry.

Of course, the sharing style cannot only be paired with the gift of evangelism, but with any other of the spiritual gifts as well, for instance, the gift of giving and the gift of voluntary poverty, but it can also be paired with the gift of service, of music, of healing, of hospitality, etc. It is helpful for every believer not only to know their spiritual style, but also their spiritual gifts, and then to spend much time contemplating the significance of the respective combinations. In order to support Christians in this process, we have published a book in the NCD Discipleship Resources series called, "The 3 Colors of Ministry." It contains, among other things, a scientifically normed Gift Test that is related to the three colors of the Trinitarian Compass.

I know a number of Christians with a sharing style who don't have an evangelistic gifting. These Christians are not usually on the front lines when it comes to aggressively sharing the gospel. They feel more at home in the background, radiating God's love rather than speaking a lot about it. Some of them may even be reluctant to share their faith by verbal means. They are concerned—which may be a consequence of their spiritual style—that this could come across as "imperialism," as imposing their beliefs on someone who really doesn't want it.

It would be helpful for these believers if their own image of evangelism were not reduced to a standard model (with prototypes such as Billy Graham or Bill Bright). There are countless ways to share God's love with other people. As they open up to God, human beings go through many different phases before they make a decision for Christ. In each of these phases they need a different type of interaction. When they are ready to make an actual decision for Christ, the gift of evangelism can be of utmost importance. During other phases, other gifts may be even more relevant.

> **Not every Christian with a sharing style has the gift of evangelism.**

The ascetic style: Developing discipline for God

enrik really doesn't like to be put into the "ascetic" box. "Is your spiritual style located between red and blue?", I asked him. "Yes." – "Is it directly opposite the green color zone?" "Yes." – "Is it positioned between the sharing and the enthusiastic style?" "Yes." – "Would you call your style 'ascetic?'" "No." I mention this because there are many Christians with similar feelings. While they can identify 100 percent with the position of this style within the Trinitarian Compass, they have difficulty relating the term "ascetic" to themselves.

Throughout church history the term "ascetic" has adopted quite different meanings, and not infrequently has it been connected with a tendency toward withdrawal from the world *(fuga mundi)*. Sometimes the term "ascetic" is almost seen as a synonym of the monastic life, which—in terms of our typology—is rather confusing. Of course, many Christians with an ascetic style will be attracted by the monastic life. But in any monastic community, as in any church, you will find *all* nine styles. The ascetic style isn't even over-represented in monasteries.

Henrik, my mentor for the ascetic style

In the past I have had very fruitful mentoring meetings with a number of monks. However, I deliberately opted for a decidedly "non-monk" as my mentor for the ascetic style, simply because most of us live our spiritual lives outside the walls of a monastery. Henrik is a typical, and also radical, representative of the ascetic style. He is a Major in The Salvation Army, which, as a whole, has a remarkably strong affinity to the ascetic style. Henrik doesn't show any appreciation for externals. They don't mean anything to him. His view is exclusively focused on the inner life and attitudes of people. I learned from Henrik that a decreasing focus on externals corresponds to an increasing focus on internal values, in other words, on the factors that ultimately count.

As we have seen, the ascetic style is at the center of what we have called the "ethical style family" (see page 55). Again one of those categorizations—ethical style family. "No," Henrik said, "I don't think that this term fits me. I really can't say that I would place ethics at the top of my value system." So I tried to translate what I mean by "ethical." "How does life transformation sound to you? Or holiness?" Indeed, these are terms that Henrik cannot only fully identify with, but which are also at the center of his own spirituality. "It is a transformation process," Henrik said, "in the course of which we become more and more Christlike." If we want to learn what holiness is about, there is no better starting place than Christians representing the ascetic style.

What fascinates me most about Henrik

Henrik expresses his spirituality extremely differently than I do, as my most highly developed style is the sacramental style, followed by the sensory style. In addition, he represents his values with relentless conviction. He's definitely not a man of questionable compromises. Though I can cheerfully drink one glass of wine in his presence, when I lift the second glass I notice him looking very seriously into my eyes, and if I were to lift a third glass, not only would he feel extremely uncomfortable, but I probably would as well. Therefore, I try to avoid such a situation. He radiates a certain rigor, but nothing legalistic. And because he is not legalistic, I am willing to open up and share about my own problem areas.

No appreciation of externals

I told Henrik how I function spiritually. Before I flew to England to meet him for our first mentoring session, I went to the opera house in Hamburg to watch Mozart's

Requiem, choreographed and performed as a ballet. I stressed that for me this was by no means "worldly entertainment" that I had taken in before we had our mentoring sessions and got involved in "spiritual things." For me, that evening at the opera house was literally an encounter with God. And it was not primarily the Latin lyrics (which are, by the way, excellent!) that spoke so deeply to me. Rather it was the way the message was expressed through the music and dancing.

Henrik's spirituality functions differently. He told me about a conference that he had attended some days before we had our mentoring meeting. While the participants of this conference were singing worship songs (to which Henrik is extremely receptive), a dancer performed on the platform (to which Henrik isn't at all receptive). "To be honest with you, I had to close my eyes in order not to have my worship ruined. I cannot relate to that at all," he said. Isn't it interesting how differently followers of Christ can function? And yet these are two absolutely authentic expressions of spirituality.

No need for symbols

Henrik told me about the history of The Salvation Army and explained why it became one of the few decidedly non-sacramental churches: "The sacraments and other externals are symbols of an inner reality. We observed the danger that symbols can take the place of that reality. You can use the symbols without experiencing the reality. On the other hand, we know that you can experience the reality without using any symbols. We aren't saying that the experience should always be without symbols, but for us it's possible."

Ascetic style:

On the one hand, the ascetic style belongs to the red style family; on the other hand, to the ethical style family. Depending on its leaning toward one of its two neighbor styles, it can manifest itself in a more sharing (red) or more enthusiastic variety (blue). For Christians with an ascetic style, it is most natural to express their spirituality through a demonstration of their independence from material and worldly concerns. The strength of this style is its focus on a sacrificial life; its peril is the tendency to withdraw from the world (escapism).

Of course, I understand what he wants to express by this. Symbols can be misused, and have been misused. However, I asked him if it would not be a better alternative to learn the proper use of externals, rather than risk throwing the baby out with the bath water. If we, in our fear of misuse, deny the use of all external aids, doesn't that simply result in making the Christian faith far more difficult than it really is? Henrik understood my questions and generally agreed that this can be a danger. However, referring to his own spirituality, he clearly expressed, "These externals have never been helpful to me. And there are many other Christians who function as I do. They are not at all touched by the things that are so important to you. So our style reaches people who respond naturally to our form of spirituality. Others may be reached through a far more sensory style. I have no problem with that."

Henrik's point is more than justified. There are many people that are attracted by the ascetic style (exactly 11% of Christianity), and 33% are attracted by the ethical style family. However, it wouldn't do justice to the concerns of the ascetic style to relate them exclusively to those who have it as a native style. All of us are called to live a holy life. We don't have to become ascetics in order to do this, but if we are serious about developing our spirituality, there is much we can learn from representatives of the ascetic style about self-discipline. The shunning of externals is, at its heart, a central means for achieving such discipline. By rejecting the pleasures of the flesh, one is able to demonstrate a single-minded commitment to the mission of God and in so doing be on the path to spiritual growth. It is an act of focus, of dedication to the task.

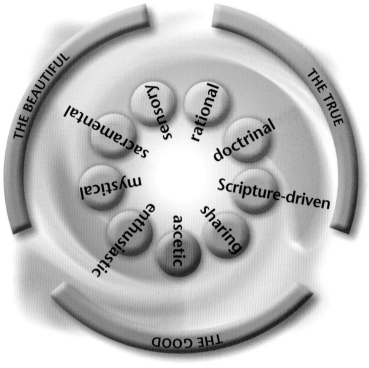

Graphical representation of the ascetic style: It is essential to understand the positioning of this style within the Trinitarian Compass. Christians with an ascetic style should take into special consideration the two opposite styles (sensory and rational) as these throw light on the dark side of the ascetic style.

I asked Henrik about the most important thing that I could learn from him or other representatives of the ascetic style, for my own spirituality. Henrik's answer came immediately. "It is the realization that you don't need anything other than God and the Spirit. Wherever you are, you can experience the presence of God, and the people you are with can experience it as well. We can simply pray, and the Spirit will manifest himself. You may not see it, but you will feel it." It is this simplicity of faith that is so important for Henrik. No, it's not only "important" for him. He literally radiates it, he lives it.

Opposite to green

Within the Trinitarian Compass, the ascetic style is the direct opposite style of the green color zone, we could even call it the "anti-green style." How does that terminology sound to Henrik? "I would agree that everything that is important for me spiritually is totally anti-green. However, I wouldn't like to be understood that I am anti those who are green. But for my own spirituality, the green component is not at all important."

Every style has strengths and dangers. Every representative of every style tends to see the dangers of the other styles, especially the opposite styles, very clearly, while they see their own dangers with far less clarity. That applies to Henrik as well. It is not difficult for him to speak about the dangers of the sacramental and sensory styles, and all of his critical observations are valuable and helpful. However, when I asked him what he sees as the dangers of his *own* style, the ascetic style, he paused, and then said, "That is probably one of the most difficult questions you have asked me. It is so much easier for *you* to answer this question, Christian. So you tell me about my dangers, and I will tell you if I agree." Of course, it was not difficult for me to spontaneously respond with a whole list of possible dangers, such as: an anti-green attitude leads to viewing the whole

To those approaching the ascetic style from the opposite side

It is easy to understand why Christians whose spirituality is grounded in the green zone (either in the sensory or rational style), have difficulty with the ascetic style. Everything that is important for your spirituality—the arts and sciences, sensory perception, symbols, etc.—is viewed with skepticism by representatives of the ascetic style. Why should you get involved with a spirituality that has such a critical view of the very things through which you experience God so concretely? How could that enrich your faith, wouldn't it just pull the carpet right out from under your feet? It would be like taking away the sacraments from a sacramental believer, the Bible from a Scripture-driven believer, or signs and wonders from an enthusiastic believer. And, without a doubt, there are varieties of asceticism (see box on page 124) that view anything green negatively.

Your starting point: either the sensory or the rational style

However, if your spirituality is green, the goal of the process is not to give up your strengths. Your ability to experience God through your sensory perception (sensory style) or through your thinking (rational style), is something that is of great value. It is not unfair to describe green spirituality as a "secular" spirituality, or even better, as a "creation spirituality." However, in spite of all of these strengths, your approach has dark sides, too. Dietrich Bonhoeffer, an advocate of both the sensory and the rational component of spirituality, didn't stop speaking about "love for the world." That same Bonhoeffer, however, could also state the following: "There is a love for the world that is hostility to God" (James 4:4). This, explained Bonhoeffer, is a love based on the world in and of itself and not on God's love for the world.

This is exactly the point at which representatives of a sensory style can learn from Christians with an ascetic style. You certainly shouldn't take over the "anti-green" view that can be found in many ascetic groups, but training in acts of self-discipline—of which the prime example would be fasting—can help you develop more independence from material things. Yes, it can even help you enjoy (and I have deliberately opted for an entirely unascetic term) God's creation in new and deeper ways.

The benefit for Christians with a rational style is similar. How easily can they forget about the sacrificial dimension of the Christian faith. Sure, in the area of asceticism you can find a lot of unthinking, self-imposed, unnecessary, and even harmful suffering. But there is also authentic suffering for Christ's sake. If you are trained in ascetic practices, you will be better equipped to lead a life according to God's standards: Expressing faith not just with your mind (green), but also with your will (red) and your heart (blue).

Christians with an ascetic style experience God most strongly when they are far away from any worldly distractions. Externals such as symbols and rites are more of a hindrance than a help in their approach to God, which is focused on living a holy life.

green area as "unspiritual," maybe even as the "enemy's territory;" the "world" is exclusively seen in a negative light; enjoying God's creation is almost viewed as "sinful." I asked Henrik if he has encountered similar dangers in his own life, to which he replied, "Yes, that is right. We have a tendency to completely abstain from those things that can be misused." He gave me countless illustrations of this from the history of his own denomination—funny ones as well as not-so-funny ones. On the other hand, he gave me countless illustrations of the proper use of this style within his denomination—examples that shaped society for the better.

The core of the ascetic style: Removing external distractions

Christians with the ascetic style deny themselves many of the pleasures common to a life lived in society, like marriage, property, alcohol, and generous food portions. The goal is to follow Christ exclusively, without the external hindrances that these pleasures so often entail. God doesn't need us to give up any of those things, but sometimes we need to learn to deny ourselves something in order to truly appreciate what really matters. Ascetic Christians don't need a lot to be able to worship God and to live. People with this style can very likely identify with the words of Teresa of Avila: "Let us love the virtues and inward goodness, and let us always apply ourselves and take care to avoid attaching importance to externals. Let us not allow ourselves, sisters, to be the slave of anyone except Christ."

Puritanism, a religious movement emerging in 16th century England which strove to build the church on the foundation of the purity of God's Word, has done much to advance the ascetic style. Significantly, historic puritanism turned against hedonism (the danger of the sensory style) on the one hand, and against the intrusion of secular philosophies into the church (a tendency of the rational style) on the other. However, puritanism hasn't only shaped the ascetic style, but has also often been a formative force (at least in Protestantism) behind the doctrinal, Scripture-driven, sharing, and enthusiastic styles.

The two wings of the ascetic style

The ascetic style is at the center of a style family that stresses holiness. Against this background, many things that play an important role within the green color zone, are viewed as "impure." This style family places a high value on *askesis*, which in Greek means nothing other than "training" or "exercise."

Different ways of viewing green

The way our spirituality expresses itself practically is strongly connected with our view of the green color zone. To simplify, we can distinguish three different tendencies:

1. The world is primarily, if not exclusively, seen as "evil," as a place of temptation, of hostility toward God. As a result, the following equation applies: The less green I am, the more spiritual. From this starting point, Level B growth—the integration of the opposite pole into your own spirituality—is all but excluded. What benefit can come from integrating into your spirituality the very things you consider "evil?"

2. The world and all of its physical expressions aren't seen as "evil," but as irrelevant, in terms of spirituality. Such believers are not necessarily against externals, but they cannot see any spiritual benefit in them either. They would say, "If some people find those things helpful, they are free to make use of them." However, with this passive attitude, we cannot expect much growth to take place.

3. The world is understood as God's creation and consequently it has received the same rating that God has assigned to it: "very good" (Gen. 1:31). Of course, if we don't stick to God's rules, there is the possibility of misusing God's good gifts. This danger of misuse should constantly challenge us to learn the right usage.

Obviously, Thomas Merton had the first tendency in mind, when he wrote: "Under the pretext that what is 'within' is in fact real, spiritual, supernatural, etc., one cultivates neglect and contempt for the 'external' as worldly, sensual, material, and opposed to grace. This is bad theology and bad asceticism. In fact, it is bad in every respect because instead of accepting reality as it is, we reject it in order to explore some perfect reality of abstract ideals which in fact has no reality at all."

However, the perils of the sort of asceticism that Merton describes must not hinder us from appreciating the benefits of the ascetic style. It is well known that poverty can destroy the body and make the soul a dump. However, an excess of possessions and pleasures can do the same. We cannot develop a sensually intense relationship to material things if they are constantly at our disposal. A child who has thirty dolls won't give a name to any of them, won't love or hate any of them, won't develop creativity while playing with them and will quickly get bored. People who watch TV five hours a day won't enjoy any of the programs, nothing will touch them in the deeper levels of their soul. They will constantly demand more and newer things without ever dispelling their inner boredom. They will learn to seek intensity in quantity, a search that is in vain. Excess destroys intensity.

Excessive asceticism and inordinate consumption are opposite ends of the same obsession. A mature form of asceticism doesn't seek domination, power, or control over creation. Rather it seeks harmony, peace, and unity with it. This approach—the praise of God by all of creation—is nowhere better expressed than in the Canticle of the Creatures composed by St. Francis of Assisi. In his prayer, Francis calls upon Brother Sun, Sister Moon and Mother Earth to praise God simply for having been created. He asks that God be praised in and through all that he has made. On this basis, the ascetic style can be linked to an appreciation for beauty and the grandeur of the physical world.

> **The danger of misuse should be a challenge to learn the right way of use.**

Training is never a means in and of itself, but always the preparation for something else. Through continuous training—ascetic exercises—you gradually become more resilient. Asceticism is not a means in and of itself, but a means to an end.

On the one hand, the ascetic style can lean more toward red, to the sharing style. When we spoke about the word for "witness" (Greek *martys*), we touched on what these two styles have in common (see page 117). On the other hand, the ascetic style can lean more toward blue, to the enthusiastic style. Both the ascetic and the enthusiastic styles share the idea that the "spiritual" is largely seen outside the physical, material, and the visible; in other words, outside the green area. Both wings reveal that the ascetic style is the one that is furthest away from the green color zone.

The strengths of the ascetic style

The greatest strength of the ascetic style is to train us in freedom from worldly things. The discipline of self-restraint puts the need for physical pleasure much lower on the list of priorities. This goes hand-in-hand with preparing us to live a sacrificial life. Historically, these are the roots of monasticism. Following the time of the great martyrs, in which believers literally gave their lives for their faith, the early monks and nuns lived a daily life of sincere self-sacrifice. Over time, monasticism came to be seen as a substitute for martyrdom.

Christians with an ascetic style have the courage to be different. Anthony of Egypt, who is regarded as the father of monasticism, exclaimed: "No! Somehow, some way, Christians ought to be different; somehow, some way the Church ought to be different!" Ascetic Christians understand this appeal. The Christian, says Paul, is not to be conformed to the world (Rom. 12:2). Dietrich Bonhoeffer wrote that if we do not have some element of the ascetic in us, we will find it hard to follow Christ. The world wants the church to be the church. The world may not agree with a church that insists on being different, but it will respect it. But it will have neither respect nor use for a church that is always trying to conform to the world.

The perils of the ascetic style

The peril of the ascetic style is clearly the tendency to view negatively everything that the green color zone symbolizes, including the ability to enjoy (see box on the counter page). Nothing would be more helpful to counterbalance this tendency than interaction with the sensory style. In groups that have been strongly shaped by the ascetic style, you can get the impression that there is no room for a land "flowing with milk and honey." Some ascetics seem to assume that Jesus lived exclusively in the wilderness, rather than just 40 days.

On this foundation, it is easy to understand the second peril of the ascetic style— its tendency to irrational suffering. As we have said before, the Bible speaks about "suffering for Christ's sake." But there is also self-inflicted suffering because of questionable theology. We can find countless examples of self-imposed suffering throughout church history. However, this irrational tendency can manifest itself much more indirectly as well. Take, for example, a church that refuses to implement a "gift-based" approach in order to avoid the possibility that it might even be fun to live in accordance with one's gifting. Or imagine a church that seeks to avoid a worship service that might appeal to all senses. Since everything must be sacrificial, all pleasure must be avoided. Nothing can contribute better to overcome this form of irrationality than interaction with the rational style, as it can help to clearly analyze the psychological backgrounds of such an attitude.

The enthusiastic style: Celebrating the power of God

When visiting with Olli, it doesn't take long before he brims over with stories about miracles, encounters with angels, exorcisms, and healings. All of this comes as naturally to Olli as it does for others to speak about the last church board meeting. Stories about amazing encounters with God's power that transcend our rationality. One of the stories that Olli has to tell is my own.

I was 26 years old when I met Olli for the first time. At that time, I suffered from an incurable disease that had been diagnosed on my 18th birthday. At the time Olli and I met, I had already planned my life under the assumption that I wouldn't be getting old. Our encounter was quite dramatic, loud, wild, drastic, extreme, "dark blue"—and definitely outside my comfort zone. However, the important thing was the result: I was completely healed.

It took some time before I realized that at that very moment God had given me perhaps 30 or 40 or even more years to live, which I now planned to make the most of. What I am doing today—including what I am doing at this very moment in writing this book—is a direct outcome of what started 23 years ago, when Olli laid his hands on me to ask for God's healing. The sensation of an incredibly powerful electric shock that raced through every cell of my body in that moment, was no hyped-up charismatic mumbo-jumbo, but an expression of a reality to which I literally owe my present life.

Olli, my mentor for the enthusiastic style

Enthusiastic style:

On the one hand, the enthusiastic style belongs to the blue style family; on the other hand, to the ethical style family. Depending on its leaning toward one of its two neighbor styles, it can manifest itself in a more ascetic or mystical variety. For Christians with an enthusiastic style, it is most natural to experience God through encounters with the supernatural. The strength of this style is its trust in God's power; the peril is an exaggerated view of human feelings (emotionalism).

Olli is the very opposite of an intellectual: A 350-pound ex-rocker, his whole body decorated with tattoos. Years ago, Christ appeared to him in a prison cell and he became a Christian. Since then he has spent a considerable part of his life among drug addicts, in red-light districts, living shoulder-to-shoulder with the poorest of the poor in order to share God's love with them.

Even though I have chosen to report on just one mentor for each style, over the past few years I have worked with a number of other mentors. Let me share with you some of what I learned about the enthusiastic style from Anthony, an Australian with Arabic roots with whom I had a series of mentoring sessions. His insights are a beautiful complement to what I have learned from Olli: the desire, or should I say, the hunger, for "more." More love. More power. More Holy Spirit. More healing. "More of God?", I asked Anthony, deliberately using a somewhat ambiguous term. People with the enthusiastic style have little difficulty with this choice of words. "Yes, more of God," he said, whereupon I immediately translated this statement as "more experience of God," which seemed to me to be more fitting.

Though people with an enthusiastic style experience a lot of God, they are never really satisfied. They constantly appear to be hungry. Anthony, for instance, pastors a quickly growing church in Sydney, which of all churches researched by NCD in Australia, is the one displaying the highest quality. He would have good reason

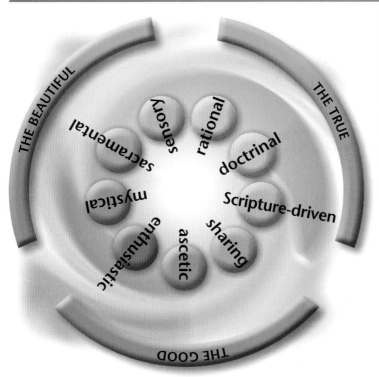

Graphical representation of the enthusiastic style: It is essential to understand the positioning of this style within the Trinitarian Compass. Christians with an enthusiastic style should take into special consideration the two opposite styles (rational and doctrinal) as these throw light on the dark side of the enthusiastic style.

to be satisfied, but satisfaction doesn't seem to be a concept in the thinking of the enthusiastic style. Rather, I sense a certain dissatisfaction in Anthony, a dissatisfaction with the "deplorable status quo," when compared with the spiritual vision of how life according to God's standards should really be.

With Olli it's similar. More than 23 years have passed since our first encounter. Olli has become a bit more composed, stable, and balanced, but his spiritual hunger is probably greater than ever. I asked him for his opinion on the hypothesis that supernatural experiences can be important at the outset of your faith, while a mature believer doesn't need them. "Very well then Christian! Coming up with these lofty ideas is just the problem of you intellectuals. You squeeze the world in such a way that you end up with no need to experience God. The secret is that your expectation of God's power should be constantly growing."

How natural is the supernatural?

One of the themes that I discussed with Olli was his recurring encounters with angels. I opened the box and once again, story-upon-story came tumbling out. "When I was in the red-light district of Frankfurt recently, I looked out at night from the fourth floor window of my room and saw an angel, probably 70 feet tall with a huge sword in his hand, clothed in a white garment, and wearing a golden belt. I asked him, 'What on earth are you doing here of all places?' The angel answered, 'I have to watch over this place, the financial district next door, and I also watch over you Olli."

I told Olli that I have never encountered an angel. "You shouldn't say that," he exclaimed, "I am convinced that many believers have encountered angels, but they just haven't been aware of them." I smiled. While we were chatting and the camera of my laptop was recording every detail, I sensed Olli's eyes turned toward the opened door. "Look, they are running through the hall again," he said. "Wonderful. These are always so incredibly relaxed moments when the angels come. There is so much love in them." I, too, could perceive the relaxation and love that Olli mentioned.

For Olli, these are two important themes. He is open to the supernatural, but he wants to approach it as naturally as possible. I recall a statement made by my mentor, Anthony: "Too many people aim for the sensational and miss the supernatural." This is a helpful distinction. The sensational is not the important point. If the supernatural appears sensational to us, so be it. But striving for the sensational and its potentially negative consequences, is the exact danger that Olli and Anthony have so often encountered and so seriously warned against.

Noise is allowed

The enthusiastic style is certainly not a quiet style. It is hard for people who equate spirituality with silence. At times you get the impression that this style only has two volumes: "loud" and "louder." If you have attended a worship service primarily shaped by people with this style, you know what I am speaking about. The music isn't quiet, the sermon isn't quiet, the prayers aren't quiet. Christians with an enthusiastic style may even regard the quietness and reverence of the mystical style (even if it is the direct neighbor style) as excruciatingly boring.

Olli doesn't need silence in order to speak to God. When praying with people, he doesn't mind if others interrupt him, or ask him questions. He doesn't need to have a "meditative attitude" in order to be close to God. "I am not afraid that the angels will fly away just because it is noisy," he said one time.

Different interpretations

It was revealing to me to observe how differently my mentors dealt with trite problems. Throughout the process of recording most of my mentoring sessions on video through my laptop, I repeatedly had problems with the cooling fan in my computer. This problem manifested itself in sudden hums similar to what I have heard in the dentist's chair. My blue style mentors' interpretation was, "The enemy wants to hinder our discussions." Hmm, could well be. When the hum appeared during a session with my red mentor, he increased his volume and continued speaking, a mechanism that he, as a preacher, is accustomed to. It worked well. My green mentor immediately headed to the nearest Apple Store to order a new fan. A great idea as well! There is no irony when I state that these different approaches are, at least in part, expressions of our different spiritual styles. All of us experience the same things, but we interpret them differently.

What fascinates me most about Olli

Olli experiences the supernatural dimension of faith so much as a normal part of his everyday life, that I would perfectly understand if he dismissed someone like me as a "hopeless rationalist." But he doesn't do that. Of course, sometimes I can sense a bit of good-natured teasing against "you intellectuals" (putting me far more into the rationalist corner than is really fitting), but I sense, throughout our communication, his honest openness, even eagerness, to learn from someone like me. When speaking to him, he doesn't react with the smile of the spiritually superior, but he begins to think, to question himself. Olli has not the slightest intention of stepping away from his enthusiastic style one bit. But he constantly hungers to learn more—even from me. And I learn new things in every encounter with him. That's what makes our relationship so exciting, so honest, and so challenging.

I asked Olli about the relevance of critical thinking in his approach to God. "I think a lot," he replied. "But usually I come up with different conclusions than you intellectuals." When he tries to listen to God, he sometimes has to "switch off his thinking," as he puts it. I said that I would deem that attitude somewhat

Christians with an enthusiastic style love to seek God in the midst of other enthusiastic believers. The focal point is the expectation that they will experience God's supernatural power.

questionable. Olli smiled. "But that is exactly what happened when I met you for the first time. The Holy Spirit told me, 'In this man, there is a spirit of death.' And then I didn't take time to think a whole lot. I just ran to you and prayed for you. And this experience has obviously had a lasting effect on your intellectual hard drive. God has smuggled a virus on it." I find his perspective interesting, even if I would probably use different words to describe the same experience.

All kinds of people

Some critics see Olli's message as something exclusively for people who are a bit more simple-minded. However, this doesn't do justice to Olli's ministry. There are many intellectuals who seek Olli's presence and cooperation. There is a photograph in Olli's office of him with Pope John Paul II. Some years ago Olli did a pilgrimage to Rome. He told me that upon arrival, the Holy Spirit said to him, "Olli, I want you to meet privately with the Pope." At first he was chased off by the "papal body guards," as Olli called the Swiss Guard. They said, "Leave the Holy Father in peace."

However, one of Olli's strengths is a considerable amount of persistence. Finally the Pope received him. Olli told him in his own, unique way: "Holy Father, I am an ambassador of Jesus Christ, I bless you with healing so that you can fulfill your office for the next seven years." Then he prayed for the Pope. As someone who knows what it feels like to have Olli pray for you, I am not so sure how the Pope must have felt at that moment. On the picture that was taken shortly after this prayer, Olli looks quite happy, just as I have known him. The Pope, however, looks a little bit perplexed. "Olli encounters" are impressive encounters. Pope John Paul II must have learned this in the same way as I did.

The core of the enthusiastic style: A God who acts

The enthusiastic style is concerned with a God who acts. Against this backdrop, it is understandable why "signs and wonders" are more important in this style than within the framework of any other style. A "sign" is a window through which light from another level of reality shines into one's room. Whenever such a sign appears, the gap between here and there, between immanence and transcendence, between rational and trans-rational has been bridged.

To those approaching the enthusi-astic style from the opposite side

If you display either the rational or the doctrinal style, it is not unlikely that you struggle to imagine learning from the enthusiastic style. Perhaps you have had encounters with people from this style, or you have heard stories about people from their "camp," and these experiences have been so unpleasant that you have firmly decided how you must evaluate this wing of Christianity. Maybe you consider Christians with this style to be "heretical," or maybe your view is a little bit more moderate: "They can live emotionally if that suits them, but it definitely isn't for me."

When I strongly encourage you to interact with the enthusiastic style (in the same way as I encourage Christians with the enthusiastic style to learn from you), I am fully aware of this tendency to skepticism. And your critical point of view is not without reason. The danger of the enthusiastic style is definitely a prevalence of the subjective, the emotional, and the spectacular, which can lead to very questionable results.

Your starting point: either the rational or the doctrinal style

On the other hand, the lapses mentioned are not a real danger for you as a representative of the rational or doctrinal style. Your own style has made you relatively immune to these perils. That is great, because on the basis of a solid, biblical foundation, you really can afford to soberly evaluate the strengths of the enthusiastic style, without the threat of being absorbed by its dangers. You have developed the ability to discriminate in spiritual matters, haven't you? You are familiar with Paul's admonition, "Test everything. Hold on to what is good" (1 Thess. 5:21). If so, you should be able to apply this principle to the enthusiastic style, for if such discrimination can be expected of anyone, most certainly it can be expected of you.

What are the perils of your style? Certainly not emotional excess. In that area you really have no cause for concern. Your potential danger is rather to neglect personal spiritual experiences and the trans-rational dimension. It probably looks neither attractive nor fitting to you to express your spirituality in the same way as Christians with the enthusiastic style. But this is not what I want to encourage you to do. We are not speaking about taking over a "whole package." Rather, your concern should be to integrate into your own spirituality those aspects of the enthusiastic style that shed light on your own shadows. Or do you honestly believe that your own spiritual style is devoid of shadows? They do exist, and encountering enthusiastic Christians can help you come to grips with those aspects of yourself that may hinder spiritual growth.

Through these overwhelming encounters with the supernatural, representatives of the enthusiastic style have a sharpened awareness of the limitations of the human mind. Frequently they have experienced that it was not human rationality which brought about a spiritual breakthrough, but openness to the trans-rational dimension. Here we encounter a motif that appeared in Rousseau's writings in philosophically reflected form. Rousseau was far away from Voltaire's "religion of rationality." He said, "The less I understand, the more I worship." Representatives of the enthusiastic style can identify with this statement.

The two wings of the enthusiastic style

The enthusiastic style can lean toward the ascetic style. One of the intersections of these two styles could be defined as "holiness." The ascetic wing of the enthusiastic style doesn't deem the green zone as very relevant for spirituality. The mystical wing of the enthusiastic style is a little bit different. This variety is somewhat closer to the green zone. An enthusiastic spirituality leaning toward the mystical style will strive to integrate contemplative ("silent") habits into its own spirituality. Very frequently, Christians who start with an enthusiastic style, later lean more heavily toward the mystical style. In other words, they move from an extroverted to a more introverted blue approach.

The strengths of the enthusiastic style

The greatest strength of the enthusiastic style is its openness to the supernatural. This attitude has solid biblical basis. It is not possible to speak about Jesus' message and to be silent about his miracles. The enthusiastic style takes seriously the reality that the miraculous effects of the coming Kingdom have already begun to shape present reality. In order to make it less offensive, a number of opposite styles tend to dilute the concept of miracles to "allow" the use of the term anywhere and everywhere. In sharp contrast, the enthusiastic style focuses on the idea that God doesn't mind offending our minds by acting supernaturally. Therefore, it considers of great importance that the miracles reported in the Bible are understood as historical facts and not just as metaphoric parables.

The goal of the enthusiastic style is to experience God's power. A God who doesn't act, is no God at all. A spirituality that doesn't experience God's activity, is no spirituality at all. Representatives of the enthusiastic style fight against all attempts to "domesticate" God. God is alive and active in our world. That's why people with the enthusiastic style are more afraid of being called boring than religious fanatics.

The perils of the enthusiastic style

The greatest peril of the enthusiastic style is to confuse the trans-rational with the irrational. There are groups that almost see it as a "quality criterion" for spiritual experiences to be inexplicable by rational means. "Rational equals unspiritual" becomes the subtle equation for their way of thinking. Representatives of the enthusiastic style could benefit enormously from interaction with the rational style in order to avoid this peril.

The high view of that which is non-rational prepares the ground for the second peril: A sometimes frighteningly naïve openness toward unbiblical practices. If someone is able to impress an audience with "signs and wonders," their teachings can be heretical, their appeals absurd, their lifestyle selfish, and no one takes notice. The glamor of the supernatural outshines everything. Their advice is sought even in areas where they have never proven to be competent. Once again it is evident that interaction with the opposite style, the doctrinal style, would help correct or prevent this tendency.

The enthusiastic style and spiritual passion

There is a widespread stereotype that understands spiritual "renewal" almost exclusively in terms of the enthusiastic style, or the culture that has been shaped by it. The stereotypical "renewed church" is very likely charismatic, has a "contemporary" worship service, favors a certain kind of music, etc. If such a church has something like a "traditional" worship service, this is not because it is regarded as an authentic expression of spirituality, but because it is a concession to the "traditionalists" in the church.

These worship services are allowed to be more liturgical, the organ may be used, and classical music can be heard. However, all of these features are definitely viewed as being outside that which is understood as "renewal." The underlying assumption is that spiritual passion is expressed exclusively—at least in its purest form—through the enthusiastic style or through a culture that has been shaped by it.

Churches that have been involved with NCD and have grown in quality, have doubtlessly experienced "renewal." Has this resulted in looking more and more like the stereotypical churches mentioned above? By no means. An Orthodox church that experiences this kind of renewal will not start to utilize guitars and drums in worship. Rather, the church members will experience their highly liturgical worship service as even more solemn, more sublime, and more majestic.

Recently I heard about an NCD consultant (who obviously was poorly trained) who dealt with an Orthodox church that had this exact experience. He commented, "This cannot be true. They do everything wrong in their worship service and have high quality nonetheless!" This consultant had an image of "quality" that was shaped by the stereotype of renewal mentioned above. Therefore, a highly liturgical worship service that was neither "contemporary" nor "seeker-oriented," was—according to such standards—completely "wrong." My guess is that his consultant training was more strongly influenced by a specific church model than by the principles of Natural Church Development.

Of course, the intention of these comments is not to say anything critical about so-called contemporary worship services. On the contrary, this form is appealing to many people and can be a wonderful way of expressing one's own spirituality. However, it is just one of many ways.

Without a doubt, the enthusiastic style has an affinity to a certain expression of spiritual passion. This form is more extroverted than introverted, prefers noise over silence. However, this is not the only way to express spiritual passion. Every style will express passion differently, but the passion needs to be expressed. Spiritual life cannot be understood in a detached way. An imperialistic nominalism that strives to downgrade the fire of Christian passion as "immaturity," is not a spiritual style, it is the opposite of spirituality. Without passion, Christian faith collapses.

Most people see the enthusiastic style as closely linked to the charismatic movement, and rightly so, since this style has shaped the movement as a whole. However, not every member of the charismatic movement has the enthusiastic style. According to our research, 26% of the members of charismatic churches display this style.

> **Each of the nine styles expresses spiritual passion differently.**

The mystical style:
Resting in the presence of God

Even his outer appearance can make one think of a "mystical guru." He has a long, wild-looking beard. His office is loaded with religious images and symbols. A large gold-plated cross rests on his chest. A soft voice communicates the idea that he is an introvert. His physical movements are far from bustling. And a contagious calmness arises from him. This man, whose main occupation is that of a Lutheran priest in Copenhagen, Denmark, doesn't only show up at Christian events, but also in the midst of esoteric spirituality fairs. I discovered online that he offers worship services at New Moon. And lately he started a Bible study group for tarot card readers in order to show them the deeper—which for Ole always equals biblical—message of the images on the cards.

Esoteric fairs, worship services at New Moon, tarot cards—I have since come to know Ole fairly well and could add countless more catchwords of the same category, all of which have one thing in common: They were—and still are— clearly outside my comfort zone. However, I deliberately *wanted* to work with mentors who are outside my comfort zone. So, with that in mind, choosing Ole as a representative of the mystical style was the perfect fit.

Ole, my mentor for the mystical style

Even today I cannot share all of Ole's views, just as Ole isn't enthusiastic about everything that I have written. Nevertheless, I have learned an awful lot from him. Interestingly enough, when speaking with other Christians about my mentoring sessions with Ole, I had the experience that, as soon as I mentioned the word "New Age" (since many of Ole's activities happen in the midst of the New Age movement), a considerable number of them stopped listening. I must admit, as I gathered information about Ole before we had our first meeting, I had similar reservations. Some of the keywords that surfaced in my research were so far outside of my comfort zone that I asked myself repeatedly if Ole really was the right mentor for me.

I asked him whether he is afraid of being labeled a "New Ager" himself. Ole looked deeply into my eyes, smiled, and became very serious once again. "I *am* a New Ager," he finally said. Then he broke into a smile again: "But I am a *Christian* New Ager." Now, that's a title that can be interpreted in extremely different ways. I asked Ole to give me his interpretation. "The fact that I am a Christian New Ager is no different to me than being a Christian Dane or a Christian member of the Lutheran State Church. I don't agree with everything that happens in Denmark. And I don't agree with everything in the Lutheran Church. However, I am a Dane and a Lutheran nonetheless. In the same way, I am a part of the New Age movement. If I weren't a part of it as a Christian, I wouldn't be able to share the gospel within it." Even Ole's strongest critics acknowledge that he is an incredibly effective evangelist in the midst of the New Age movement.

What fascinates me most about Ole

In my encounters with Ole, I rejoiced in some things while I was confused about other things. But there was one thing in particular that deeply moved me: The sincerity with which he seeks out the image of God in every human being—in literally every person regardless of how esoteric or sinful or heretical they may be. This image may be blurred in some people, even to the degree that it is no longer recognizable, but Ole's eyes are able to see it nevertheless. And he wants to help these people transform this image into the original beauty that the Creator intended. Ole's eyes are trained eyes. They see things that other people don't perceive. The focus on the image of God in other people has transformed Ole's eyes into loving eyes.

Since I was still not completely satisfied with Ole's answer, I went on to ask, "Do you teach Jesus' claim, 'I am the way and the truth and the life?'" "Yes," he said, "this is what I teach. As I said before, I am a *Christian* New Ager." I asked him how his New Age friends react to such a statement. For them, his approach must be unbearable. Again, Ole smiled in his most winsome manner. "That is right, they don't like that statement. But again, I am a Christian New Ager, not just a New Ager. They know that I am not their enemy, but that I am a friend and part of the movement. On the other hand, they know there are differences between us, and we are honest about them. They appreciate what we Christians have. They sense that there is a presence in us which they may not interpret as the presence of the Spirit of God, but they sense there is something very strong and full of light. Of course, that doesn't make them Christians immediately, but it has often been the first step."

Between enthusiastic and sacramental

Ole is someone who knows my work fairly well and views it positively, even if he is not really a friend of tests and typologies similar to those used in my ministry. In that area he simply reacts like a typical mystic. He is afraid that these tools could place people into boxes and predetermine certain behavior, while their openness for new, different, unaccustomed things may be hindered. In this area he shares the typical mystical skepticism toward systems, including dogmatic systems. Mystics have the impression that these patterns of explanation obscure more than enlighten.

Even if Ole approaches a typological tool such as the Trinitarian Compass with certain reservation, it is not difficult for him to relate to this typology. He sees his own spirituality "between the enthusiastic and the sacramental style," as he said. At the same time, he can identify with the concerns of many of the nine styles, even within the red zone that is opposite him. The values behind the Scripture-driven and sharing styles (see his evangelistic ministry) are of great importance for Ole.

Mystical style:

On the one hand, the mystical style belongs to the blue style family; on the other hand, to the aesthetic style family. Depending on its leaning toward one of its two neighbor styles, it can manifest itself in a more enthusiastic or sacramental variety. For Christians with a mystical style, it is most natural to express their spirituality through a focus on the inner person ("Christ in us"). The strength of this style is its appreciation of the mysterious dimension of faith; the peril is an overestimation of inner enlightenment (spiritualism).

Symbols and liturgy

In Ole's spirituality it is noticeable that his mystical style leans more heavily toward the sacramental than toward the enthusiastic wing. In his spirituality, images play an important role. Even as a child, images in fairy tale books had a great impact on him. At that time, when little Ole attended a worship service, he often didn't understand the sermons and wasn't overly interested in them, but instead was more fascinated by the altarpieces. *They* preached to him.

His love for liturgy is something that distinguishes him from most representatives of the enthusiastic style. Deeply moved, he shared how he increasingly learned to appreciate the liturgical dimension during several encounters he had with the Coptic Church in Egypt when studying theology. After he had learned the Coptic language, this love grew even deeper. While many Christians are tempted to associate a strong focus on liturgy with "lifelessness," in Egypt, Ole experienced the exact opposite. "The life of the church was mind-boggling," he said. "While we Europeans—it was the late sixties—declared the miracles of Jesus to be pure myths, in Egypt I was experiencing the charismatic dimension

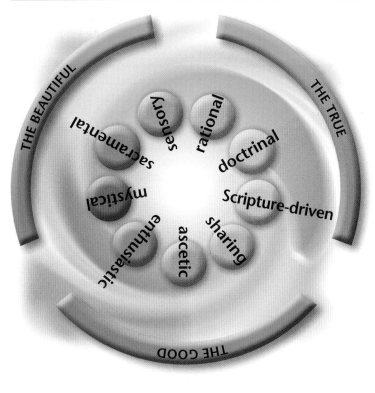

Graphical representation of the mystical style: It is essential to understand the positioning of this style within the Trinitarian Compass. Christians with a mystical style should take into special consideration the two opposite styles (doctrinal and Scripture-driven) as these throw light on the dark side of the mystical style.

in the midst of the Coptic church, including healings, exorcisms, etc. I would like to see this integration of the sacramental and the charismatic dimension in the church of Denmark as well."

Reluctance to set boundaries

Ole has clear dogmatic convictions, and in that sense he isn't much different from my doctrinal style mentor. "I believe that the central doctrines of Christianity are necessary. They are the best way of describing our collective experiences with God. The doctrines have never been my problem. What I don't like is the use of doctrine or the Bible to judge others." Representatives of the mystical style don't like to set boundaries. I wanted to know if he sees members of his Lutheran State Church who don't have a personal relationship with Christ, as non-Christians. "I don't like that language," he said. "If we define people by what they are not, we draw a line. I prefer to speak of potential disciples of Jesus. I want to focus on the potential in people. I want to invite them to become what they have been created to be."

Seeing the image of God in others

When Ole encounters people, whether Christians or non-Christians, the first thing he is interested in is discerning the image of God in them. "This doesn't mean that I agree with all that they say. I don't believe in re-incarnation, for instance, I believe in resurrection. But people holding this view are still created in the image of God, and in their experiences they express something which is true insofar as it describes an authentic spiritual longing. I don't believe that original sin totally destroyed the image of God. This image has been blurred so that it doesn't shine through clearly. It must be cleansed, it must be healed. The prodigal son was still the son of his father. The father was waiting for him."

To those approaching the mystical style from the opposite side

If you have the doctrinal or the Scripture-driven style, defining boundaries is definitely important to you. The boundary between truth and error. Between life and death. Between light and darkness. If there were no error, we wouldn't have to speak about truth; if there were no death, we wouldn't have to broach the issue of life; and only on the background of darkness can we appreciate light. In your spiritual style this boundary is strongly stressed—not in order to exclude people, but to motivate them to cross this boundary—from error to truth, from death to life, and from darkness to light.

Since this is important to you, you have difficulty with spiritualities that either don't set any boundaries or at least don't stress them very much. The mystical style is just such a spirituality. It is a spirituality in which borderlines are blurred, dissolved. At its center, mystical spirituality is the experience of oneness, of unity. In addition to this, in mysticism the subject—and consequently, subjectivity— plays a far more prominent role, when compared with your own spiritual style. Maybe the encounter with mystical experiences will even confirm you in your view of how important it is to set clear boundaries!

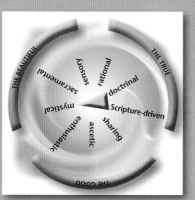

Your starting point: either the doctrinal or the Scripture-driven style

Your skepticism toward the mystical approach is not unjustified; rather, your criticism hits the mark: These are the exact dangers of mysticism, as can be studied in church history. However, at this point we don't want to speak about the dangers of mysticism, but about your own dangers, the dangers of the doctrinal and Scripture-driven styles. Even in your case, the dangers are nothing other than the downside of your strength. The legitimate emphasis on the objective element in the Christian faith—faith is not to be confused with our changing feelings and moods—can lead to a neglect of the inner life. The exclusive focus on God speaking to us through Scripture can result in no longer perceiving God's voice within us.

Your starting point, when exploring the mystical style, is an ideal one. Your own style has fixed, clear, objective standards at its center. On this foundation you are not in danger of sinking into the ocean of a mystical experience of oneness. Rather, interaction with the mystical style can help you correct the one-sided approach of your own style. In other words, this learning process aims at making you a better representative of the doctrinal or Scripture-driven style. Since the biblical standards are deeply rooted in your life, you can afford to take your own subjectivity more seriously than you have in the past.

Christians with a mystical style experience greatly the work of the Holy Spirit within them. Mystical spirituality is characterized by practices that advance inner contemplation.

This concept pervades the way Ole does evangelism. "In the early years, when I dealt with people who believed in re-incarnation, I used to say, 'If you don't leave your false belief, we will have to stop meeting.' But people cannot simply leave what is a strong personal experience." Today Ole takes a different approach. He mentioned the story of a woman who told him about her "experiences in a former life." She had been part of a group that was with Jesus in which she became a witness of his crucifixion, but not his resurrection. "I didn't argue with her about re-incarnation, instead I told her that what was missing in her memory center was an experience of the risen Christ. I told her, 'What I will do now is to pray that Jesus as risen and alive will reveal himself into your memory center.' Two months after this prayer, the lady came back to me. She said: 'Now I am ready, please pray with me that I may receive Christ in a humble heart.' Little by little, the presence of Christ grew in her, and all of these re-incarnation images gradually withered away."

The core of the mystical style: Discovering "Christ in us"

The Greek term *myein* that is at the root of the word "mystic," simply means "close." You close your lips and your eyes. What happens next—in your soul and in your heart—is your encounter with the supernatural. Mystic spirituality stresses that, just as he abides in heaven and over the earth, God also dwells within the believer. In contrast to the enthusiastic style, the mystical style doesn't thrive on visions and extraordinary experiences. Often it is expressed very quietly and can sometimes be remarkably rational and sober. In contrast to the enthusiastic style, a certain "dryness" in one's prayer life is not interpreted as an "absence of the Holy Spirit." Representatives of the mystical style can feel close to God even if they are momentarily not excited or enthused.

Mistrust in systems

Mystics have the tendency to prefer the fragmentary. Mystical thinking cannot be easily categorized theologically. It doesn't offer elaborate systems in which every element finds its place. Rather, it is an expression of an intense religious experience that resists being classified verbally. For a mystic, God remains invisible—not only in the physical, but also in the intellectual sense.

I am well aware that in the past few paragraphs I have repeatedly spoken about "mystics" rather than sticking to the terminology that I committed myself to use

The mystical wing of all religions

In the same way as any religion has its fundamentalist and its liberal wings, almost all religions have a mystical movement. The mystical experiences that can be gained from different religions are amazingly similar—whether we are dealing with a Hindu yogi, a Persian Sufi poet, a neoplatonic philosopher, a medieval monk, a representative of the Jewish Kabbala, or with a contemporary who has turned away from the rationalism and technocracy of Western civilization.

Phenomenologically, the experiences that mystics of different religions have, can be assigned to the same category. That doesn't mean, however, that they are theologically identical. The content of a mystical experience can differ considerably from religion to religion. The common element is how this content is approached. The same is true of the fundamentalist wings of various religions: Their content differs considerably (that is why they battle against each other so relentlessly). The way this content is approached, however, is almost identical.

There are mystical varieties where belief in God is not even a prerequisite for the mystical experience. Mysticism knows theistic, pantheistic, and atheistic varieties. What, then, is the common denominator?

The common denominator is the experience of "oneness." Within non-theistic religions this state is usually referred to as "illumination," within theistic religions, it is referred to as the "unification of God with our soul," unio mystica. This experience of unity overrides the subject-object separation. People don't necessarily idolize nature, but they experience the absolute through nature.

> **Mystical experiences that can be gained within different religions are amazingly similar.**

All strains of mysticism have a certain tendency toward esotericism. The mystical mystery is only accessible by the "initiated." The mysteries are secret teachings or secret cults that are not discussed in the presence of the "non-initiated." Generally, words are not seen as adequate tools to communicate mystical experiences. Mystical spirituality doesn't have any visible body of control. Mystics—whether they are Jews, Muslims, or Christians—don't need outer assurance, since they are conscious of God's presence wherever they are.

Often mystics are in tension with the orthodox representatives of their respective religions. However, in most cases they don't attack the traditional orders and doctrines. Rather, they formally agree with them, without it really meaning an awful lot to them. Sticking to words, dogmas, and rules is regarded as a hindrance to moving forward to the actual meaning of what they have been intended to communicate.

If the result of the Spiritual Style Test has revealed the mystical style as your native style, this doesn't imply that all of these descriptions apply to you. It simply means that you have a stronger affinity to these tendencies than other Christians. You may use completely different terms—such as, "contemplation," "meditation," or perhaps simply "prayer"—to describe the same experiences that other people describe as "unity," "illumination," or "unio mystica."

Hans Küng observed correctly: "Mystics of completely different religious backgrounds can be closer to each other than they are to the average believer within their own religion."

within this book—"representatives of the mystical style" (see page 32). When using the word "mystic" here, I am referring to that which has been labeled "mysticism" throughout church history, where we can find many themes that are characteristic of mystical style representatives as well.

The two wings of the mystical style

When the mystical style leans toward the enthusiastic style, it places more stress on the supernatural and comes relatively close to a charismatic style. Also in this variety, nature and matter are less important. On the other hand, if the mystical style leans more toward the sacramental style (i.e. toward green), as in Ole's case, the physical realm that can be perceived through the senses is given greater spiritual significance.

What both wings have in common is a focus on the mysterious. Mystic spirituality doesn't strive to dissolve nor to explain the mystery. Rather, it loves the mysterious and draws its energy from it. The downside of this is that those things that are not mysterious are in danger of not being seen as truly "spiritual."

The strengths of the mystical style

Since faith is essentially a mystery, the appreciation for the mysterious dimension can be seen as the greatest strength of the mystical style. This has nothing to do with ignorance, but with being aware of the limitations of human knowledge. In theological discourse this is referred to as *via negativa*: It is easier to describe what something is *not* than to define what it *is*. This is expressed in prefixes such as un-, over-, trans-, and out-, or in expressions such as "more than," "higher than," "beyond." In Greek, constructions with *hyper* have been the model, in Latin, those with *super*. This spirituality doesn't want to be irrational, but trans-rational—*more* than rational.

Mystical spirituality is critical toward all attempts to functionalize the Christian faith. The mystic Meister Eckhart put this concern in the following drastic words: "Some people want to look at God through the eyes with which they look at a cow, and they want to love God, just as they love a cow. You love the cow because of the milk and the cheese and your own advantage. This is like people who love God because of outer prosperity or inner comfort."

The perils of the mystical style

This appreciation of the mysterious dimension may lead to an exaggerated view of the mysterious: Things that are logically explainable—that fit into a doctrinal system—lose their fascination. One may not fight against them (mystics usually don't fight at all), but instead smile about them in a slightly condescending way. However, there is no reason for this kind of smile, as we are speaking about a very serious danger of the mystical style. Rather than smiling about the doctrinal style, it would be far more helpful to interact with it and to learn from its concerns.

The interest of the mystical style is with the subjective, explored by the question, "What happens within me?" This focus doesn't necessarily imply a disinterest in the objective, rather one asks for the *effect* of the objective on one's own life. However, the danger of this approach is that people actually lose sight of the objective. In the end, one's own pious feelings may be confused with God. Faith, as it is perceived in one's inwardness, has become the highest standard by which everything else (such as the critical questions of other Christians or the words of Scripture) is measured. To counteract this danger, nothing would be more fruitful than an involvement with the Scripture-driven style.

The sacramental style: Expressing the incarnation of God

When Jonathan and I discussed the sacramental style for the first time— since I had the impression that he is a typical representative of this style—his reaction was rather skeptical. He expressed that he didn't really feel comfortable with the terminology of the spiritual styles. "The sacramental dimension," he told me, "isn't just one of nine styles. It's concerned with the whole of the Christian faith. All of life is sacramental." If it were up to Jonathan, I would have to place what I call the sacramental style right at the center of the Trinitarian Compass.

For me, this reaction was the best proof that Jonathan *is* indeed a typical representative of the sacramental style—a fact that was later confirmed when he did the Spiritual Style Test. All representatives of a specific style tend to place the very aspects that are important *for them*, at the center of the Christian faith. After all that we have learned so far about spiritual styles and their different theological centers, this mechanism seems to be perfectly normal.

Jonathan, my mentor for the sacramental style

Jonathan is an Orthodox priest. For that reason I don't address him as "Jonathan," but as "Father Jonathan." The first time I came across his name was when studying a Wikipedia article on the Orthodox Church. There he was quoted as a critic of attempts to present Orthodoxy in North America on the basis of exaggerated numbers. Jonathan views the situation of the Orthodox Church quite realistically. He sees Natural Church Development as a way to help Orthodox churches experience qualitative and quantitative growth.

Sacramental style:

On the one hand, the sacramental style falls exactly on the interface between the blue and the green style families; on the other hand, it is at the very center of the aesthetic style family. Depending on its leaning toward one of its two neighbor styles, it can manifest itself in a more mystical (blue) or sensory variety (green). For Christians with a sacramental style, it is most natural to express their spirituality through a connection between sensory perception and spiritual reality. The strength of this style is its appreciation for symbols and tradition; the peril is to perform the respective rites without inner participation (ritualism).

Since I also have the sacramental style, it was important for me to find a mentor who practices this style far more radically than I am accustomed to. Even if not every Orthodox Christian displays a sacramental style (in the Orthodox Church, just as in any other church, all nine styles are represented), a Christian who has *both* the sacramental style *and* is part of the Orthodox tradition, is sure to be a radical representative. In this respect, Jonathan didn't disappoint me.

Of course, the sacramental style can be displayed in the midst of the most puritan evangelical churches. However, in those environments, it seeks other expressions than in the Orthodox Church. There is no other church tradition that, as a whole, represents the sacramental style quite as strongly as Orthodoxy. The term "Orthodoxy" is sometimes translated as "correct belief," which is certainly not wrong. Yet it points, in terms of the Orthodox Church, in a somewhat misleading direction. This church regards itself, first of all, as the church of "correct praise" of the Triune God. *Orthos* means correct; and *doxa* comes from *doxazein*, which means "praise." Of course, Orthodoxy sees itself also as a church of "correct doctrine" (from *doxa* = opinion, conception). However, the element of correct praise and worship is the more basic one within Orthodoxy.

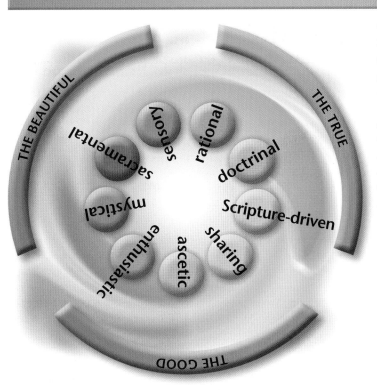

Graphical representation of the sacramental style: It is essential to understand the positioning of this style within the Trinitarian Compass. Christians with a sacramental style should take into special consideration the two opposite styles (Scripture-driven and sharing) as these throw light on the dark side of the sacramental style.

East and West

Since the beginning of Christianity—not just after the so-called "schism" in 1054—there has been a "Western" and an "Eastern" wing of Christianity, both emphasizing different aspects of the Christian message. While many of the Western church fathers were educated primarily in the law, a philosophical and scientific background prevailed among the Eastern teachers. That, of course, shaped theological work. While in the West, Christianity was largely interpreted in legal categories—the focus was on topics such as sin, guilt, and atonement—the Eastern tradition likened the church more to a hospital—human beings are sick and need to be healed. Of course, it also spoke of sin, but sin in that context was understood more like a disease that has to be healed.

Such typology is a gross simplification, but it expresses tendencies that can be detected in the churches of the East and the West even today. While the sacrifice of Christ is seen as the pivotal element within Western churches, in the Eastern churches, it is the incarnation ("The Word became flesh..."). While Eastern and Western traditions together stress the importance of *both* the incarnation *and* the crucifixion of Christ, the different emphases are noticeable. Interestingly enough, this was the "homework" that Jonathan assigned to me: For one whole evening I was to contemplate the two images—church as courtroom and church as hospital. For Christians like me, there is no question as to which image we prefer!

Physical expressions of a spiritual reality

Repeatedly Father Jonathan and I discussed the physical side of spirituality. I told him about other Christians—among them, some of my mentors—for whom "externals," as they call them, are not important. "I agree that these are externals," Jonathan said. "But they are needed externals, we shouldn't do without them. Externals are nothing more than reflections of internal core values and beliefs of who and what God is." On the other hand he clearly sees the danger that these externals can turn from being "external expressions of the inner faith" into the equivalent of paganistic rituals; that they become a means in themselves, rather than being seen as outer expressions of an experienced inner reality.

The sacramental style, as understood in our typology, has little in itself to do with what different church traditions have labeled "sacraments," or with how many there are. Though these sacraments can become an essential part of our spirituality, at its center the sacramental style is concerned with something different: In all areas of life, spiritual mysteries shall find a physical expression. It is not by accident that the sacramental style is located right on the interface between green and blue. It is not bound to a specific form of worship service or church tradition. On the other hand, it is clear that certain traditions and forms of worship services speak more to people with this style than to others.

Jonathan explained to me the importance of not reducing the sacramental life to one sacred act. Rather, it should permeate our whole life. "It's not ideal to live six days of the week like pagans, and then to light a candle on the seventh day," he said. Sacramental expressions are supposed to shape the whole week, which encompasses the study of Scripture as well as fasting, daily prayers, acts of charity, saying grace, the sign of the cross, or fulfilling your responsibilities as spouse and parent.

What fascinates me most about Jonathan

When asking Father Jonathan if NCD was suitable for the Orthodox Church, his answer was clear: "Yes, because it has worked. The results of those churches that have been involved with NCD are very encouraging." In the past few years he has inspired quite a number of Orthodox churches to launch the NCD process. I have visited some Orthodox churches—those in which the NCD Survey revealed a high quality, and those that have a relatively low quality. In both cases, the things happening in the worship services were exactly the same. It is the same liturgy. People light candles, chat with their neighbor, pray in front of an icon, or remain silent in God's presence. Externally, the quality increase hasn't changed anything about the worship service. And yet, the differences between churches with high and low quality are almost physically palpable.

The meaning of liturgy

While in non-sacramental churches the term "liturgy" is largely seen as a synonym for a "sequence of events," in sacramental churches the term has an altogether different meaning. The goal is actually the "correct praise and worship of God," the forms of which we are not free to decide. Essentially, liturgy is the "ritual of the open heaven." According to Orthodox understanding, liturgy takes place in heaven, and within a worship service we become part of the heavenly dimension—we access that which happens from eternity to eternity. Pope Benedict XVI describes the essence of liturgy as "letting the heaven shine into the earth." Jonathan loves to describe liturgy as a "window" into heaven: "The goal of worship is to open a window into the majestic worship that continuously takes place in heaven, to give people a taste of that experience."

This understanding of liturgy explains why in the Orthodox worship services children are not taken to separate rooms for special programs. While the majestic liturgy takes place, it's not a disturbance when kids run through the church, play, or sometimes even cry. "The children have to get used to being in their father's house," Jonathan said. "The majestic worship of heaven, that is our home. We can be free to act naturally because we are at home. It wouldn't be natural to stand like statues for two or three hours. Thus, crying kids and the majestic liturgy don't necessarily stand in tension."

Moreover, an Orthodox worship experience can be quite attractive for kids, as it is full of audio-visual extravaganza. There are colors, there is movement, there are candles, there is incense. Most kids love that. And over time, they learn the meaning behind it all.

Christians with a sacramental style love to express spiritual realities in physical ways. Among other things, this makes them very receptive to symbols, rites, and architecture.

Most Orthodox worship services have a sermon (in Father Jonathan's church it is a relatively long one), but the sermon is not the focal point. People don't attend in order to listen to a sermon. The worship experience would be complete even without it. Words are not seen as the best way to communicate divine truth, they are seen as just one way among many others to communicate that truth.

Icons as a typical example

As someone who is receptive to sacramental expressions, I listened with joy to Jonathan's sermon, but the beautiful icons of his church spoke to me even more. During the liturgy my eyes wandered from icon to icon, pausing at times for several minutes on some, and longer on others. Each one had its own "sermon" for me. No preacher can prepare a sermon that well, can know my personal situation that well, can relate the eternal to my worldly problems that well... in comparison to what I experience when contemplating the icons. As Solrunn Nes, one of the most distinguished iconographers of our time puts it, "The icon is not an illusion of the physical, visible world, but a vision of the spiritual, invisible world."

Of course, not every Christian with a sacramental style is spoken to by icons. This has less to do with the style itself and more to do with developments in church history that banned the use of icons within a considerable part of Christendom. Icons aren't immediately or easily accessible. They require some practice, just as liturgy does, before the message moves to the deeper levels of one's soul. However, Christians with a sacramental style are more than happy to get involved in studying these backgrounds. Nothing bores them more than a sermon that could be found in a do-it-yourself guide ("Seven Steps to Wealth"). Such a message, which hovers at the surface of spiritual truth, quickly wears out its welcome, while interaction with symbols and liturgy will never get boring for people with a sacramental style.

People who have understood the concept of iconography have also understood the essence of incarnation, which is the core of the sacramental style. God became man in Christ. He became visible through him. While we can and must not make images of God himself, it is not only legitimate, but also helpful to have an image of Christ. Iconography is a testimony to the fact that the Lord took on flesh. An icon enables a sensory experience of the spiritual truth that it symbolizes.

To those approaching the sacramental style from the opposite side

If you represent one of the two red styles—Scripture-driven or sharing style—it is unlikely that symbols, traditions, and rituals, which are at the heart of the sacramental style, speak to you very much. It is even likely that some features of the sacramental style not only appear strange to you, but downright superstitious. Isn't it true that in this spirituality, material things take a place that only belongs to God? Isn't there an almost magical understanding assigned to mere externals? And aren't many of these rites that are so difficult to access (at least for newcomers), more of a hindrance than a help?

If these are your questions, they are justified ones. There are historical reasons why some churches have stripped statues and banned crosses from their walls. There has been misuse of material objects and it is, even

Your starting point: either the Scripture-driven or the sharing style

today, one of the real dangers of the sacramental style. Therefore, your questions are by no means off target. On the other hand, we must clearly see that absolutely everything can be misused. There isn't just the possibility of approaching sacraments in a magical way, but we can also have a magical approach to the Bible. There isn't just a traditionalism that is blind to the needs of the unchurched, but also a puritanically flavored imperialism that led to the iconoclastic excesses belonging to the saddest chapters of church history. The externals that are at the center of the sacramental style, can be either lifeless rituals or life-altering encounters, depending upon how we approach them.

An attitude that generally deems material expressions of spiritual truth as superstition or idolatry, hasn't understood the essence of the incarnation. The Word became flesh. God merged with matter, therefore matter should not be despised. Isn't the cross matter? Isn't the body and blood of Christ matter? Isn't the Bible matter?

As I try to challenge you to take to heart the concerns of the sacramental style, I am not wanting you to take on this style. However, it is definitely my goal that you abandon a view that suspects idolatry whenever people express spiritual secrets in physical ways. The meaning of the visible sacraments is to highlight an invisible truth, to make it sensually approachable. Most likely, the five senses don't play a central role in your own spirituality (with the exception of hearing and of a kind of seeing that is exclusively concerned with words, thus being just another variety of hearing). However, other believers function differently. What is so wrong with expressing central statements of the faith through means that God's creation offers us and which appeal to all five of our senses?

The core of the sacramental style:
The link between the green and the blue

Incarnation, in essence, means that the invisible becomes visible, the unlimited lets itself be limited. God voluntarily let himself be confined within time and space when he became human through Jesus Christ. For the sacramental style this event is central. Therefore it is natural for representatives of this style to use the physical world (green) to express nonphysical, spiritual truth (blue). The spiritual and the material are not in opposition to one another. God manifests himself to us through material means. The invisible Father has a face in the Son. We humans can now hear, see, and touch the incarnated Word with our hands.

The two wings of the sacramental style

It is no accident that the sacramental style is right at the center of what we referred to as the aesthetic style family. People who are responsive to artistic expressions often have an affinity to the sacramental style. On the one hand, this style can lean more to green (sensory), and on the other hand, more to blue (mystical). In the first case, the stress is more on the physical, material aspects; in the second case, on their spiritual meaning.

However, it is characteristic of the sacramental style that these two dimensions aren't separated. While many Christians view the sensory style as almost "worldly" and the mystical style as "extra-worldly," within the sacramental style, mystical and sensory elements are blended together in a way that transcends the usual categorizations.

The strengths of the sacramental style

The greatest strength of the sacramental style is its physical expression of faith. For that reason, groups that have been strongly shaped by this style, love to make use of material means such as water, bread, wine, oil, etc. Matter is not devalued, but seen as a bridge to spiritual secrets. The aesthetic element—expressed, for instance, in the celebrative clothing of the liturgist—plays an important role.

This leads us to the second strength of the sacramental style, its appreciation of traditions and rites. The focus is not so much on the individual, but on the community—including the community with those who have preceded us in faith. This creates respect for traditions; it is not ours to decide how we deal with them if we want to take the community of the body of Christ seriously.

The perils of the sacramental style

The greatest peril of the sacramental style is the attribution of a magical aura to the sacraments. Albert Schweitzer recorded a good illustration of what is the core of magical thinking from his jungle experiences in Lambarene, Africa. When he would write a medical prescription for the natives, they often *ate* it up in front of him. They were convinced of the healing power of the prescription, rather than seeing it as an access to the desired remedies. Magical thinking is the confusion of symbol and object. Thus prayer can become a spell; a religious symbol, a fetish; a sacrifice, a magical ritual. Nothing would be more helpful in correcting this tendency than a serious interaction with the Scripture-driven style.

The second danger is insensitivity toward outsiders: The believers are so focused on their own forms and traditions that the needs of unchurched people are no longer perceived. Sacramental-style Christians may demand that others adapt to existing forms, in order to be part of Christianity. Nobody can better show them how to avoid this peril, than representatives of the sharing style.

My Three-Color Icon

Since I have the sacramental style, it is not surprising that icons speak to me very strongly. Some time ago I approached Solrunn Nes, one of the most accomplished iconographers in the world today, in order to discuss with her the possibility of a Three-Color icon.

Iconographers are not free to just implement their own subjective ideas (or the ideas of a sponsor) in an artistic way. According to Orthodox belief, an icon is theology written in images and color. Every newly created icon is based on an ancient archetype. Iconographers don't have the right to change an icon just to be different. They are simply co-authors, part of a collective endeavor. Of course, no icon is a pure duplicate of the archetype. To a certain degree every icon is unique; but this uniqueness has clear limitations, comparable with the formulation of dogmas within Western churches.

I was amazed to learn that in iconography the three colors, green, red, and blue, have basically the same meaning as within the Trinitarian Compass. Green usually represents aspects of God's creation, e.g. vegetation or fruitfulness. Red is the color of blood and symbolizes Christ's sacrifice—in most icons, Jesus'

The "Christ the Savior" icon in my office

inner robe is red. And blue is associated with heaven, mystery, and the mystical life—Christ's cloak is often depicted in blue.

We found an old Greek archetype of a "Christ the Savior" icon that displays exactly these three colors. It was important to me that, in the new icon Solrunn Nes was going to create for me, all three colors were reflected within the gems of Christ's halo. If Christ is the perfect image of God, we should recognize all three colors in him. In the Christological hymn of Colossians 1:15 we hear: "He is the image of the invisible God." If you take a closer look at the halo, you will detect nine white dots—for me, symbols of the nine spiritual styles and therefore for the nine mentors with whom I have worked over the past few years.

For me, this icon is extremely expressive. When sitting opposite one of my mentors, I surely can perceive something of Christ's light, but this light is broken. However, when considering all nine mentors together (viewing all nine dots simultaneously), the full glory of Christ reaches me.

Whenever I have a conversation with one of my mentors, the image of the icon emerges in my mind, and I experience how the message that I hear from this mentor is complemented by the messages of the other eight. The image of Christ unites them. For me, this icon has become an enormous help in understanding the messages of my nine mentors, which sometimes sound so contradictory, like broken reflections of the one light that emerges from Christ.

This icon throws light on the invisible reality that is behind it. Through the senses, it communicates a certain notion of the eternal dimension that wouldn't be present without the image. For me, there is no other medium that expresses the plurality of the spiritual styles and their unity in Christ more effectively, nor theologically more correctly.

Who is right, who is wrong?

Throughout the last 63 pages we have dealt with each of the nine spiritual styles, and I have deliberately applied the exact same criteria each time: Nine times we have highlighted the strengths of the respective styles; nine times we have spoken about their greatest perils; nine times we have seen why interaction with the opposite styles is the key to dealing with our own shadows; nine times we have approached each style from the viewpoint of those who, as representatives of the opposite style, are most distant from the style in question.

I am well aware that there may be fancier ways of introducing the individual styles, but my goal was not just to describe these styles. I wanted to familiarize you with the dynamics of the Trinitarian Compass. My expectation is that once you see how I have applied this scheme to, say, six different styles, you will be able to do this with the remaining three styles on your own. If, while reading my writing, you should have had the increasing impression that you knew exactly what I was going to say next, that would indicate that the Trinitarian Compass has started to take effect.

Not wrong, but incomplete

Take a look at the graphic on page 149. By now you should be familiar enough with the Trinitarian Compass to guess what my contribution to the headline of this chapter ("Who is right, who is wrong?") will be, or what it must be. Each of the nine styles focuses on a different aspect of truth (mind you, an aspect of the *one*, biblical truth!) and places this aspect at the center of its value system. At the same time, the large, dashed circle in the middle of the graphic indicates that our own view of things may be correct, but it is not yet complete. You may be absolutely right in what you know, but there may be things that you don't know yet. In order to learn from other styles, you don't have to give up your knowledge, but add to it. You may be 100 percent correct in your concerns, but blind toward other concerns.

In our world of experience—and the nine spiritual styles are dealing with the world of our experience—we can only perceive portions of the universe, never the whole. The philosopher Wilhelm Weischedel writes: "You cannot and must not make one specific aspect of reality an absolute, because then the other aspects will rebel." Large parts of church history reflect nothing other than the "rebellion of the other aspects." It can be easily demonstrated how much more creatively we could have dealt with these conflicts if the dynamics of the Trinitarian Compass had been observed. The spiritual styles aren't mutually exclusive, but rather complementary aspects of our capacity to encounter the Divine.

The two most common patterns

The majority of attempts (or should I say non-attempts?) to deal with the diversity of spiritual approaches within Christianity, can be assigned to one of two tendencies: Either we lean toward an *imperialistic* view ("I am right, you are wrong") or we lean toward a *relativistic* perspective ("There is no right or wrong"):

1. Imperialism

With imperialism, you regard your own style—or the church tradition that has been primarily shaped by a given style—as already complete and in no way in need of being complemented by others. Diversity beyond your own style or your own style family is seen as a threat. People who talk about "unity," from this position, inevitably understand it as a call to others to become like them. Philosopher Hannah Arendt describes this attitude as *totalitarianism:* "Human beings are organized as if they didn't exist in the plural, as if there were only one gigantic human being on earth."

2. Relativism

At the other end of the spectrum is relativism. Everyone defines for him or herself what "truth" means, so that there is no absolute truth. This form of relativism can adopt features of totalitarianism, at which point it is not allowed to call anything false, evil, or ugly. And since nobody dares to make any binding statements, all of us simply utter our "opinions" or express our "feelings," which of course could be easily questioned, but remain unquestioned because they are not supposed to be questioned. Within this paradigm, there are countless truths, and a demand to show equal respect to all moral and metaphysical ideas. This leads to a cocktail theology devoid of any transformational Christian substance.

Two levels of integration

Though I am aware that some critics will regard the approach of this book as a cocktail theology as well, the Trinitarian Compass doesn't have much in common with relativism; rather, it is an alternative to relativism. On the previous pages, I have tried to show that we can integrate different aspects of truth, without hiding our own identity or conviction. There are two levels of this integration:

1. Level A Integration

If you have reached this level, you generally accept other styles. You see them as legitimate, while regarding your own style implicitly or explicitly as superior. This is similar to some Indian religions that don't regard their own truth as the only one, but see it as the "highest" or "deepest" one; the truths of others are pre-stages or aspects of their own truth (which is often overlooked by Westerners who are so much taken with the "tolerance" of these non-exclusive systems). The others are virtually absorbed and integrated into one's own system, which due to this process becomes even more powerful. The others are no longer "enemies;" they become spiritual novices that are looked down upon with benevolence.

Relativism:

A world view that doesn't know any absolute truth: everyone defines their own "truth" and accepts the "truth" of others. In contrast, the Trinitarian Compass is based on the reality of absolute truth; the problem is simply that every spiritual style merely illuminates one aspect of truth, often believing it is the "whole truth."

2. Level B Integration

Level B Integration—the theme of part 3 of this book—takes an important step beyond Level A. At this point you have understood that God can only be fully met at the center, therefore all styles are essential expressions and should be equally appreciated. You are well aware of your own specific style, and know, at the same time, that you are out of balance. In order to become complete, you depend on and need to learn from people who display other styles, especially in the area of your danger zones.

I am convinced that only on the basis of Level B integration does the nice, but highly abstract, formula of "plurality with a unifying center in Christ" make sense. People with an imperialistic or relativistic mindset may use the same formula but mean something altogether different: either converting the other person to their own paradigm, i.e. to that which they themselves have defined as the "unifying center in Christ" (in the case of imperialism), or dissolving this "unifying center" into a foggy "something" devoid of any clear content (relativism).

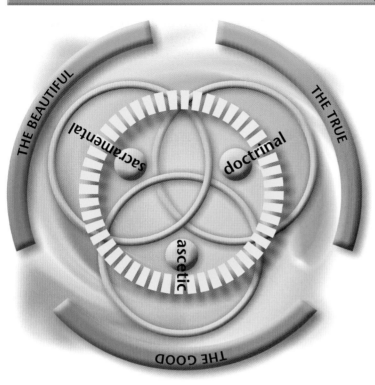

We have already used this diagram on page 81 to demonstrate that the centers of each spiritual style (symbolized by the yellow dots) are outside the intersection with other styles (for the sake of visual clarity, I have again reduced the presentation to three, rather than nine styles). The dashed circle shows that a form of unity is possible that includes the centers of all nine spiritual styles, while excluding their one-sided tendencies.

The consequences of Level B learning

If you have done the step leading up to Level B (not just intellectually, but in practice), your question is no longer, "Which of the nine styles is the right one?" Rather, you understand the following:

a. Your own native style is exactly the right one for you.

b. Likewise, the other spiritual styles are the right ones for those who have them.

c. Every style needs to be complemented.

d. The style opposite your own style is necessary for your spiritual growth and therefore of special importance for you.

The decisive progression from Level A is this: You not only *accept* the other styles, but you are *happy*—which is an emotional category—that they exist. You know that you need the others exactly in their "otherness" in order to grow spiritually. Therefore, you proactively seek interaction with them.

As we have previously seen (page 79), it would simplify things too much to distinguish between center and fringe and then claim that we are united at the center and only separated at the fringe. The problem is that everyone defines the terms "center" and "periphery" altogether differently, which is absolutely normal given the fact that we have different spiritual styles. And even the size of the circle drawn around the center ("Where do the essentials end, and where does the periphery begin?") can be drawn narrower by some people and much wider by others. The same things that are peripheral for one person may be central for others, and vice versa. If we don't understand these dynamics, we may continue indefinitely to seek "unity at the center." It will never work; it can never work.

No relativism

As I mentioned earlier (page 43), approaching different spiritual styles in this way is complicated by the fact that throughout church history some styles have not only been presented imperialistically, but have also been linked to respective imperialistic theologies. Within the logic of these teachings, something is "good theology" only if it is in line with your own style. Everything else is either "bad theology" or even "false theology." If you study theology books that describe the different styles from the viewpoint of their own self-perception—as I have done extensively—you will encounter this structure at every turn.

However, it is not only the imperialistic theologies that have had a devastating effect on our handling of the different spiritual styles; a totalitarian relativism, as described before, may present an even greater danger. This approach makes it virtually impossible to live one's own style with passion and to share one's experiences with enthusiasm. It makes it impossible to present your own values as you interact with other styles. This sort of relativism kills passion, even before it has had a chance to emerge.

Every style—if it is not viewed as an idealized abstraction, but as an empirical reality—is a mixture of dubious religiosity and authentic Christian faith. Many people have difficulty learning about something if, in reality, it can only be approached in such a mixture. In our attempt to avoid the dark side of a specific style, we are in danger of throwing the baby out with the bath water. Since we know that Hitler loved Richard Wagner's music, the Alps, and the German Shepherd, we ban Wagner, the Alps, and the German Shepherd. Is the German Shepherd henceforth suspected to be a "Nazi in disguise?"

Neither Level A integration nor Level B integration should be seen as "relativism." The Trinitarian Compass does distinguish, and quite precisely, between false and true, between dark and bright. However, the false and dark dimension is not projected on the opposite pole by itself. Rather, it is seen:

a. in the *opposite pole* (or in any style other than your own) that moves in the wrong direction—away from the center—in which the questionable aspects aren't even seen as questionable.

b. in your *native style* that moves in the wrong direction—away from the center—as it rejects any integration and thus becomes blind to its own deficits.

Is that relativism? Certainly not. It is a pursuit of truth so strong that it doesn't end in your own comfort zone. Level B learning takes seriously the fact that Christ himself is the truth of Christianity. Therefore he—and not your own style or theology—is placed at the center.

Starting point:

No matter what kind of developmental process we are speaking about, the first step should always be to identify your present starting point. Only when you know your starting point, can you lay out the appropriate steps you need to take in order to reach your desired destination. Because of that, there are no "wrong" starting points. In NCD the concept of the starting point plays a central role. This explains the multitude of tests developed by NCD International. Their goal is none other than to reveal to individual believers and whole churches, as clearly as possible, their present position within the development process.

A symphony rather than just noise

The individual spiritual styles can be compared to instruments in a symphonic orchestra. To perform a symphony we need musicians who can play different instruments, and every musician has to play the different musical notes that have been written exclusively for their particular instrument. Within a symphony, there are not only harmonious sounds. In fact, it is especially the dissonance that makes a piece of music more suspenseful, and thus more attractive. However, all

A picture that I use in all of my seminars and in most of my books. The individuals displayed here move in different—even opposite—directions, and yet they move in exactly the same direction, i.e. closer to the center. Their different starting points determine if this "same way" leads one person from right to left, or from left to right.

of the musicians have to stick to a common score that indicates all of the different voices. They have to submit to a conductor whose goal is to draw out the giftedness of each member of the ensemble and to motivate them to excellence. In my view, the Triune God himself is the conductor of the symphony we are trying to perform. The Trinitarian Compass can be seen, metaphorically speaking, as a score that strives to combine the different voices that exist within Christianity.

Every style occurs in a disintegrated and in an integrated variety. Integrated styles aren't only coherent in and of themselves, but also compatible with others; disintegrated styles are also coherent in and of themselves, but not compatible with others. Soloists can perform wonderful music as well. But only those musicians who have made their specific contribution compatible with the contributions of other musicians, are able to take part in a symphony.

Strengthening your own identity

The Trinitarian Compass doesn't outline a universal theology, but a paradigm in which different styles and traditions—including different theologies—can flourish and cross-pollinate each other. Unity and plurality in the church are not in opposition. They complement and complete each other.

This is, again, one of those nice-sounding phrases that remains meaningless as long as we cannot precisely say when and where all of this takes place. Is it in ecumenical committees where a theology of the least common denominator is worked out? In ecumenical worship services where a Catholic and a Protestant minister do their best to produce a joint venture that is perfectly endurable, but definitely not what anyone would wish for every week? In theological declarations that hardly make us more passionate and effective in ministry, but rather lead us to communicate only halfheartedly the things we believe in? In abstract trains of thought that may look convincing, but simply do not resonate at the grass-root level and consequently don't move anyone?

Or does it take place wherever Christians—whether in a local church or on a regional level, whether within one denomination or inter-denominationally, whether nationally or internationally—get involved with their heads, hands, and hearts in exactly those learning processes that are symbolized by the Trinitarian Compass? Part 3 of this book will show you how you can put this into practice.

Is the Pope your spokesman?

The question, "Is the Pope your spokesman?", is easily answered. If you are a Roman Catholic, it is self-evident that the Pope is your spokesman. That is true whether you like the incumbent Pope and share all of his views, or not. The Pope speaks for the Roman Catholic Church, as nobody else does. That is his job and responsibility. He was elected to do just that.

If you aren't Catholic, the question is just as easily answered: No, the Pope is not your spokesman. In this case you are part of another church—maybe you are Baptist or Pentecostal or Lutheran—and it is not the job of the Pope to represent Baptists or Pentecostals or Lutherans. He is neither commissioned to do this, nor would he be competent to do it. For that reason you should never expect the Pope to speak for you. He has enough to do in representing Catholicism in all of its diversity. Would you seriously expect him to learn the ropes of Baptists, Pentecostals, and Lutherans in order to represent them as well?

Again and again I have experienced that non-Catholics feel "excluded," "hurt," or "degraded" by statements made by the Pope. If you analyze the psychological mechanism that lurks behind such a response, you almost always find the expectation that the Pope "should also speak for us." But, why should he?

When the Pope speaks about "the church," of course he always refers to the Roman Catholic Church and its self-conception. This concept includes the conviction that only the Roman Catholic Church is Church in the "full sense" (i.e. in the sense of Roman Catholicism). Is that so illogical? As a non-Catholic, I perceive this statement neither as discriminatory, nor as hurtful. The Pope doesn't speak for me, nor does he speak for other churches. He speaks exclusively for his church, the Roman Catholic Church. In the same way, I find it absolutely legitimate for representatives of Baptist, Pentecostal, or Lutheran churches to speak only for their respective churches. This, and nothing else, is their job.

It is altogether normal that the concept of "unity" differs from one church tradition to another. Some stress more institutional unity, others stress doctrinal unity, and still others emphasize the unity that is expressed by the actual lives of the believers. Basically, we come back to the same three motifs again and again.

I have an entirely different task than the Pope or the World Pentecostal President. It is not my job to speak for a specific denomination. My task is to serve believers of all traditions—regardless of the church they are associated with. That's an entirely different task than one of representing a denomination. No representative of a denomination, including the Pope, represents the whole of Christianity. I am convinced that they can only meet this challenge if they stress the specifics of their tradition—that which distinguishes them from others.

Everything else would be downright grotesque if taken to its logical conclusion. The Pentecostal President would have to constantly check his statements to ensure that they represent every Catholic, and the Pope would have to have all of his statements counterchecked to make sure that they reflect all of Martin Luther's concerns in their fullest glory. People who seriously desire for this to happen, are confusing ecumenism with comedy.

> ## It is not the job of the Pope to represent Baptists, Pentecostals, and Lutherans.

Part 3

Level B growth: Explore your opposite pole

Few believers have experienced the conscientious, pro-active learning from their opposite styles that we call "Level B growth." The majority of people who read this book will be content with Level A growth; many will find the most important message of this book to be how to identify their own spiritual style. However, it is on Level B that things really start to get interesting. In terms of spiritual development, a person who remains on Level A for their whole life resembles a person who has never really left adolescence.

The essence of Level B growth

As you are going through the process of Level B growth, you must always remember that your goal is not to abandon Level A. The discovery of your native style, which is one of the goals of Level A growth, is nothing other than the discovery of your home. This home remains your home, even if you set sail to explore new and foreign territory. You will leave your home repeatedly, always knowing that you can return. The two circular arrows in the middle of the graphic express this interplay between Level A and Level B.

Nine worlds or one world?

Take a closer look at the graphic. At the beginning of the process (left column) you only perceived one world, namely your own. You believed that this was the whole world. When you reach the end of the process (right column) you will again perceive *one* world, but you will know that what you believed to be "the world" before, is merely one of many cultures within a greater world. Since you will always remain a member of your native culture, your growth process will take place continuously between the pole of your native identity and the pole of the broader world (middle column).

These dynamics of Level B learning create a lot of tension. This tension can either be perceived as exciting—like a journey into an unknown country—or evoke feelings of insecurity and anxiety. Usually there is a mixture of the two feelings, and the negative ones can prevail. This is the major reason why many Christians don't want to enter into the territory of Level B learning. They want to avoid negative feelings.

Insecurity is normal

Interaction with the opposite pole makes us feel insecure. But it is exactly that feeling of insecurity that is a prerequisite for maturing spiritually. It is a sign of wisdom to be resourceful in the face of uncertainty and to tolerate ambiguity and disappointment in your connection with God. On Level A you basically do what is fun; and there is nothing wrong with that. On Level B you do what is right, whether it is fun or not. On Level A you primarily pray, "Lord, bless me, protect me." On Level B you will increasingly hear yourself praying, "Lord, show me the obstacles within me, even if it hurts. Reveal my shadows. Lead me directly into the problem areas, so that I can grow." It goes without saying that a certain level of maturity is needed before we can pray such a prayer.

Many spiritual leaders complain about how "immature" Christians are, and I assume that in many cases their assessment is appropriate. However, the question then arises: What have they—the leaders—done to assist people in becoming spiritually mature? Spiritual maturity doesn't emerge out of the blue; it depends on a climate in which it is continuously and systematically promoted.

NCD Cycle:

A 6-phase-process within NCD. Among other things, it is characterized by the following features:

1. It is a spiral rather than linear, i.e. within each cycle you move through all of the phases, then you go up a layer and repeat the process.

2. Every phase of the Cycle describes universally valid biblical principles rather than just programmatic ideas or tools, i.e. it's not for us to decide whether or not we want to get involved with these phases.

3. For each of the eight quality characteristics of NCD there is a different version of the Cycle, i.e. it is a process designed to be applied in many diverse areas of your personal life as well as a church's life.

4. The Cycle is based on the Trinitarian Compass, i.e. concepts such as radical balance, opposite pole, and the assignment of the six growth phases to the colors of the Compass are essential elements of the Cycle.

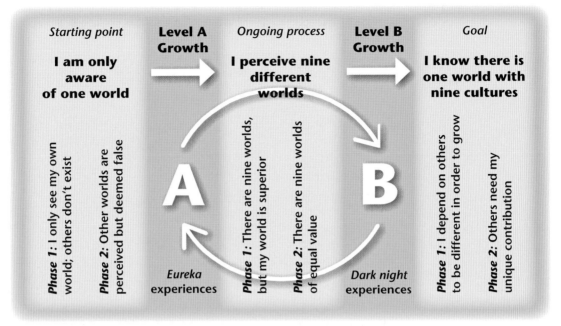

Within the continual interplay between Level A and Level B growth (middle column), different spiritual cultures virtually perceive each other as different "worlds." Whether you lean more toward A or toward B will determine if you regard your own world as being superior to others (phase 1) or as of equal value (phase 2). The realization that there is only one world—encompassing nine different cultures—is the goal of the process (right column). From your starting point (left column) you also perceive only one world, but this is not the whole world as seen in the right column, but merely your own culture which you erroneously believe to be the "whole world."

If Level B is never reached

It is by no means the privilege of just a few chosen ones to reach Level B. It should be the goal of every Christian. However, I am realistic enough to recognize that only a relatively small percentage of Christians—including the readers of this book—will start this journey. It is the "negative feelings" connected with Level B growth (more precisely, those feelings *interpreted* as negative) that prevent many Christians from taking this crucial step toward spiritual maturity—especially those who tend to confuse feelings of well-being with being "close to God."

We have to live with the fact that many Christians will remain on Level A for the rest of their lives, though we must never forget that this represents tremendous progress compared to the starting point of Level 0 (see page 47). However, I believe it is disastrous for Christian leaders and teachers to remain on Level A. The willingness to get involved with a Level B learning process (which doesn't mean you have to be a world champion) is one of the most important criteria for Christian leaders and teachers. If they aren't *willing* to deal with their shadow areas they can do a lot of harm, despite all of their committed and well-meaning ministry.

According to Søren Kierkegaard, human beings are characterized by the freedom to not necessarily choose the truth, but also to prefer untruth and ignorance. To remain on Level A is to flee from the truth, to flee from one's own shadows, to flee from oneself—it is even to flee from Christ, at least from those aspects of Christ that don't really fit into our "feel-good" paradigm.

Learning from individuals or churches?

One way to learn from the opposite style (or another style foreign to you) is to attend well-known churches that are shaped by this style. When traveling, I am regularly interacting with churches of very different traditions. I have been greatly stretched through these encounters over the past 25 years. Nevertheless, I don't want to recommend this procedure to you without reservation—at least not if you seriously want to get involved with Level B growth. My reservations are primarily based on the following three reasons:

First, while it is true that a whole church can be shaped primarily by one specific style (or family of styles), we cannot conclude that most of its members have this style themselves. Based on our research, it is safe to assume that the majority of believers (markedly more than 60%) don't have the style that shapes their church. Moreover, in these churches you will encounter a disproportionately high number of Christians who practice the favored style (simply for a lack of alternatives), without actually having this style.

For anyone who takes the process of Mutual Mentoring seriously, this presents a notably awkward situation. In a Mutual Mentoring relationship, the decisive factor is not the "tradition" of which we are a part, but rather whether we have the respective style ourselves. Especially in churches that are famous for a specific style, the ability to make this distinction is not very strong, to put it mildly.

Second, if the church you attend doesn't reflect its experience in the categories of the Trinitarian Compass, an encounter with such a church can have the opposite effect of what was originally intended. One of the goals of interacting with the opposite style is to reduce prejudices about that style. Many Christians who attend a church characterized by their opposite style come to the following conclusion: "It's really much worse than I would have imagined in my wildest dreams." Churches known for a specific style tend to project that style on others, or even expect it of everyone. This is not exactly what you are looking for in your learning process. It could even lead you to say, "I've had all I need of that for the rest of my life."

Third, if a church is known for a specific spiritual style, the probability is relatively high that many of the church members who have that style have stopped their growth at Level A. This doesn't mean that you cannot learn from them. It does mean, however, that you should exercise caution. There are Christians who are on Level A because they are presently involved in that phase of their spiritual growth process. As soon as they feel secure enough in their identity, they will proceed to Level B. There are other Christians, however, who are on Level A because their spiritual growth has stagnated at that level. In five or ten years they will still be on Level A, since neither they nor their church expect anything else from them. These are less than ideal conditions for mutual learning.

Of course, in expressing these reservations, I am not suggesting that you should never attend a church with a style that is not your own. If you keep these three points in mind, there is a good chance you will benefit from such a visit. Be persistent.

> **The encounter with such a church can have the opposite effect of what was intended.**

The problem is that these people aren't willing to subordinate to the will of God. They would prefer to project their own will on God. "The result," according to St. John of the Cross, "is that something that isn't in line with their will and taste, isn't—in their opinion—the will of God; but conversely, whenever they are content they believe that God is content. They measure God according to their own standards, rather than measuring themselves according to God's standards." I couldn't describe Level B growth more precisely. Neither you nor your theology nor your spirituality should be at the center, but God and his will.

Allow sufficient time for Level A growth

As mentioned before, reaching Level A is an absolute prerequisite to entering the Level B growth process. People who are only now in the process of discovering their Level A identity, shouldn't begin to pursue Level B learning. It must be postponed until later. However, waiting doesn't mean waiting until pigs fly. Perhaps you need more time—a week, three months, even one year—to overcome your "Level 0" frustrations. But you certainly don't need to remain on Level A for several years.

Most of our lives should be spent within the creative cyclical interplay between Level A and Level B, as expressed in the graphic on page 155. If this should never happen, the reason is not that the Level A phase demands so much time. The reason is simply that people don't *want* to reach Level B. If you have completed the Spiritual Style Test and found out that you have lived confidently in your native style for a number of years, you can launch Level B growth right away.

Not a linear growth process

Especially in the Western world, Christians have to learn that spiritual growth is not a linear process (from point A to point B). It is a cyclical process involving ups and downs, crises and breakthroughs, negative feelings and positive feelings. There is no growth without pain. If you have never felt anything like "spiritual pain," chances are high that you are still far away from Level B.

Expressed in biblical language, Level B growth has a lot to do with repentance. The biblical word for repentance, *epistrepho* (literally, turning) is a very dynamic term. I don't become increasingly more of what I already am (Level A), but I am literally transformed (Level B). My horizon will be enlarged, my value system renewed, my awareness of sin (of *my* sin) sharpened, my ability to endure pain increased, my readiness to tolerate phases of ambiguity expanded. Level B growth restrains us from misusing faith for our own selfish purposes. It is a process that liberates us from an image of God that is fully in line with our favorite ideas, in which all displeasing features are excluded as well as all uncomfortable demands, whose only function is to serve our spiritually clouded selfishness.

Linear growth:

Many people—especially in the Western world—have difficulty understanding a cyclical growth model such as the one that NCD promotes. They are accustomed to a linear understanding of growth. When they think about growth, they imagine a line that stretches from point A to point B, not the image of a spiral, in which each cycle moves to a higher level. However, all organic growth processes are cyclical in nature, not linear. Because of this, an understanding of cyclical dynamics is important for understanding how we grow in our relationship with God.

C.S. Lewis didn't explicitly reflect on Level B growth, but he made a statement that summarizes precisely what Level B growth is all about: "It may be hard for an egg to turn into a bird: it would be a jolly sight harder for it to learn to fly while remaining an egg. We are like eggs at present. And you cannot go on indefinitely being just an ordinary decent egg. We must be hatched or go bad."

Don't worship your style

What is an idol? When hearing this term, many people think of a pagan statue made of stone or wood. Others think of the idol of money, that has brought so many people under its spell, especially in the Western world. Some call to mind the idol of sex. The idol of power. The idol of science. The idol of one's political party. The idol of one's nation. It is true that all of these things can become idols for us. An idol is something that takes the place of God in our lives.

Spiritual styles can become idols

However, we would be simplifying things too much if we reduced this peril exclusively to pagan or materialistic dangers. If it is true that everything that takes the place of God in our lives becomes an idol, this also implies that we can commit idolatry even with all of our committed spirituality. This happens when we begin to worship the things that are of special value within our spiritual style. Instead of viewing these things as what they really are—tools to facilitate our encounter with God—these tools take the place of God. We virtually turn them into God and so, biblically speaking, they become idols.

For the sacramental style this could be the sacraments. For the enthusiastic style, signs and wonders. For the ascetic style, the simple life-style. For the Scripture-driven style, the Bible. No style is immune to this danger. In every single case, what Scripture warns against can take place: We worship and serve created things rather than the Creator (Rom. 1:25).

The center: your style or God?

As long as we remain on Level A, our own spiritual style is the center of our universe, metaphorically speaking. We see the other styles, but we place them at the fringe. Therefore, I call Level A *style-centered.*

On Level B, the situation changes radically. This stage still contains all of the Level A ingredients: our native style, the other styles, and God. On Level B, we still represent our native style, perhaps with even more confidence than ever before, but we and our style are no longer the center of the universe. The Trinitarian Compass assigns an important place to us and our spirituality, but not a central place. The central place is occupied by God alone. Therefore, I call Level B *God-centered.*

At first glance, this distinction may seem a little bit abstract, but it isn't. Only by getting involved in a God-centered approach can we avert the danger of making an idol of our style. At the beginning of this book (page 2), I spoke about a *philosopher* (as a representative of the dogmatic style family), a *practitioner* (ethical style family), and an *artist* (aesthetic style family) and their respective love of God. Could it be that in the end, that love is more the love of philosophy, ethics, or the arts? That is the question of all questions: Are you in love with the arts and simply express this in a religious manner? Or are you actually in love with God and express that love in an artistic way? In like manner, this holds true for people who have a primarily dogmatic or ethical antenna to the Divine: Is their love focused on God and does that love find a primarily doctrinal or life-transforming expression, or is it nothing more than the love of philosophical reflection or a specific life-style clothed in religious terminology? The very thing that is so valuable in our personal style, is that which most threatens to become our idol.

A Copernican change

Metaphorically speaking, in the style-centered approach God revolves around you (of course, this isn't true, but that is how you perceive it). In the God-centered approach, you revolve around God. This change from a style-centered to a God-centered approach can be rightfully called a "Copernican change."

Copernicus was the first person who realized, first, that the sun doesn't revolve around the earth, but the earth revolves around the sun; and second, that the stars don't revolve around the earth, but the earth revolves on its own axis. The philosopher Immanuel Kant wrote about Copernicus' discovery. He said, "When he didn't succeed in explaining the movements in the sky by assuming that the whole host of stars rotates around its audience, he wondered if it wouldn't make more sense to have the audience rotate while leaving the stars in peace."

This discovery was loaded with consequences: It implied the expulsion of humanity from the hub of the universe and the relocation of our place in the cosmos from the center to the orbit. That went against human pride and immediately provoked the most vehement resistance, primarily on the part of the church, sadly enough. That's worth pondering.

A counter-intuitive paradigm

Copernicus' problem was that his discovery, while being correct, contradicted sensory perception. We can see with our own eyes how the sun "rises" in the morning, and how it "goes down" in the evening. We enjoy sunrises and sunsets—why should we allow Copernicus to destroy such a beautiful illusion?

Copernicus, while achieving acceptance in our minds, didn't achieve acceptance in our feelings. Although we know that the earth revolves around its own axis and around the sun, we stubbornly stick to our pre-Copernican language: "The sun rises, and the sun goes down." Strictly speaking, we would have to say, "*We* rise, and *we* go down," since it is we who are moving, together with the whole planet. The sun, though our senses perceive it to be moving, doesn't move an inch. It is a fixed star.

We can apply this to spiritual styles. On Level A, we perceive ourselves to be at the center of the universe. On Level B, we learn that neither we nor our spirituality is at the center, but God. God does not revolve around us, but we revolve around God. However, this rational knowledge doesn't correspond to what we experience through our senses. What we experience—or what we believe we experience—is based on an illusion.

Solid ground?

We, as humans, don't stand on solid ground. In reality, we stand on extremely shaky clods of earth, dashing in circles at a breathtaking speed, constantly rotating and flying through space. In the same way, our own spirituality doesn't stand on the solid ground that our sensory perception and the theologies aligned with that perception make us believe. Level B learning leads us to the realization that it is not our clod of earth (i.e. our spiritual style) that must function as this "solid foundation." Rather, it is God himself who has the whole rotating system remarkably well under control. God is our foundation. He sets things in motion. Do we allow him to move us?

Integrated styles:

Depending on the degree of spiritual maturity, we can distinguish two growth phases for every spiritual style: People whose growth process stopped at Level A tend to place their own style at the center of their universe, and to pit it against other styles. In contrast, those who are at Level B acknowledge the value of the other styles, while being confident in their own style. On Level B, believers strive to integrate into their lives those aspects of the opposite style that highlight the deficits in their own spirituality.

Theoretical versus practical polytheism

Christianity, together with Judaism and Islam, is one of the three monotheistic world religions. The same creed that devout Jews recite every day, applies without restraint to Christians as well: "Hear O Israel, the Lord our God, the Lord is one" (Deut. 6:4). On page 36, when considering the "Jesus rule," we looked into this creed.

Sometimes, the two other monotheistic religions accuse Christians of stretching our understanding of monotheism too far. They are referring to the Christian doctrine of the Trinity (Father, Son, and Holy Spirit). They would say, "Could it be that, in spite of all your verbal appeals to monotheism, you Christians have nothing other than a small Christian pantheon of Gods?"

In response to such an accusation, Christians stress, and rightly so, that the confession of one God most certainly applies to them. We, as Christians, don't worship three Gods, but the one true God. All of the dogmas and teachings about this question, have put this fact beyond reasonable doubt.

However, it seems to me that we as Christians don't take the Jews' and Muslims' questions seriously enough if we flatly reject their criticism by pointing to the monotheistic orthodoxy of our written creeds. Could it be that, while vehemently confessing with our mouths that there is only one God, on a psychological level, we have started to treat the Trinity almost like a small pantheon of Gods?

It is one thing to work up a written creed that stresses the oneness of God. It is altogether different to interact with the Trinity spiritually and psychologically. To put it bluntly, the less we focus on all three colors of the Trinitarian Compass and the more we place our respective "favorite colors" at the center, the more we are in danger of slipping into what I would like to call "practical polytheism," even if we maintain the orthodox confession of one God. In the end, we treat the Trinity almost like three Gods from which—based on personal preference—everyone is free to choose his or her favorite God. For conservative or evangelical Christians this would probably be Jesus; in charismatic or mystical groups, the Holy Spirit; and for liberals, God the Creator.

I am deliberately exaggerating a little bit in order to make my point clear. Whether we are monotheists or polytheists is not merely a matter of what we verbally confess. Our confession is also, and primarily, expressed by our actual behavior. And a separation of the three colors of the Trinitarian Compass into three areas that are hostile to each other, comes close to a separation of God. In the end, three or even more forces, whose hostility is rooted in a pluralism of incompatible claims, confront each other with dire consequences. This is a situation that we could, with good theological basis, call "practical polytheism."

Could it be that the Trinity has become for many of us a small Christian pantheon of Gods?

Of course, with our one-sided concepts of faith we don't really separate God, but what we do separate is our human capacity to encounter God in his wholeness, as the "one God" (see page 36). This is the challenge of the Trinitarian Compass and especially of what we have called Level B growth: that God becomes one, not just in our verbal creeds, but also in our own spirituality—understood, believed, and expressed.

Your own style and your opposite style

I s it really best to deal with our areas of weakness, as is characteristic of Level B learning? Wouldn't it be better to focus on our strengths (our native style) and simply forget about our weaknesses? This is a good question. To be constantly preoccupied with one's weaknesses would be both psychologically unhealthy and highly ineffective. As I tried to demonstrate on page 54 ("The power of purple alligators"), attempting to avoid a negative habit can result in being possessed by that very habit.

On the other hand, the solution should never be just to ignore our dark sides. The goal of spiritual growth is much more than simply learning to think positively, and in the process risk putting to sleep both our ability to self-criticize and our ability to suffer. In vast parts of spiritual growth literature, the constructive role of negative feelings is neglected. Sometimes we get the impression that "spirituality" and "feeling well" are almost synonymous. But feeling well has nothing whatsoever to do with our spiritual maturity. After having evaluated empirical studies and his own pastoral experiences, the psychologist Steven S. Sandage concluded, "If I have an index of a person's present spiritual or psychological well-being, it tells me nothing about their level of spiritual or psychological maturity."

> **Minimum factor:**
>
> *The NCD term for the quality characteristic that is least developed, and therefore in need of special attention. Focusing on the minimum factor is the key to qualitative and quantitative church growth.*

Minimum factor or opposite pole?

Before we take a closer look at the implications of working on the opposite pole, we should clearly distinguish this approach from two possible misunderstandings:

- As mentioned earlier (page 72), Level B learning is not concerned with focusing on the style that is least developed, but on the style opposite your native style. They could be the same but they don't have to be. Your "minimum factor" (i.e. the least developed style) can be very different from your opposite style.

- Interaction with the opposite pole doesn't imply a "shift" to another spiritual style. Such a suggestions would be asking people to deem their actual experiences with God as invalid or inferior, just for the sake of a theory that defines as "authentic" only those things that fulfill a list of predetermined criteria.

The challenge of Level B growth is to integrate into your own spirituality, on the basis of a strongly developed native style, those aspects of your opposite style that can help you minimize your own dangers. As a result, you don't abandon your style, but you develop additional abilities at the other end of the spectrum that automatically lead you closer to the center.

The function of negative feelings

It is a highly counterproductive, but widespread view to exclusively associate "positive" feelings with God. But he can also speak to us, sometimes especially so, through our negative feelings. Many people condemn themselves because of their negative feelings of anger, worry, and weariness. Sometimes they try to fight these feelings "with God's help." They pray that God will take them

Leaving your comfort zone

Often an organizer of a seminar will beg me, "I can rely on you not to confuse our people, can't I?" My stereotypical answer is usually, "I would hope that some confusion takes place. Whenever we learn something new that has deep personal consequences, we cannot avoid phases of confusion." Our spiritual comfort zone limits our range of experiencing God; in a way, it limits God.

In Christianity there is a frightening preoccupation with safety and security, with comfort and convenience. In order to enter Level B growth, we must leave our comfort zones. It is in the nature of the growth process to feel uncomfortable at times. However, phases of discomfort are the key to spiritual maturity.

As far as spiritual styles are concerned, the reality of discomfort is complicated by the fact that our comfort zone indicates the area where we feel closest to God. On the flip side, leaving our comfort zones means setting sail into areas in which we feel distant from God. Who really wants to do that?

Before you leave your comfort zone, you must know what that comfort zone is. And you need to be aware that this is simply your spiritual comfort zone, no more and no less. From that comfortable place you can then dare to move to the uncomfortable, but you must have this security first. You must have a safe place before you can have the freedom to feel unsafe. When I try to motivate people to leave their comfort zones, I deliberately appeal to their value systems. When dealing with red spiritualities, I say: "If you want to grow in Christ, you must be willing to make the sacrifice of leaving your places of comfort." Representatives of red spirituality know what it means to sacrifice. When encouraging blue spiritualities, I say: "If you want to experience God in his fullness, you must be open to follow the Holy Spirit, wherever he leads you." Representatives of blue spirituality know what openness to the Holy Spirit means. When dealing with green spiritualities, I say: "You must be tolerant toward approaches that are unfamiliar to you." Representatives of green spiritualities know what it means to be tolerant.

If we want to gain experience outside our comfort zone, nothing is as ineffective as over-stretching. The best way is through small, controllable steps. In terms of training—spiritual training is not exempt to this rule—the following principle applies: We grow by burning energy beyond our normal limitations (more on page 167). The problem is that when we begin to feel uncomfortable, we are tempted to avoid those feelings. On the other hand, the intensity of satisfaction that we draw from certain activities decreases over time. As threatening as change processes may be, our deepest satisfaction arises from our readiness to face them.

> **Your spiritual comfort zone limits your range of experiencing God; in a way, it limits God.**

What motivates people to leave their comfort zones? We could demand, "You simply have to do that." That would be a correct, but fruitless statement. Much more promising is to learn from Antoine de Saint-Exupéry: "If you want to build a ship, don't summon up people to buy wood, prepare tools, distribute jobs, and organize the work," he said. "Rather teach them the yearning for the wide, boundless ocean." People who have sensed this yearning are willing to stretch beyond their comfort zone in order to draw closer to the goal of their yearning.

away. It is often much more constructive to ask yourself why you have those feelings, or even, why you need those feelings. What would you miss out on if you no longer had them? People who simply cover up their negative feelings, or suppress them by means of positive-thinking ideology, will never learn the lessons that can only be learned through contemplating the questions that these feelings raise.

Difference to other approaches

A good way to learn about other spiritual styles is to study books. Over the past few years, I have read countless books on spirituality and have benefitted enormously from them. As you do so, it is helpful to distinguish between the following two categories of books (I am exclusively referring to decidedly Christian contributions to spirituality):

*   The majority of books don't treat the whole spectrum of Christian spirituality, but focus on that which this book calls a "style," a "style family," or a "color segment." In most of these books you will get the impression that the respective subdomain of spirituality represents either the whole of spirituality, or that it is superior to other approaches. Sometimes this is openly stated. In other cases it is conveyed with more subtlety. In these books, you will find more about the dangers of other approaches than about the perils of the portrayed spirituality.

*   A few books have an integrative approach, i.e. they describe a multiplicity of spiritual approaches based on the assumption that different people have something like different "antennas to God." These books have a similar approach to this book. The major difference is in two areas: First, in most of the books the styles are not arranged in a cyclical continuum as in the case of the Trinitarian Compass. This makes a huge difference when it comes to practical work (consider concepts such as neighbor styles, opposite styles, etc.). Second, the typologies that I have studied in such books have a somewhat narrower focus than the one presented in this book. For example, in the language of the Trinitarian Compass, instead of radically exploring the nature of all three colors, some of them seem to distinguish three different shades of red (or green or blue).

> **Neighbor style:**
> *Every spiritual style is surrounded by two neighbor styles, which are clearly different from that style on the one hand, and have a considerable area of overlap with it, on the other. If direct interaction with the opposite pole seems to be too challenging for you, you can start your growth process by focusing on one of your two neighbor styles.*

Learning a little to learn a lot

If you deal with a style that is not your own, you will notice that the very things you learn from interacting with that style will help you deal with other styles as well. It is not necessary for you to interact with all nine styles. People who have worked with two styles foreign to them won't have overwhelming difficulty understanding the essence of the remaining styles. Many of the lessons learned from working with one style, can be transferred to the other styles as well.

Incidentally, this doesn't apply only to learning spiritual styles. Interaction with a culture other than your own (language, customs, habits, etc.) trains exactly the same "muscles" that you need in order to deal with a spiritual style that is strange to you. People who have multicultural experience (in the sense that they have approached them with an attitude of mutual learning) will find the dynamics of the Trinitarian Compass easy to grasp.

Level B and the "dark night of the soul"

Many books on spirituality explicitly refer to that which the Spanish monk, St. John of the Cross (1542-1591), has called "the dark night of the soul." Richard Foster writes, "To desire spiritual maturity without the dark night is like an athlete hoping to become a champion without training." If a tree is not shaken by wind, it doesn't develop deep roots. If we cannot stand up under temptation, we won't mature.

According to my experience, that which St. John of the Cross describes as the "dark night of the soul" has a close affinity to what we have labeled, in the dry language of this book, "Level B growth." Level B learning inevitably includes dark night experiences; in fact, it can directly trigger such an experience.

The teaching of St. John of the Cross

The writings of St. John of the Cross are so demanding that to study them can be exhausting. He writes about the dark night of the soul: "There will come a time when God will bid us grow deeper. He will remove the previous consolation from the soul in order to teach it virtue and prevent it from developing vice." A little bit further he explains: "This darkness has to last until the habits that we have formed in ourselves over a long period of time through our way of understanding things, will be expelled and destroyed, and their place is taken by God's illumination and light."

Dark night experiences are phases of our lives where we don't experience God's presence. However, it is especially through these times that we can learn to trust God unconditionally. In his writings John distinguishes three different experiences that he relates—in his unique metaphoric language—to three phases of the night:

- *The beginning of night,* dusk: This is the night of the "senses." Those things that meant a lot to us before (e.g. enjoyment of God's creation), become meaningless. This night cleanses and purifies our senses, and our scale of values is reset.

- *Midnight,* complete darkness: This is the "night of the spirit," the night of distance from God. This non-experience of God is not a sign of his absence, but, in reality, an experience of God's increasing care for us. It is probably one of the most intense growth phases imaginable, since it results more than anything else in purification and maturity. It is the night proper, which is what John refers to when speaking about the "dark night of the soul." The preceding day no longer exists and a new day is not in sight. It is absolutely dark. This phase often follows intense experiences of God's closeness.

- *The beginning of the new day,* dawn: This experience of night, which was not labeled by John, could be described as the "night of faith." It is not so much a time-limited phase as something that permanently accompanies the Christian. Although it is dark, the dawn of the next day is always on the horizon.

Darkness due to an excess of light

Many authors use the imagery of light and darkness to describe spiritual fights. To avoid confusion, we need to make a distinction between two kinds of darkness:

1. Darkness as a symbol for sin, disobedience, and separation from God. This is the meaning of darkness in the figurative language of the Trinitarian Compass. The further away we are from the center (i.e. from God himself), and the less God's light is illuminating us, the greater the darkness.

2. In St. John of the Cross' writings, however, the term "night" has a different—almost opposing—meaning. The fullness of God's light blinds people so that it is dark for them. Their inner eyes are not accustomed to such brightness and they experience as darkness, what in reality is light. "The brighter it is," John writes, "the more it blinds and darkens the pupil... The more openly one looks into the sun, the darker the world around us becomes."

Mountaintops and valleys

John's figurative language is a fitting way to describe experiences Level B growth experiences. God's light shines into areas where it hurts. In reality, the light illuminates our darkness, but we experience it as darkness. We feel distant from God. And yet these are the very moments that lead us to maturity.

Spiritual growth is not a linear process. We may enjoy the mountaintop experiences, but it is in the valleys where our faith is formed. Even though we know that we have to go through valleys, we don't like it. But it would be unhealthy to bypass these experiences. Jean Lafrance describes these dynamics in the following words: "Jesus hasn't set up a stepladder of perfection, which we could climb up step by step to finally own God. Rather, he has shown us a way that leads into the depth of humility. At the crossroads we have to choose which way we will take to approach God: the one leading up, or the one leading down."

God isn't playing with us when he inflicts a dark night experience upon us. There is a clear goal behind it; namely, to lead us to maturity. Reinhard Körner, an expert of St. John of the Cross' writings, describes the fruit of this process as follows: "Our concept of faith and our image of God have left their previous narrowness; and along with them the image of ourselves and other human beings, of the world and of the church. It is as if our spirit and soul now have an entirely new, never imagined breadth to approach God, his truth, his creation, his sons and daughters."

> **Dark night experiences:**
> *A concept that originated with St. John of the Cross that is frequently used in classical works on spirituality. It describes experiences of seeming "remoteness" or "distance" from God that don't result from sin or disobedience, but are positive elements of a spiritual growth process.*

How to deal with this phase

When experiencing this phase we must be ready to let it happen. We should not try to repress it nor to "counsel it away." And the last thing we should do is to "pray against it." As we go through this process God is at work within us.

The problem is that a person who experiences a dark night tends to believe it will never end. This is what John describes as "midnight." In contrast to dawn, when you see a light on the horizon, at midnight you experience nothing but complete darkness. You may tell yourself as often as you wish that this phase won't stay for all eternity, but you will find it hard to believe yourself.

However, this applies to mountaintop experiences as well. People who have reached the mountaintop tend to believe that there has been a breakthrough, that all "negative feelings" have been dispelled for ever. But in reality a dark night experience often occurs immediately after a spiritual mountaintop experience. Those who are accustomed to thinking about learning as a linear process, will especially have difficulty in dealing with these waves that are characteristic of an organic growth process.

My own "dark night" experiences

St. John of the Cross describes the experience of the dark night of the soul as "bitter and terrible," and as "horrible and awful to the spirit." These are hardly words that a publisher would like to use to promote the process laid out in this book. And yet, these are fitting words. Though they don't describe the whole process of spiritual growth, they are a precise description of phases that take place within this growth process.

I, personally, have lived through two such dark night experiences. Both times were direct results of Level B growth. I should add that I got involved with Level B growth much more intensely than I would recommend to others. I literally interacted with all nine styles simultaneously, and not in a detached way, but by getting involved in them very personally.

Given my own experiences, terms like "terrible" and "horrible" are rather harmless expressions. I sensed that my encounter with the other styles threw so much light on my own shadow areas that the "blinding effect" was unbearably strong. I felt ridiculous. What's more, I realized that not only did I feel ridiculous, but that I was ridiculous. Ridiculous toward God, and ridiculous toward myself. What makes a dark night experience so painful is this discovery: Prior to it, you were convinced that the "enemies" were outside your doors. But now, they enter your own world; indeed, you realize that they are part of you.

My most recent dark night experience took place about six months ago. At that time, I wrote in an e-mail to one of my mentors: "Presently, I am in a really peculiar phase, difficult to explain to outsiders.

I am not really 'depressed,' this would be a very misleading term (even though I don't know how a doctor would view me and which pills he would probably prescribe). However, I am strangely inaccessible to many things that usually mean a lot to me. I am untouched by the beautiful things of life, but also untouched by spiritual disciplines. This is annoying to me, since I want to be accessible, but I can't succeed. Emotionally, God has moved far away from me. You don't have to be afraid that I am in danger of quitting my Christian faith, definitely not. But emotionally... I don't feel God. Usually I can feel his closeness strongly and that means a lot to me. For weeks, I haven't experienced anything like that. Yet in the midst of this emotional darkness, I sense a clarity of thought, especially in my thinking about spiritual things, that is not available to me at normal times. It is as if I don't think, but 'something' thinks in me. I make enormous progress in my spirituality project and feel miserable nevertheless."

During that time I was well aware of everything that St. John of the Cross wrote about the dark night, and what I had developed about Level A and Level B growth myself. But emotionally, it was of no use.

St. John of the Cross wrote, "The fight is so deep, since the peace waiting for us shall also be deep." This is how cyclical, wavelike growth works: When the night is especially dark, the day will be experienced as especially bright. And I know that God isn't only with me in the light of the day, but he was also with me in the midst of the deepest night, and will certainly be with me in the next phase of darkness as well.

> Given my own dark night experiences, terms like "terrible" and "horrible" are rather harmless expressions.

How training works

When I talk with Christian leaders about Level B growth, they frequently respond with a good-natured smile, accompanied by a comment like, "In theory that is excellent; however, people are simply not resilient enough to get involved with such a process. It would be too challenging for them." Let's assume these leaders are right. The only constructive response would be to come up with a way to help the people who aren't resilient today to become resilient by tomorrow.

At some point, we must join the dots. On the one hand, we complain that people are not resilient enough; on the other hand, we oppose the training that would make them more resilient. If you feel challenged by anything—it doesn't really matter what it is—one way of dealing with it is to reduce the demands on yourself. The result is that you will continue to feel overchallenged by the same things for the rest of your life. Alternatively, you can participate in a training program until the very things that you experience as overchallenging right now, will no longer be a challenge for you. That is the basic rule of any kind of training, including spiritual training.

Spiritually trained or untrained?

People who are spiritually untrained are overwhelmed by everything beyond their personal comfort zone. Unfortunately, most Christians are spiritually untrained. Only a small minority has ever gone through a systematic spiritual training process similar to that of body-building. Consequently, a book like this may look too challenging. However, this can change. Much like physical training, this kind of spiritual training will enable us to bear burdens in the future that we are unable to bear today.

If you feel overchallenged by some of the chapters in this book, don't give up prematurely saying, "This is too hard for me." Rather, you should ask, "Is it my trained or my untrained self that is wanting to throw in the towel?" If it is your untrained self that holds this opinion, don't take your reaction too seriously, or at least don't allow your future to be determined by it. Instead, say, "Dear untrained self, you will soon be a trained self, and then I am going to ask you this question again." You should never forget that it is only your trained self that is able to recognize the full potential that God has placed within you.

Spiritual training in churches?

In many churches the members are either strongly *overchallenged* (since untrained people are expected to do things that can only be expected of trained people), or they are permanently *underchallenged* (since all activities are focused on spiritually untrained people and nobody dares to increasingly raise the bar). Thus, those who haven't done any running training for years, get the impression that they are constantly expected to do a spiritual marathon (and consequently withdraw); while those who are impatiently looking forward to their first or tenth marathon, find themselves getting bored with endless warm-up exercises that are never followed by the main event.

What does spiritual training that continuously strengthens your spiritual muscles, that enables you to shoulder heavier burdens, that makes you more resilient, more teachable, more able to receive criticism, and ultimately more loving, more tolerant, and more powerful, look like? That is what level B growth is all about.

Training in godliness

John Ortberg wrote, "There is an immense difference between training to do something and trying to do something." This difference is crucial for dealing with spiritual styles. It is not very effective, for instance, simply to try to understand the opposite style. That would be the same as trying to run a marathon without having trained for a marathon. You could try to do it, but would end up more frustrated than ever, saying "I knew it would be too hard for me."

In 1 Corinthians, Paul clearly describes the spiritual significance of a continuous training process: "Do you not know that in a race the runners all compete, but only one receives the prize? Run in such a way that you may win it. Athletes exercise self-control in all things, they do it to receive a perishable wreath, but we, an imperishable one. So I do not run aimlessly, nor do I box as though beating the air; but I punish my body and enslave it, so that after proclaiming to others I myself should not be disqualified" (1 Cor. 9:24-27). Level B growth is nothing other than "training ... in godliness" (1 Tim. 4:7).

The right dosage

Medical research has helped us discover how muscles develop. If we want to strengthen our muscles, we have to systematically stress them so that they expend energy beyond normal levels. This results, literally, in microscopic tears in the muscle fiber. At the end of the training session muscle capacity is *reduced*. In other words, training initially results in chaos. You might say that the opposite effect of the training occurs. However, after 24 to 48 hours of rest, the muscles are already stronger and can meet the next challenge better than before.

These dynamics apply to all areas of life. Management trainers Tony Schwartz and Tim Loehr write in their book, *The Power of Full Engagement*, "We build emotional, mental and spiritual capacity in precisely the same way that we build physical capacity. We grow at all levels by expending energy beyond our normal limits and then recovering. Stress a muscle too much, and you risk severe injuries. Expose a muscle to ordinary demand and it won't grow. With age it will actually lose strength. The limiting factor in building any 'muscle' is that many of us back off at the slightest hint of discomfort."

The secret is the right dosage. It must be high enough to activate our systems, but not so high that it results in injury. At any rate, normal stress is not training; we have to exceed the normal amount. We have to live—even if only periodically—over and above our strength. Otherwise the training effect equals zero. In addition, the phases of physical or spiritual stress must be followed by phases of recreation. As we have learned in the area of muscle increase, muscle fiber isn't built up in the actual training sessions, but in the rest periods in between the sessions.

Churches as spiritual training centers

It is helpful to group all church activities into one of the following three categories:

1. Those that are targeted on continuous spiritual muscle formation. In these activities, Christians are challenged just enough to result in those microscopic tears in their spiritual muscles, which leads to a strengthening of the muscle during periods of rest. In order to be effective, these opportunities must take into consideration each individual believer's stage of development.

2. Those that offer rest, i.e. opportunities that have the sole purpose of letting people recover spiritually. These phases of regeneration only make sense and will only be experienced positively if they follow phases of intense spiritual training.

3. Those that are not concerned with either training or resting, but fall outside of these categories.

The function of rituals

In any kind of training, regularity is of utmost importance. No fitness program works if you only exercise once a week. This applies to spiritual training as well. Why do so many Christians complain—for years, maybe even decades—that they haven't experienced any spiritual growth? The answer to this question is so trite that it's almost embarrassing to give: because they have never been involved in any systematic spiritual training.

In order to have a lifestyle of spiritual training, rituals may help. They assist you in doing what willpower in and of itself cannot accomplish. People who use a ritual don't have to ask what they need to do when confronted with a new situation. The need to make new decisions continually consumes enormous amounts of energy and often ends up in negative results. The secret of training is not to wait until you are in the right mood. You do your exercises independently of your current mood, and consequently experience that the discipline of such a continuous process has a positive influence on your mood. Positive feelings do play an important role in training; however, they rarely emerge at the beginning, but at the end of the process. Rituals help ensure that the things that are important for us, will happen "automatically."

Contrary to willpower, which *pushes* us to a certain behavior, a ritual virtually *draws* us. Apart from guaranteeing continuity, rituals assist us in bringing about emotional change in ourselves. At first, we might feel miserable while carrying out the ritual. But after a certain time, we may feel miserable if we miss it.

Spiritual training:

Just as the human body needs regular training to give us our full potential of physical energy, so does our spiritual life. Without continuous and systematic training we will either experience no growth at all or, if we are fortunate, "accidental growth." The key to training, both in the physical and in the spiritual realm, is to challenge ourselves regularly such that we built up our muscle mass. Attempting to avoid those deliberate phases of high intensity makes training virtually impossible.

Time for training

As beneficial as it is to read a book like this, it can only be seen as a part of an overall training process. If we are serious about spiritual growth, about placing God at the center of our life, about becoming more and more Christlike, about achieving "the measure of the stature of the fullness of Christ" (Eph. 4:13), continuous training should be firmly rooted into our daily lives.

The good news about spiritual training is that it doesn't necessarily demand additional time investment. The time that an average believer invests in Christian activities is already considerable. The goal should be to use the activities that we are already involved in for spiritual training. For instance, you could experience a grim argument at a church board meeting and cultivate your negative feelings about it. But you could also use that opportunity to apply the concepts of the Trinitarian Compass and explain them to the rest of the board, enabling all of you to experience spiritual growth. In the end, you may even say, "Thank you, Lord, for this wonderful fight."

Physical, intellectual, and spiritual training

During the time that I was working on this book, I got involved in regular, disciplined training in the following three areas:

First, with the assistance of my spiritual mentors, I began a spiritual training process to help me through the challenge of working with all nine spiritual styles. As much as I benefitted from it, it led me continuously beyond my comfort zone.

Second, due to health issues, I launched a strict physical training program. I ran one and a half hours every other day, and did two and a half hours of weight-lifting on the alternate days. I trained so intensely that some people believed that the "A." in my name stood for "Arnold" and "Schwarz" was merely an abbreviation...

Third, due to the needs of our ministry I did extensive language training—grammar, vocabulary, and pronunciation. Usually I did this while simultaneously sweating on the treadmill or working out my muscles with weights.

None of these workouts were particularly "fun" for me; I simply did them because I had to do them. But that is not surprising. The purpose of training is not to have fun, but to achieve results. And I can clearly see the results in my life. My experience during the three years in which I trained so intensely, was surprising: All the three training areas melted into one big training effort. I had the impression that it didn't really matter whether I was sweating on the treadmill, studying Spanish grammar, or working with my mentors— everything was contributing to strengthening my "spiritual muscles." I now know that this was not just a subjective feeling. Indeed, the same "muscles" are strengthened by all forms of training.

Learning languages took me out of my comfort zone and challenged me to understand others within the framework of their own mindset. Did that help me in my spiritual life? Very much so. It prepared the ground for my interaction with foreign spiritual styles.

Physical training continually stretched me beyond my comfort zone as well. For most of my life, I have been the absolute "anti-sportsman." As my physical muscles grew, I literally sensed the influence this had on my emotional and spiritual muscles. I learned to overcome my longing for physical comfort. The lessons I learned in the gym were more important to my spiritual life than many of the things that I learned in seminars or worship services.

After all that I have shared in this book, the fact that working with my spiritual mentors affected my spirituality doesn't need explanation. But maybe it is appropriate to add that this was real training as well. When I had a session with one of my mentors, especially with one who was far outside of my comfort zone, I imagined myself being in the gym lifting weights. I realized that when I manage to stretch myself in one area, I am also able to do it in other areas.

Why do I share this? To show off my training progress? No. The purpose is quite the opposite. I write this in order to share how difficult training has been for me in all three areas, but also to share the wonderful revelation that the lessons I learned in each one of the three areas influenced the other areas as well. Before doing it, I would never have imagined that pumping iron in the gym and learning Indonesian vocabulary would positively affect my spiritual resilience!

> *The lessons I learned in the gym were more important to my spiritual life than many of the things I learned in seminars.*

28 days of discipline

T here are different ways to transfer Level B growth to a practical training plan that fits your own situation. In the long run, the most effective way is to get involved in a Mutual Mentoring relationship in the areas of both your native style and your opposite style. On page 182 we will discuss what this looks like practically.

I assume that, over time, quite a number of Christians will get involved in this kind of process. NCD International will do everything possible to further these activities, especially through the Trinitarian Monastery. However, I recognize that only a relatively small percentage of those who read this book will get involved in a process of Mutual Mentoring. For many, this kind of learning is simply too unfamiliar to start with straight away. I expect that five years from now the situation will be quite different. By that time, it will be far more natural to speak with someone from your opposite style, either in person, or on the other side of the world, via video conferencing. But we haven't quite reached that point yet.

Daily E-mails

To help you ease into Level B learning, we have developed a *28 Days of Discipline* process. This is to enable you to get involved with the process on a somewhat lower level than within a Mutual Mentoring process, and to prevent you from confining your "spiritual training" to the reading of this book, or, worse yet, to the completion of the Spiritual Style Test.

After registering online for this free process, you will receive daily e-mails as part of a 28 day cycle that includes some simple repeated rituals, as well as a more demanding once-a-week challenge. You get to choose whether you will receive training that relates to your native or opposite style. Ultimately, you can even grow your way through all of the styles over a nine month time period. (www.3colorsofyourspirituality.org).

This whole process is developed in such a way that every reader of this book, including those who don't have any contact with a local church, can take part in it. That said, if you work through the disciplines at the same time as a friend, a group, or your whole church, there is greater opportunity for growth and life transformation as you share your experiences and learn together. These times of sharing can make the learning experiences particularly intense and fruitful.

Journeying with your small group

For those who would like to take a whole group on the spiritual style journey, we have developed a companion guide to this book called, *How to Embrace the 3 Colors of Your Spirituality in Your World.* With the help of clear instructions, the leader guides the group (e.g. Bible study group, choir, leadership team, best friends, married couple, etc.) through this book according to a very flexible reading guide that allows for different levels of studiousness. This process is punctuated by weekly group meetings where experiences can be shared and mutual learning can take place. The guide also includes tips for how to involve your whole church in the spiritual style discovery process.

It is one thing to read about all of these learning options. It is something altogether different to experience how they work in practice. And launching such processes is far less difficult than most of us might imagine.

Feeling spiritual versus being spiritual

In today's world of media, people aren't concerned about getting informed, but they do want the feeling of being informed. Likewise, most people aren't concerned about healthy living, but having the feeling of healthy living. There are whole industries that live exclusively from infusing people with this feeling.

My experience is that the same applies in the area of spirituality. Many Christians aren't concerned with being spiritual, they just want to have the feeling of being spiritual. Or worse yet, they simply want to have spiritual feelings. For such people these feelings, whenever they occur, are the epitome of God being close to them. There are whole industries that live exclusively from infusing people with these feelings, too.

From this soil, the phenomenon of consumer Christianity, that has shaped the Western world and has undermined the substance of Christianity so strongly, has emerged. This doesn't just apply to the Western world. Those who profit from this system work globally. Thus consumer Christianity was exported to the ends of the earth and has found native imitators, who apply the same principles in a culturally-adapted way.

My concern is not that you "feel spiritual" while reading this book. My goal is that you will be challenged to strengthen your spiritual muscles. Therefore, you cannot afford to pick out those aspects of the learning process that you sense as pleasant (e.g. Level A learning) and ignore the more troublesome aspects (e.g. Level B learning). Training shouldn't be confused with wellness. Offers of wellness are targeted at giving us temporary "feel-good" moments, but they don't train us. In training, however, you may feel overloaded, stressed, and exhausted at the outset, while feeling good usually only follows after some time.

As I mentioned previously (page 44), the publisher of this book will be frequently asked if it is possible to purchase the Spiritual Style Test separately, without the "extra weight" of the Trinitarian Compass and the opposite pole, of Level A and Level B learning. People would like to utilize the survey in a church group as a type of spiritual wellness offer, since the feel-good moment is virtually pre-programmed into the survey results. Everyone will go home with the feeling of having done something spiritually meaningful. But, a whole book?! For heaven's sake, nobody expects that any more. Too much thinking, too much time, you must be joking! Christian, what planet are you from?!

There are a number of books whose explicit goal is to produce positive spiritual feelings within their readers. Sometimes this process is referred to as "spiritual reading." I don't want to criticize it, since these feelings can be very nice (I, for one, like them very much). And there are times—for instance, during recovery phases between two challenging training units—in which this kind of reading can be extremely useful. I simply want to make it very clear that this is not the goal of the book you are holding in your hands.

The same things that Thomas Merton writes about "meditation" apply to all spiritual disciplines. He writes, "We should not, however, judge the value of our meditation by 'how we feel.' A hard and apparently fruitless meditation may in fact be much more valuable than one that is easy, happy, enlightened, and apparently a big success."

> **Many people are more concerned with feeling spiritual rather than being spiritual.**

The essence of spiritual maturity

W hen George Barna speaks about the state of Christianity, we can be pretty sure that his observations are based on hard facts. Presumably there is no other person who has collected as much empirical data on Christians and churches in North America as he has. Recently I asked him what he would regard as the most alarming result of his research. He didn't need much time to think about it. "We are still a church nurtured by milk rather than solid food," he said, and in the eyes of this thoroughly sober man I could sense deep concern. Should this be the depressing net result of all Christian activity over so many years?

Of course, it is not wrong for some believers to get "milk rather than solid food" (1 Cor. 3:2). That is what Paul gave the Christians in Corinth, whom he regarded as "infants in Christ" (1 Cor. 3:1). Infants should be given milk. However, if after 10 or 20 years we still think that the time for "solid food" has not yet come, and if we still see and treat these people as "infants," we have a clear indication that something has gone completely wrong. Or is it possible that the obsession with milk products, on the side of those who have been believers for many years, is the intended goal of the Christian "milk industry?"

The goal of spiritual maturity

With pointed clarity, Ephesians describes the goal of spiritual growth as "the equipping of the saints for the work of service, to the building up of the body of Christ; until we all attain to the unity of the faith, and of the knowledge of the Son of God, to a mature man, to the measure of the stature which belongs to the fullness of Christ. As a result, we are no longer to be children, tossed here and there by waves and carried about by every wind of doctrine, by the trickery of men, by craftiness in deceitful scheming" (Eph. 4:12-14). This goal of spiritual maturity, according to Ephesians, doesn't apply to a few chosen ones, but clearly and explicitly to "all."

Spiritual maturity manifests itself in the ability to tolerate the stress and suffering that are often part of a growth process. This includes the willingness to display uncertainty. Confusion and indecision are often interpreted as weakness. But in actual fact, they are the door to improvement, to creative solutions. While working on this book, I grew the most during phases of confusion. Decisiveness, in the sense of being able to come up with superficially plausible solutions quickly, should not be regarded as a virtue. Guy Claxton, Director of the *Centre for Real-World Learning*, expresses it well: "Always retreat from uncertainty and you will end up the prisoner of a very limited range of knowledge and know-how. Always dive into the unknown, and you are likely to have a short life (but an exciting one)."

> **Maturity Scale:**
> *A 5-stage-model of describing the relationship between your own spiritual style and your opposite style. The Maturity Scale is designed to help you see Level B growth as a constantly progressing, dynamic process. Every advancement on the scale (even from –2 to –1) is real progress toward spiritual maturity.*

The way to maturity is to change your diet increasingly from "milk" to "solid food." In other words, expect people to grapple deliberately with difficulty for a while. They will soon learn that this is not something to worry about. And with each experience their "spiritual muscles" will get strengthened and they will be enabled to bear even greater burdens in the future.

Don't expect everything from your church

It would be wrong—and in fact, highly immature—to expect your church to support you systematically both in your native style and in your interaction with your opposite style—and everything in the exact dosage that you need at your present phase of development. And woe to the preacher whose sermon doesn't exactly address your spiritual style! If you expect such, you (a) are probably sulking, (b) deem your church either "unloving" or "unspiritual," and (c) are beginning to consider if it wouldn't be better to join another church.

If you really have such an expectation, you must be fair enough to think it through from the viewpoint of representatives of the other eight styles. Most likely they would have the same demands of your church. No matter what the church does—at least in the area of public events—the majority will deem it wrong, since the very things that are appealing to one style, aren't appealing to the others. This kind of "please-me" attitude pre-programs church members to be constantly sulking.

Throughout my whole life, I have never belonged to a local church that corresponded to my own spiritual style. Now one could say, "Christian has constantly gone to the wrong church." But that is not the way I see it. I have constantly belonged to churches that represented either my opposite style or a style that is far away from my native style. That has made my own spirituality far more balanced, and both my ministry and myself have benefitted from that.

I have formed the habit of using techniques to translate the expressions of spiritual styles that are foreign to me in such a way that I can benefit from them. For instance, when I listen to a sermon whose whole paradigm is shaped by a spiritual style that is strange to me, I ask myself, "Christian, what exactly is it that disturbs you so much? Which sore spot in your life does your reaction reveal? What would you have to do to make progress in this area?" Applying this method, I develop a new sermon in my brain, tailor-made for my situation and full of ideas for Level B growth. That is far more constructive than being angry with the preacher or saying in resignation, "That simply doesn't speak to me."

I apply this same procedure in other contexts as well. It is extremely helpful to have the image of the Trinitarian Compass in mind as I do this. It enables me to integrate everything I encounter into this frame of reference, thus making it useful for my spiritual growth. Once you become accustomed to this habit, it happens almost automatically. You are no longer angry, no longer grumpy; you simply learn.

Whenever I attend a worship service with friends that is foreign to our own spirituality, I sense that my training in this area has enabled me to draw much more out of the unfamiliar things than they do. Somehow most seem to expect that every public expression of spirituality must address their spiritual style. But even statistically, this is an absolute impossibility.

It is a sign of immaturity to expect your church to constantly focus on your personal spiritual style. You should not expect your church to provide everything you need for your spiritual growth. There are countless other sources of spiritual learning at your disposal.

> **You should not expect your church to provide everything you need for your spiritual growth.**

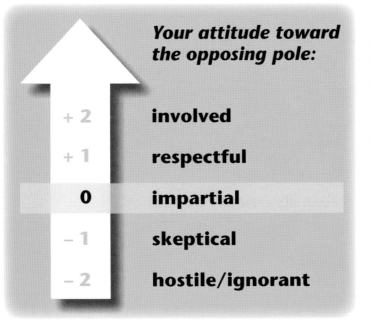

Your attitude toward the opposing pole:

+ 2 **involved**

+ 1 **respectful**

0 **impartial**

– 1 **skeptical**

– 2 **hostile/ignorant**

The Maturity Scale distinguishes five stages that describe your relationship to the opposite pole. The further you progress on this scale, the more balanced you will be spiritually. By means of this scale, you can monitor how far your spiritual maturity has advanced over the course of your learning process. In order to get started with a Mutual Mentoring process, you should at least be at stage 0 (impartial attitude).

Maturity and Level B learning

While Level A learning helps you grow from childhood to adolescence, Level B learning leads you from adolescence to maturity (see page 46). Constructive interaction with the opposite pole is an *indication* of maturity, on the one hand, and the *way* to maturity on the other. How do we prepare people for "solid food?" By expecting them to consume food that is increasingly more solid.

Take a look at the graphic. The Maturity Scale describes the relationship that you have to your opposite pole, with the span ranging from "hostile/ignorant" (stage –2) to "involved" (stage +2). This graphic shows that the question of whether or not you have integrated the concerns of the opposite pole is not a "yes" or "no" issue. There are different degrees of integration. Maybe you will never reach stage +2, which actually wouldn't be a catastrophe. The sheer fact that you have stage +2 in mind, can help you move from stage 0 ("impartial") to +1 ("respectful"). That would be significant progress!

The Christian life as constant movement

Spiritual growth is all about movement. It was Isaac Newton who corrected a far-reaching error made by the Greeks. He noticed that it is not the state of movement, but the state of rest, that demands an explanation. It became clear to him that a body continues in its movement as long as there is no force that hinders it. Movement, not rest, is the natural state of a body. In spirituality, the same applies: Standing still is unnatural; movement is natural.

If you are working with the Maturity Scale, you should notice that both ups and downs on the scale can be "normal." It may be that in your interaction with the opposite pole you open your heart widely and embrace new things enthusiastically. Later on, however, skepticism may take root, which is then indicated by a downward move on the scale. This is exactly what happened when I dealt with some of the spiritual styles. The scale helps us monitor these ups and downs.

Spiritual styles in a Three-Color Church

Not only individual Christians, but also whole churches have spiritual styles. Of course, what we are referring to as "church style" is shaped by various factors (such as tradition, theology, and the styles of the church leaders). However, as we have previously seen, the nine styles are not equally distributed among the members of a given church. Sometimes one or two of the styles clearly prevail, which will have a strong influence on the church climate.

Your style and your church's style

It is eye-opening to compare your own spiritual style with the most frequently represented style of your church. When doing such a comparison it can be helpful to focus more on the style family (i.e. dogmatic, ethical, aesthetic or green, red, and blue) than on the fine-grained breakdown of nine different styles. Strongly simplified, three different relationships are possible:

1. By and large, your church represents **your own native style** or at least your style family. In this situation, chances are high that you get plenty of input for your Level A growth (provided that continuous spiritual growth is the distinct goal of the church so that enough challenges are provided).

2. Your church represents one of **your opposite styles**. Though you may suffer in this situation in terms of your Level A growth, you need to realize that this situation provides the opportunity of enabling permanent Level B growth. Properly handled, your spiritual life could benefit from that environment.

3. Finally, it could be that your church represents neither your native style nor your opposite style, but rather one of **your neighbor styles** (or a style between your neighbor style and your opposite style). In this scenario you encounter elements that are familiar to you (providing chances for Level A growth) and elements that are more difficult for you (Level B); however, neither is as radical as could be expected in the first two situations.

Each of the three relationships mentioned has its advantages and disadvantages. Option 1 should by no means be seen as the "ideal fit." On the contrary, most Christians who have never grown beyond Level A have lived all their lives in an environment such as that.

Three categories of churches

The chances of experiencing spiritual growth are not only determined by the three relationships mentioned above, but also by your church's attitude toward different styles. Roughly speaking, there are three possibilities:

1. Within the church, exclusively one style (or style family) is appreciated; the others are dismissed or viewed with hostility.

2. The church has a clear tendency toward one specific style (or style family), but is generally open to all of the other styles and approaches them with respect, even if not every style can be supported actively.

3. The church displays—not just verbally, but through concrete measures that permeate all of church life—equal appreciation toward all nine styles.

What your church should do

Perhaps one of the most important tasks of a church is to create an atmosphere in which it is possible to share honestly about spiritual styles. Such a climate, in which people can openly speak about their own strengths and weaknesses, and their hopes and fears, is a precondition for all kinds of spiritual growth processes. If the Spiritual Style Test has been conducted at the level of the whole church, those churches that favor a specific style will discover that all nine styles are in their midst, even if in differing quantities. Those members who have the "favored" style, will be glad to discover that there are others within their own church who represent the opposite style, providing them the possibility for Level B growth.

The power released by a paradigm such as the Trinitarian Compass, should not be underestimated. The very same discussion that may be fruitless and frustrating without this paradigm, can become extremely constructive and inspiring on the basis of the Trinitarian Compass. The same "squabblers" who have continually tortured themselves and others with the same argument, can get involved in a Mutual Mentoring relationship in order to learn from each other. Is this unrealistic? Absolutely not. I have countless examples of how fruitful these processes can be. We may start with the same conflicts; but approaching them from a different paradigm makes all the difference.

I am not aware of any reason why church leadership should be absolved of the responsibility of helping all of their members identify their spiritual style. If a church were to actively support its members in their Level A and Level B processes, that would be wonderful. However, as a church member you shouldn't expect this to happen (see Box on page 178). There are countless other opportunities for Level A and Level B learning, even without the explicit support of a church.

What you should do

It is the responsibility of every believer to establish permanent personal growth processes both in the area of their native style and of their opposite pole. This is not a task that you should delegate to your church.

> **Three-Color Church:**
> *Churches that have deliberately placed the Trinitarian Compass at the center of their ministry. Rather than using terms such as "evangelical," "liberal," or "charismatic" for a description of their identity, an increasing number of churches within the NCD network label themselves "trinitarian" or "Three-Color Churches." By this they want to express that they are striving to reflect all three colors in the life of the church.*

- Take care that you don't only practice your native style, but also that you grow continuously in that area. You need training, challenges, incentives, and last but not least, interaction with other Christians who have the same style as you. Even if your church, as a whole, cannot support you in your native style, very likely there are other members who share the same style. Get together with them. Share your experiences. Learn from each other, inspire each other, encourage each other, challenge each other. You need not look for another church in order to benefit from Christians who share your native style.

- Take care, as well, to get enough incentives for growth in the area of your opposite pole, even if you should invest far less time in this area than in practicing your native style. If, by and large, your church represents your opposite style, theoretically, everything that you need for this process is at your disposal. Your challenge is to filter and process this input in a way that becomes beneficial for your own growth.

The power of red shoes

Some time ago, Dave Wetzler, our American NCD Partner, gave me a red pen with his company's logo. "Christian, you should use it so that you never forget which color zone you have to work on," he said. Since Dave knows me quite well, he is aware that my personal minimum color is "red."

I accepted the pen and with it the challenge of asking myself, every time I use it, "What do I need to do in order to grow in the red color zone?" Since I also know Dave quite well—his own color profile is at the junction between red and green—I asked him if he would be willing to use a blue pen in his daily work. He smiled, reached into his front pocket and pulled out a blue pen. "I have done it for weeks now," he said. "I know that blue is the color area in which I still have a lot to learn."

Dave has had his company's logo printed on hundreds of green, red and blue pens. He uses them regularly in his training events. At the beginning, each participant receives one of these pens along with the rest of the conference materials. Later the participants conduct a color profile and find out which of the colors is least developed in their lives. Then they are asked to find another participant with a pen the color of their own weakness, so that they might exchange pens.

As a result of this small exercise there are many informal encounters. There are jokes, there is laughter, people pat each other on the back. In the end, every participant not only has the right pen, but there have been—even if in a deliberately playful setting—countless conversations about very personal themes. The ice has been broken.

> ## We depend on concrete symbols in order to visualize the dynamics of the Trinitarian Compass.

I am convinced that we need these kinds of symbols if we are serious about integrating the dynamics of the Trinitarian Compass into our daily lives. Therefore it excites me to see the creative solutions that many churches have found to create their own symbolic language in order to communicate these dynamics.

In a rural Anglican church close to Sydney, during their participation in an NCD Campaign, every member wore a name tag that displayed their personal color profile result. This tag provided a glimpse into the "heart" of each believer. Everyone has strengths, and everyone is imbalanced at the same time. Even the imbalance of the pastor was made known for everyone to see. He told me, "If we want to help each other grow in faith, we have to know where each one of us presently is in our spiritual life."

As symbols speak strongly to me, some time ago I bought a pair of red shoes. Since in my culture red shoes are seen as almost abnormal—for reasons I will never understand 99% of the men prefer the colors black and brown—people are constantly asking me about my red shoes and I have to explain why I wear them. I simply cannot avoid sharing my personal growth areas with other people.

Each time I put on my red shoes, I combine it with the following thought: "Christian, throughout this day, stand on the Word. That is your foundation." No, there is no magical power in red shoes. But they help me tremendously in my effort to feed my head and my heart with continual reminders that challenge me in my personal spiritual growth process toward becoming a more balanced Christian.

How to explore your opposite style

A s I teach, whenever I sense a conflict that can be traced back to a difference in spiritual styles, I take the opportunity to literally put this conflict "on the platform," deliberately dramatizing it. My goal is to demonstrate how we can deal with these conflict situations constructively, i.e. in a way that each of the opponents can take benefit for the sake of their own spirituality.

Looking for learning opportunities

When you hit the road of learning from the opposite pole you shouldn't make the mistake of thinking exclusively about "official" learning settings (such as seminars, mentoring processes, etc.). If you keep your eyes wide open, you will encounter learning opportunities wherever you go. Usually these are the very situations that would have made you angry in the past. However, rather than getting angry in the future, you can use these situations as learning opportunities. It's effective; it doesn't cost you a minute more time; and it has a remarkably positive effect on your emotional life.

Conflict situations, in particular, are excellent learning opportunities. Hardly anything is a greater obstacle to deep personal learning than complete satisfaction with the status quo. Substantial conflict is far better. If we learn how to deal with conflicts on the basis of intelligent rules (for instance, those behind the Trinitarian Compass), the learning effect is much greater than what might come out of the most ingenious seminar.

10 Steps to explore your opposite style

If you seriously want to interact with your opposite style, follow these ten steps:

> **Energy transformation:**
> *One of six "growth forces" taught by NCD. Rather than fighting against that which may be interpreted as "hostile," this principle strives to utilize the energy of the "opponent" to one's own advantage.*

1. *Be sure that you are confident in your own style.* You should not only have a clear knowledge of your spiritual style (which can be identified in less than 30 minutes), but also feel secure in it. If you have just discovered your native style, but never really lived it, it could be good to wait awhile before getting involved with Level B growth.

2. *Address the dark side of your style.* Every style has strengths and dangers. The overview on page 52 lists, among other things, the two main perils of your spiritual style. Enjoy the strengths of your style, but be aware of its perils as well.

3. *Re-read the sections about your opposite style.* In the second part of this book every style is extensively portrayed. You have probably read the text about your native style with special interest. Now re-read—maybe even two or three times—the text on your opposite style.

4. *Express your own spiritual experience in the categories of your opposite style.* In the chapter on your native style there is a box with a message for people who approach this style from the opposite side of the Compass. This text can inspire you to summarize the experiences that are important to you, in the categories of your opposite style. Do this in writing. Describe your spiritual

My own pilgrimage

It took a while before I realized that I have the sacramental style. Since I have lived all of my life in churches that display very different styles, I was never actively encouraged in my native style.

Actually, it was my involvement in this spiritual style project that brought me to the realization that I have the sacramental style. If someone had asked me four years ago what my "spiritual style" was (what a strange term!), I probably would have assigned myself to the word-centered area, i.e. the red color zone. Today I know that this area is of great importance to me—of theological importance—but it doesn't really speak to me personally. It is not the way my antenna to God functions.

From my own experiences I learned how questionable it is to assign people to one of the nine spiritual styles on the basis of their published books. Of course, after this book has been written, everybody will say, "Sure, Christian has the sacramental style, we should have known that before." But that is complete nonsense. Based on my previous publications nobody could have known that. Not even I knew that. Because of that, I am aware that I don't have the slightest idea which spiritual style Christians such as Augustine, Martin Luther, John Wesley or others may have had, and I am always astonished how well other authors seem to know this. I regard it to be highly questionable to extrapolate an author's spiritual style from his or her theological works.

My own spirituality is always on the interface between green and blue. God's promptings, for instance, which I access through the blue part of my spirituality, are for me a far more "real" reality than, say,

Does the professor who criticized me work just as hard on the blue zone as I work on the red?

the figures on my bank account, which I treat largely as a "virtual reality" (my wife says that the balance of my bank account is pretty much the "most red" element of my spirituality; but this is an exaggeration). I am shaped by the sensory (green) dimension as well: Encounters with other people, their laughter, their tears—these are things that influence the way I lead my life much more than, say, scientific deductions.

I know that I am one-sided in this area, unhealthily one-sided. Therefore, I want to grow in the area of my opposite pole. People who have only known me superficially would never guess how at risk I am: A single dream could change the course of my life (even without biblical evaluation). Personal encounters with other people move me extremely (far more than abstract "goals"). The supernatural dimension of faith attracts me very much.

Some time ago, I shared very honestly about this imbalance at a conference. Some weeks later, I received an article from a theology professor who had attended the conference. He stated that I had definitely "come out of the closet." I had clearly declared that I don't take the Word of God seriously, that I would give any wild dream, any emotionally loaded conversation priority over biblical standards.

Actually, I had tried to communicate the exact opposite. I had shared that I take the red area extremely seriously and work very hard on it, but also that this doesn't come easily for me. Therefore I try all the more to grow in this area. I wonder if the professor who criticized me works just as hard on the blue zone as I work on the red?

experiences in a way that would communicate to a representative of the opposite style.

5. **Be sure that you have reached "stage 0" on the Maturity Scale.** In order to get involved with Mutual Mentoring, it is essential that you have at least reached the stage of an "impartial attitude" (see page 175). If you sense that you are still on stage –2 or –1, please don't initiate a Mutual Mentoring process.

6. **Get involved in a relationship of Mutual Mentoring.** Find a mentor who represents your opposite style and start the process. The next chapter (page 182) describes how this can be done in practical terms.

7. **Start all practical activities with a "warm-up" exercise in the area of your comfort zone.** Whenever you do something related to your opposite pole, you should first connect to God in a way that, in the framework of your native style, is most natural to you. Perhaps for you this means to listen to worship songs that touch your heart, before dealing with the doctrinal style; or, you may need to connect with God in a highly sensory way before you take a fast. Since through your native style you *are* already connected to God, it is the ideal launch pad from which to explore other ways of connecting with the same God.

8. **Plan time for recreation.** As we have seen in the chapter on spiritual training (page 167), every phase of training must be followed by an appropriate rest period, if the training is going to be effective. It is not in the training phases themselves, but in these periods of rest, when the spiritual muscles are built up. You must plan time for it from the outset.

9. **Integrate your learning experiences into your own style.** Never forget that the goal of the process is not to become like your partner in the Mutual Mentoring relationship. You should not switch to his or her style, but rather integrate those aspects of your opposite style that are helpful for your growth.

10. **Share your experiences with others.** Everything you learn—and you will learn a lot within this process—is not your personal, private property, but something you have to pass on to others. Only by giving it away can you keep it alive. Think about how you can share your experiences with other Christians (your small group leader? your pastor? your bishop?). You may be surprised how receptive people are to hear messages that aren't characterized by a "know-it-all" mentality, but are rooted in authentic processes of mutual learning.

A new self-awareness

The goal of Level B learning is not to give up your identity, but rather to strengthen it. If you deliberately work on your perils, you become a better representative of your native style—more trustworthy, more loving, more powerful! Throughout these processes you should never forget that there are many other Christians who have the same style as you do. To be even more precise, exactly 11% of the Christians worldwide have the same style as you do, and a third of all Christians share your style family. If you defend the specific concerns of your style, do not see this as an opportunity for an ego trip, but as an opportunity to be an ambassador for 11% (or 33%) of Christianity. To be sure, you are not an ambassador of the majority, but of a significant minority—a minority that deserves to be listened to, whose voice needs to be heard by representatives of other styles.

How spiritual mentoring can help you grow

I could well imagine that a number of readers will be disappointed that there is not a section containing "practical tips" of what we should do in the area of every style, such as, "Light a candle. Now close your eyes. Breathe deeply." Without a doubt, we need concrete applications. The reason that this book doesn't offer tips of this kind, is not that practical applications are unnecessary, but that there are far better ways to communicate them, specifically adapted to the needs of each individual situation.

The idea of Mutual Mentoring

The most effective way of launching Level B learning is to enter into a Mutual Mentoring relationship with a person who represents your opposite style. In such a mentoring relationship learning takes place primarily in a conversation, through questions and answers. The mentor is not the "enlightened" Plato, but more the inquiring Socrates, who tries to reassure his own thinking by identifying increasing levels of dubiousness. Socrates compared his task with midwifery—his mother's profession—and said that it was not his job to birth wisdom, but solely to help others birth their own ideas.

This reference to Socrates is not meant to imply that in Mutual Mentoring we depend on geniuses of that kind. The great thing about Mutual Mentoring is that it works with average Christians. Nobody needs special training for it. Within the mentoring relationships we propose, which usually aren't overly spectacular, an old philosophical claim is realized, namely the communicative search for truth.

Mutual Mentoring:

One of the major working methods within the Trinitarian Monastery. Instead of being based on a hierarchical relationship of mentor to client as found in classical mentoring, a Mutual Mentoring relationship is based on the principle of mutuality: Each of the two partners strives to learn from the other. The classical application of Mutual Mentoring is learning from the opposite style. However, it can be applied equally well to growth processes within your native style.

The Trinitarian Monastery

In order to help initiate this kind of mutual mentoring processes, we have founded the Trinitarian Monastery. This is nothing other than a web-based learning community that in many respects can be compared to a "real" monastery (see page 10). The main task of the Trinitarian Monastery is to help readers of this book implement its contents. In this way, the Monastery is part of the book. However, within the Monastery implementation takes place, not through the study of books, but through encounters with real people.

We must be aware that, until recently, truly "ecumenical learning" (the Greek word *oikumene* means nothing other than "encompassing the whole world") was extremely limited. It largely referred to the gathering of several experts meeting in remote places and brooding over documents in search of theological consensus. Since our world has jumped from Gutenberg to Google, entirely new possibilities of worldwide learning have emerged. Now the Sunday school teacher in Detroit can connect with a Russian-Orthodox priest; the Baptist pastor in Belgium, with a house church coordinator in Guatemala; the leader of a pantomime group in Jakarta, with a bishop in Australia—not to discuss abstract documents, but to learn from each other spiritually. Up to now, this possibility simply wasn't a realistic option.

Global consciousness

During the 16th century in Nuremberg, Germany, the first globe was manufactured. After that time humanity possessed a visible, symbolic image of global consciousness. People could literally hold this model in their hands. Almost 500 years later astronauts looked down on the real globe for the first time. Since that moment, humanity has grown accustomed to this image of planet Earth. That was probably the moment of the birth of modern global consciousness. Now, it may seem a bit over the top for me to place the Trinitarian Monastery in this same line. However, I am convinced that its long-term relevance for *Christian global consciousness*, could result in a comparable quantum leap.

For global learning of this kind, it is not sufficient simply to have Internet access. In addition to technology, we need at least two more ingredients in order to learn practically about spirituality from one another:

1. We must be brought in contact with the **right people**. You cannot wait in a chat forum until a representative of the ascetic style coincidentally turns up, with whom you then agree to start a Level B Mutual Mentoring relationship. There must be an intelligent system through which you can find exactly the right partner for your needs. That is one of the functions of the Trinitarian Monastery—to help you find representatives of your opposite style who are eagerly waiting to learn from your native style. You can decide whether these people come from your own denomination or a different one, whether they live near you geographically or far away, whether they speak your native language or your second language, etc.

2. In order to cooperate in a meaningful way, we need a **common paradigm** that is shared by everyone. This paradigm is the Trinitarian Compass, which provides both the language and the rules for the learning process. If you have a Mutual Mentoring relationship with a Christian in another part of the world, you can be certain that this person holds the exact same book in his or her hands as you do (even if it is in a different language). Page 183 in their book has exactly the same contents as page 183 in your book, and this person—just like you—is committed to the 10 Rules of Mutual Mentoring (see next page).

The Trinitarian Monastery is designed to unburden the local church. As we have seen (page 178), it would be unrealistic to expect every local church to put into place all of the processes that are described in this book. Through the Trinitarian Monastery this task can be "outsourced," so to speak. This is one way it strives to minister to existing churches.

Altruism forbidden!

Perhaps the most important rule of Mutual Mentoring is that altruism is not allowed. You must not get involved with a Mutual Mentoring relationship in order to "be of help" to others, but solely to learn *yourself*. Since your partner joins the process with the same attitude, your interaction will be mutually helpful. However, helping others is not the goal. Such an attempt leads—in the area of spiritual styles—almost inevitably to an imperialistic mindset.

NCD Discipleship Resources:

The book series in which "The 3 Colors of Your Spirituality" has been published. Each book in this series covers one of the eight quality characteristics of growing churches and is marked, among other things, by the following features:

1. It is based on the Trinitarian Compass.

2. It contains a scientifically standardized test that helps you assess your own starting point.

3. It applies the "growth forces" (biotic principles) of NCD, usually without explicitly mentioning them.

4. It is addressed to every believer, not just to church leaders.

Accept your responsibility!

Far too many Christians are accustomed to delegating the responsibility for their spiritual growth to others—to their home church, for instance. While there are things in life that can be delegated to other people, our own spiritual growth doesn't belong in this category. It is the responsibility of each individual to make sure that there is continuous progress in his or her relationship with God.

Taking responsibility for your spiritual growth also implies taking over the responsibility for your own mistakes. It implies taking the initiative to change things, rather than demanding that others have to change. It implies viewing yourself, not as a victim of circumstances, but as a shaper of tomorrow's world.

Of course, we can't expect people who have just started their Christian journey to take over this responsibility from the outset. Responsibility is strongly related to spiritual maturity. Maturity doesn't emerge over night, and it doesn't develop all by itself. Therefore we need churches that won't take this responsibility away from the individual Christians, but will teach them how they can take responsibility for themselves.

Nevertheless, this is a vicious cycle. Since countless churches have actually taken the responsibility for spiritual growth away from their members, many people feel at a loss when they are supposed to name concrete measures that help them in their spiritual development. There are church and parachurch structures that deliberately further a dependency in spiritual things, rather than helping Christians develop a mature, responsible faith. Responsible Christians aren't necessarily easy to work with. If comfort is your highest goal, you can forget about responsibility.

As I mentioned earlier (page 177), I definitely regard it as part of a church's responsibility to assist their members in identifying their spiritual styles, even more so as this is really not an exceedingly difficult or time-consuming task. But once you have identified your spiritual style, you shouldn't expect others to organize your continued spiritual growth process. Both in terms of Level A and of Level B growth it is your job to set up a concrete training plan with all the measures that fit you.

The Trinitarian Monastery will support you in this process. The insight that responsibility for your spiritual growth is up to you does not imply that you are left to sink or swim. That would be an individualistic misunderstanding of responsibility. As you pursue growth, you can benefit from the experiences of thousands of others. Within the Trinitarian Monastery these experiences are easily accessible, so that you can find exactly those things that are most helpful to you.

Within the Trinitarian Monastery you won't encounter any "gurus." If you are looking for someone like this (or are even in need of it), you may be disappointed by what you find there. In the Trinitarian Monastery there is no hierarchy. Here it is not possible to delegate your responsibility to other people. Here the professor learns from the construction worker; the bishop, from the small group leader; the manager, from the unemployed. Here you will find a climate that cultivates responsibility.

"The old paradox applies," Guy Claxton writes, "when people are given no responsibility, they tend to act irresponsibly; when they are treated as responsible, they tend to behave responsibly."

> *If comfort is your highest goal, you can forget about responsibility.*

The 10 Rules of Mutual Mentoring

The one precondition for participating in Mutual Mentoring is that you agree to the following ten rules:

1. *I am in this relationship, not to teach, but to learn.* This is the practical application of the "altruism-forbidden" principle. Many Christians will have enormous difficulty sticking to this rule. Don't forget, your only goal is to change yourself, not to change others. This rule must be strictly applied.

2. *I expect neither to be understood nor to understand.* If the other person should understand you, or the other way around, wonderful! But don't expect this to happen. Expect that you won't be understood. In order to reach your goal—i.e. to change yourself—deep mutual understanding is not a prerequisite.

3. *I have the right to be respected in my spiritual style.* The fact that you want to learn from someone who has a different style than you do, doesn't mean that you should talk down your own style or yourself. After all, 11% of all Christians represent the same style as you do, and one third have the same style family. Your mentoring partner doesn't have to understand you, but he or she must respect you.

4. *My mentoring partner has a right to be respected in his or her spiritual style.* This is the inversion of the rule three. Approach the other styles with respect, whether you understand them or not.

5. *I will only share critical observations about my mentoring partner if she or he has asked me to do so.* The principle of focusing on your own learning doesn't mean that you are not allowed to share critical observations about your partner. But you are only allowed to do this if your partner has explicitly asked you to.

6. *We both have the right to discontinue our interaction at any point in the process.* As a rule, you should anticipate a series of Mutual Mentoring sessions, but if you decide that you should leave the process, you can do so at any time, without explanation.

7. *The focus of our interaction is not to discuss theology, but to share how we encounter God.* Of course, these dimensions cannot be completely separated from one another, but the main focus of your interaction should be how each of you experience God.

8. *I commit to speaking honestly about my feelings.* In a Mutual Mentoring session you shouldn't share pre-fabricated statements, but rather honestly express what you feel, including your insecurities and doubts.

9. *The mentoring relationship is based on the assumption that we both need each other in order to grow our natives styles.* Your goal is not to change styles; neither is that the goal of your partner.

10. *I will treat my mentoring partner exactly as I would have him or her treat me.* This is the application of Jesus' "Golden Rule." Implicitly, rules one through nine have taken this concern into account already. Rule ten simply covers any situation that is not explicitly addressed by the first nine rules.

The goal of the Trinitarian Monastery is that the Christian world would truly shift from being a *pluriverse* to a *universe*, in which the plurality of spiritual styles can be bundled up into a universal approach that makes each of us more effective. You can access the Trinitarian Monastery through *www.3colorsofyourspirituality.org*.

The fruit of Level B growth

Throughout the whole third part of this book I have spoken about Level B growth. In doing so, I have deliberately highlighted the difficulties of the process, those aspects that stretch us beyond our comfort zones. Level B growth is not meant to increase the fun factor of our lives. At the same time, Level B growth does result in benefits that strongly enrich our lives and will cause us to become more joyful Christians.

Benefits of the process

What, then, are the benefits of Level B growth? When contemplating this question, every Christian, depending on his or her personal value system, will highlight different aspects. For me, the following ten points are the most important:

1. *It expands the way we experience and express our faith:* While God "broadcasts" on all nine channels, we may have only set up one or two receiving channels. From our perspective, the other channels don't even appear to exist. In reality, we simply have never learned how to switch them on. The more we learn to tune in to other channels, the more we will experience God. Level B growth enables us to find the sacred anywhere, and everywhere.

2. *It increases tolerance:* If you are only familiar with one style or one style family, you will be tempted to regard it as *the* approach to God and presume that Christians who display different styles may not have authentic experiences with God. Level B growth expands our tolerance toward the experiences of other Christians, which will have a positive effect on our ability to display tolerance in other areas as well. Most importantly, this is by no means a form of tolerance that sacrifices the truth.

3. *It strengthens your own style:* Even though you will go through phases of insecurity, at the end of the day, interaction with your opposite pole will have strengthened your own style. Level B growth enables you to view yourself through the eyes of others. As you interact with other styles, you will begin to discern the weaknesses and dangers of your own style.

4. *It improves psychological health:* One of the saddest developments in Christianity is that which psychologists call "ecclesiastically induced neuroses," i.e. diseases that are produced by church affiliation. If we took a closer look at what was happening, we would be able to detect that many—though certainly not all—of these neuroses have something to do with the fact that spiritual growth stagnated at Level 0 or Level A.

5. *It better equips us to communicate our faith to non-Christians:* Though the purpose of this book is not to describe how to share the gospel with unchurched people, it is worthwhile mentioning that as long as we are only familiar with one spiritual style, our presentation of the gospel will be limited. It will only appeal to people who are like us. The same dynamics that apply to sharing our experiences with God inside the church, apply toward outsiders as well.

6. *It gives us a more objective understanding of truth:* I am aware that some people believe that the Trinitarian Compass does just the opposite, since they identify their style with what is "objectively true." However, it is the goal of Level B growth to move beyond the subjectivity of our own style and, with the help of other believers, to acquire a more objective image of God.

7. *It breeds intercultural competence:* Interaction with other spiritual styles strengthens the same emotional and intellectual "muscles" that we need to deal with other cultures. As a result, our interaction with people of a different cultural background will be more thoughtful, more sympathetic, and more competent. You may not fully understand them, but at least you are aware that you shouldn't impose your own point of view on them.

8. *It prevents our spirituality from becoming rigid:* An alert mind and a willingness to embrace new ideas keeps you mentally alert. Age itself shouldn't bring any marked intellectual decline, but a static mindset does. Level B learning activates a process of constant self-renewal.

9. *It helps us observe leaders as constant learners:* Level B growth doesn't happen hierarchically. Everyone in this process gives and receives at the same time. Therefore, leaders who want to initiate Level B learning can only do this if they become a part of the process themselves, i.e. if they become constant learners. When others can clearly see both the imbalance of their leaders and their eagerness to grow, they are given more spiritual wisdom than the most powerful sermon could hope to give.

10. *It results in church growth:* I have not mentioned this point earlier in this book, since the focus of NCD is not on numerical growth, but on increasing church quality. Our research in 60,000 churches on all six continents has clearly revealed that if we invest in the quality of a church, we no longer have to be concerned about its quantitative growth. It happens all by itself, which is a very pleasant, and by no means an unimportant, side effect.

Spiritual fruit:

In a narrow sense, this term describes the "fruit of the Spirit" that is mentioned in Galatians 5. In a wider sense, the term can be used to describe the results of various forms of qualitative and quantitative growth within the church.

Your identity in Christ

I believe that any one of the above-mentioned benefits provides sufficient reason to get involved in Level B growth. Yet, the sum of all ten points barely touches the surface of why we should. Even if Level B growth had no visible benefit for us, we should still pursue it, for this is exactly what Jesus expects of us when he calls us to love God "with all your heart and with all your will and with all your mind" (Mark 12:30). Without Level B learning, we would be in danger of alternatively choosing between heart, will, and mind, which would be the very opposite of Jesus' intentions.

Level B growth enables us to experience what "unity in Christ" means at a practical level. We experience it especially with those who seem foreign to us, those Christians we don't really understand or even like. This feeling of foreignness is part of our unity in Christ. It would be an extremely superficial concept of Christian unity to seek it exclusively among like-minded people, among those with whom we share the same values, among those with whom we have "chemistry"—unity within our extended circle of friends, so to speak.

Level B growth opens up the door to a love for God that says, "God, you are the God that you are—the close God, when you reveal yourself as near; the remote God, when you allow us to feel distant from you; the hurting God, when you know we need pain; the God who heals wounds, when that is your desire—the one who doesn't comply with my pre-fabricated image, the one who is worthy to be sought, to be loved, and to be worshiped for your own sake."

Process versus breakthrough

In my work on spirituality, I have encountered two categories that I would like to refer to as breakthrough and process spiritualities. In breakthrough spirituality everything is focused on the one decisive moment that brings change: The laying on of hands. The conversion. The confession. The pilgrimage. The consecration. The blessing. The vow. The baptism in the Holy Spirit. The one mystical experience.

On the other hand, process spirituality, while acknowledging the relevance of mountaintop experiences and decisive moments, puts them into perspective by treating them as waves within an ongoing journey. The focus is not on a specific moment, but on progress, and this progress doesn't happen linearly, but with successive ups and downs.

When studying books on spirituality, the approach can usually be easily categorized. Some of the spiritual styles have a closer affinity to breakthrough spirituality, while others lean more toward process spirituality. Usually the extroverted versions thrive on breakthrough, while the introverted versions focus on process.

Without a doubt, Level A growth has an affinity to breakthrough spirituality. For some Christians the mere completion of the Spiritual Style Test becomes a mountaintop experience. That is good and valuable. My point is not to communicate that breakthrough spirituality is bad and process spirituality is good. Rather, my goal is to relate both experiences to each other. In our context this means Level A growth (breakthrough) should be followed by Level B growth (process).

Level B growth is a typical example of process spirituality. In processes, the focus is not so much on a certain decisive event, but on the development, the growth, the movement. We should never try to convert Level B growth into breakthrough spirituality, for that would thwart what Level B growth is all about.

In every process there are breakthrough moments (mountaintop experiences), but they are by no means more important than the process itself. Significantly enough, the first of the 95 theses which Martin Luther nailed on the Castle Church in Wittenberg in 1517, was this: "When our Lord and Master, Jesus Christ, said 'Repent,' he called for the entire life of believers to be one of repentance." In other words, repentance is not to be seen as a momentary event, at least not exclusively, but as a lifelong process.

Scot McKnight provides a helpful comparison: "Conversion, like wisdom, takes a lifetime. For some, conversion is like a birth certificate while for others it is like a driver's license. For the first, the ultimate question is 'What do I need to do to get to heaven?' For the second, the question is 'How do I love God?' For the first, the concern is a moment; for the second, the concern is a life."

Process spirituality necessarily demands more time. Nevertheless I am extremely reluctant to see the criteria of "duration" as a "quality criterion." This could lead to the fatal argument that quick equals bad, and slow equals good. But not everything that proceeds slowly, should be seen positively. Slowness can also be the result of laziness, procrastination, passivity, lethargy, or fatalistic attitudes. You can run away from God even by means of impressive-sounding process vocabulary.

> **You can run away from God even by means of impressive-sounding process vocabulary.**

Change is possible

The dynamics described in this book can be applied by any church, independent of denomination, theological position, and philosophy of ministry. They can be applied independent of culture and financial possibilities. However, they do demand a certain minimum of openness to engage with that which goes beyond the familiar.

None of us has to wait to get involved with these processes just because our church as a whole isn't ready for it. Each of us can start the process on our own, subsequently inspiring other believers to get involved as well. Though both Level A and Level B growth are easier when they have local church support, they do work even without it.

The ultimate goal: Expanding the kingdom

Scripture only minimally speaks about church growth, but it has a lot to say about the coming of the kingdom of God. In Jesus' own teaching this topic emerges in many variations. The kingdom of God is where his authority is acknowledged, where his will is accepted, where his reign takes visible effect. Jesus could probably have spoken simply of God, instead of God's "kingdom." The kingdom of God describes the way God works in us; the way God works in the world; the way God will reveal himself at the end of all time. What makes heaven heaven? God. What brings heaven to earth? God's presence. How do we experience more of God's presence? That has been the contents of the last 188 pages of this book.

Take a look at the graphic on page 191. It distinguishes three different dimensions of God's kingdom. As you reflect on this image, you must never forget that, in the end, Jesus himself is the kingdom of God. The kingdom is not a "something," it is a person. If Jesus is seen in our lives, the kingdom has come into our heart; if society bears his mark, it is a foretaste of the kingdom to come; if we receive access to God through Christ, heaven has already become a reality for us. Our present life is a foretaste—albeit weak—of the heavenly glory awaiting us.

Time and again, Jesus himself pointed to the apparent meagerness of the kingdom. It is like a mustard seed, the smallest among all seeds. It is like leaven, a tiny speck compared to the quantity of the whole dough. It is repeatedly compared to the seed that is scattered on the soil of this world. That which appears insignificant, bears the power of the kingdom.

Multiplication:

One of six growth forces that is taught by NCD. While methods that are based on addition can lead to insignificant and energy consuming growth (2+2+2+2+2) in the best case, applying the principle of multiplication releases exponential growth (2x2x2x2x2). Every believer should constantly evaluate his or her own life as to what degree it contributes to multiplication.

Constant multiplication

Even when Jesus spoke about our mission mandate, he used metaphors such as light, salt, and leaven. On the surface these metaphors seem quite different from one another. However, all of them speak of penetration. As Richard Foster writes, "Light exists to penetrate the darkness; salt exists to penetrate the meat; leaven exists to penetrate the dough. And we exist to penetrate the world!"

Jesus hasn't spoken about church development, but he has called us to "make disciples." Disciples are people who strive to become more and more Christlike, which involves both Level A and Level B growth. They are people who have learned what it means to love God with all their heart, with all their will, and with all their mind. Since churches are made up of people, the community of these disciples is what church is all about. Church development is essentially disciple development.

Discipleship is the key to multiplication. Win five people with whom you set out to love God with your heart, will, and mind. Subsequently, each of them wins five more. That isn't really difficult to achieve. Compared to many resource-hungry Christian programs, it seems virtually insignificant, but it is the way the leaven penetrates the dough, the salt penetrates the meat, the light of God penetrates the darkness. What counts is not the input, but the impact.

It can be done

Some things described in this book may seem far away from what you are presently experiencing. The question of all questions is: Do you really believe that people can change? Many don't believe it is possible. They base all of their plans on the assumption that people never change; that in the future each of us will continue to strive for the same material possessions; that each of us will continue to use the same destructive energy to destroy the environment; that each of us would prefer to be spiritually entertained rather than spiritually transformed. Brothers and sisters, there is evidence that people can change!

Some people teach that history determines our future. But this assumption is wrong. History explains your present; it makes where you are today understandable. But it doesn't determine the future—where you will be tomorrow or the day after tomorrow. That is determined by our present. By you and me. By what we decide to do right now. And each person who is willing to make changes becomes the maker of the map for others to follow.

Qualitative growth:

Rather than setting numerical growth goals (such as, "By May 2014 our church will have 230 new members"), NCD is focused on qualitative growth. It involves constant work on increasing the quality in eight essential areas. Progress is evaluated at least once a year by means of the NCD Survey. Our research indicates that this focus on quality is the most effective way to experience numerical growth as well. However, quantitative growth is not the strategic goal of the development process; it is its natural fruit.

The chance of a crisis

Epoch-making changes are always born in times of crisis. I view the current global crises as tremendous opportunities, especially opportunities to see changes in Christianity. From that perspective, crises fill my heart with joy. They make it overtly clear that there is an urgent need for a genuine Christian contribution in the world. In order to make this contribution, however, we have to come back to our quintessential strengths rather than seeing ourselves merely as the Christian arm of a commercial entertainment industry. In the introductory chapter (page 6) I mentioned that Karl Marx called religion the "opium of the people;" Friedrich Nietzsche, "platonism for the people;" and Sigmund Freud, a "collective neurosis." Given the realities that each of these critics had in mind, their assessment was not all wrong. Even today, Christianity—at least parts of it—gives still too great an impression of being opium, platonism, and neurosis. That has to change, and it can be changed.

Back to the basics

In this book we discussed the Trinitarian Compass, native styles and opposite poles, neighbor styles and style families, Level A and Level B growth. If I were to reduce the net message to three simple points, I would say the following: Love God. Love others. Make disciples.

1. *Love God:* Love him with all your heart, with all your will, with all your mind. Be radical in that love ("with all your strength"). Don't leave out any one of these areas.

... in a changed society

green

The kingdom of God manifests itself ...

blue

red

... within you

... in heaven

According to the Bible, spiritual growth is not an end in itself. The goal is that the kingdom of God takes shape. Different strains of Christianity stress different aspects of God's kingdom. Red spirituality identifies the kingdom primarily with heaven; blue spirituality stresses the growth of the kingdom in ourselves; green spirituality is focused on a changed society. All of these are, indeed, different aspects of God's kingdom that are inextricably linked.

2. *Love others:* Much is implied in this command, and it is not all treated in this book. However, Level B learning is one of the best ways to train yourself in love, since love demands the ability to see the world through other people's eyes.

3. *Make disciples:* This implies that you give away what you have received. Share your discoveries with others. Share it with both believers and non-believers. Even among those who call themselves Christians there are many "undiscipled disciples." Plant Jesus' love in their lives.

Unrealistic?

Does this sound unrealistic? Absolutely not. You can start right away. You don't have to ask others for their approval. You don't have to win majorities. The kingdom of God can take effect in your heart immediately.

Again and again I am puzzled to hear Christian leaders say that the concept described in this book is "desirable," but "unrealistic." Leadership, they tell me, is the "art of the possible." Therefore, it is misleading from the outset to strive to achieve things that "overburden ordinary believers." I disagree. Leadership is by no means the "art of the possible." Leadership is the art of making possible what appears to be impossible today. Ordinary believers are by no means overburdened by the concepts described in this book. I am constantly working with ordinary believers, and with none other than ordinary believers. They can do it. Of course, we may have to explain things a bit. That may take an hour, a whole weekend, or even a bit longer. Most believers are extremely responsive to explore radically ("with all their strength") what it means to love God with all their heart, with all their will, and with all their mind.

This is an invitation for everyone who hasn't given up the goal of radical Christianity, who doesn't shy away from self-criticism, who trusts that a healed Christianity will be able to lead seeking people into a more hopeful future.

Two hours to change your church

Do you recall the image of the six figures on top of a dartboard (page 151)? Every single one is moving in a different direction (one from right to left, the other from left to right), and yet all of them are moving in the same direction, namely, closer to the center. At almost every conference I use this graphic to show what the Trinitarian Compass is all about.

When working with a group of people, I constantly keep this image in my mind. The dynamics expressed by the dartboard image are exactly what we want to see happen. In my case, reflecting on this image tends to cause it to materialize in real life. Once I have seen it long enough in my mind, I long to see it with my physical eyes as well!

Ever since the Spiritual Style Test was made available, I like to do the following in my seminars: I have all of the participants complete the test, and calculate their results. During the half hour that they are taking the test, I affix large tags with the names of the nine styles around the four walls of the room, in the same arrangement that is found within the Trinitarian Compass. Then I ask the participants to place themselves underneath the tag that corresponds to their native style. At this point, the first light-bulb moment occurs: "It's true, all nine styles are represented in this group!"

I let the participants stand in this arrangement for a few minutes, just to allow them to sense what has happened. The very things that people have previously seen on the dartboard image ("There he goes again, Christian and his graphics!") start to materialize in front of their eyes. We don't see six virtual figures any longer, but maybe 50 or 100 real people with real faces. All of the prejudices toward the opposite styles, all of the light that the opposite pole throws on our own shadow areas, all of the curiosity to explore these processes—all of that is reflected in the faces of these people.

I then ask everyone to look into the eyes of a person standing opposite him or her. This eye-contact ignites an almost magical moment. It is the exact moment at which the Trinitarian Compass leaves the abstraction of a graphic and starts to take effect in our hearts. I let the participants experience this special moment with all of their senses. Sometimes I interview two or three of them. Sometimes we spend these special moments in complete silence.

Then I repeat the message that the participants already knew up to this point, at least on an intellectual level: "You need the person opposite you exactly in his or her otherness in order to grow spiritually." Afterwards everyone approaches the person with whom he or she has had eye-contact. One person crosses the room from right to left; the other, from left to right, and all of them meet at the center. What a moment!

While in these groups of two, I give the participants thirty minutes to share their answers to the following questions: How does your style express itself in concrete ways? What do you experience in your relationship with God that I have not experienced? How could we help each other to experience God more fully?

The whole exercise takes less than two hours. Of course, these two hours in and of themselves don't transform the whole church. Yet this experience marks a point of no return. People who have experienced how marvelously the Trinitarian Compass works in one area, are eager to see these dynamics take effect in other areas of their lives as well.

> **This eye-contact ignites an almost magical moment.**